D1544124

	DATE DUE		

The Firm and the Market

For Catherine

The Firm and the Market

Studies on Multinational Enterprise and the Scope of the Firm

Mark Casson

The MIT Press
Cambridge, Massachusetts

First MIT Press edition, 1987
Published in Great Britain by Basil Blackwell Ltd

Library of Congress Cataloging-in-Publication Data

Casson, Mark, 1945–
The firm and the market.

Bibliography: p.
Includes index.
1. International business enterprises.   I. Title
HD2755.5.C392   1987   658′.049   86-27199
ISBN 0-262-03129-9

Phototypeset by Dobbie Typesetting Service, Plymouth, Devon
Printed and bound in Great Britain by Butler & Tanner Ltd, Frome and London

Contents

Preface

Modern economic analysis of the multinational enterprise (MNE) relies heavily on the theory of internalization. This book is firmly with the tradition of internalization theory – a tradition that can be traced back to the pioneering work of Ronald Coase. Its aim is, quite simply, to widen the subject area to which the insights of this theory are applied. This is effected by taking the modern theory of the MNE – which encapsulates most of the insights of internalization theory – and developing it further, to give it a wider range of applications. The new applications lie at the interface of sub-disciplines within economics which have traditionally remained isolated from one another. Using 'intellectual arbitrage', it is possible to revitalize these sub-disciplines by importing into them insights derived from internalization theory and from the theory of the MNE.

Within the broad aim of this book, three specific objectives can be distinguished.

1 To extend the analysis of the MNE to accommodate contemporary phenomena such as strategic rivalry between multinationals and the restructuring of their global operations. This involves synthesizing internalization theory with other theories – such as the economic theory of strategic entry-deterrence and the statistical theory of quality control.
2 To demonstrate that, when extended along these lines, analysis of the MNE provides the basis for a general theory of corporate organization over space. It suggests a vision of the MNE as a nexus for a diverse set of contractual arrangements. These arrangements co-ordinate activities at different points in space. Viewed in this way, the theory of the MNE has important implications for conventional theories of the firm, and for new theories of industrial organization.

vii

3 To show that the ramifications of the theory of the MNE go well beyond the areas to which it has traditionally been applied. The theory has policy implications which have so far gone unrecognized. It is relevant, for example, to issues in industrial policy which concern not only the operations of multinational firms, but the operations of purely national firms as well. The theory provides a framework of analysis which lends itself particularly well to case study applications. This book illustrates in detail how the theory can be used in case study investigations, and in policy appraisals, in a range of different industries.

The first two chapters of the book review the existing state of the theory of the MNE. Chapter 1 emphasizes the strengths of the theory by synthesizing its insights in a novel way, whilst chapter 2 focuses on its limitations. Chapter 1 identifies the analytical core of the theory as a set of principles governing choice between alternative contractual arrangements. Business operations involve a composite collection of interrelated activities, which include not only routine production, but also research and development, advertising and promotion, and the physical distribution of the product. These activities are linked by flows of intermediate goods, the most important being services derived from intangible assets such as knowledge. The co-ordination of these activities poses intriguing strategic problems, and the way these problems are resolved determines the scope of the firm. Some firms operate internationally with a narrow range of products based upon the same technology, whilst others supply a variety of products within just a few national or regional markets in which they have special knowledge or reputation. Some firms produce the same product throughout its life cycle from innovation to maturity, whilst others specialize in groups of products at particular stages in their life cycle. The multinationality of the firm therefore, is just one of several characteristics which are simultaneously determined by the strategic problems encountered in its operations.

Chapter 2 critically examines the most influential recent writing on the MNE. The literature is criticized for the persistence of some fundamental logical errors, for the exaggerated claims advanced for the theory, and for the over-zealous attempts of authors to 'differentiate their products' from those of others. More work needs to be done if some of the claims recently made for the theory are to be validated. Some of the necessary steps are taken in chapters 3 and 4, which extend the theory in new directions.

Chapter 3 analyses oligopolistic rivalry between MNEs in global markets. Under certain conditions, rivalry will lead to an exchange of threats. The credibility of such threats is enhanced by the multinationality of the firm. This is a refinement of an idea due to Monty Graham and Raymond

Vernon; it is closely related to recent developments in the theory of imperfect competition and international trade. It has important implications for monopoly and merger policies, and for the international political economy of protectionism.

Chapter 4 highlights the crucial importance of quality control in the operations of both national and multinational firms. It shows how internalization of intermediate product flows can establish a 'chain of confidence' linking the earliest stage of raw material or component production to the distribution of the final product. Internalization helps to overcome some of the administrative problems in implementing quality incentives within a multi-stage production process. The theory has wide ramifications. It has particularly important implications for trade in services.

Chapter 5 marks the transition from theory to empirical evidence. It develops a methodology for testing internalization theory using case study evidence on individual firms. It demonstrates that, unlike certain other branches of economic theory, internalization theory works well not only in explaining the behaviour of a population of many economic agents, but also in explaining the behaviour of specific decision makers in specific situations. Drawing upon evidence from business histories, it shows how the application of the theory can shed new light on the interpretation of historical evidence.

Chapter 6 applies the analysis of quality control presented in chapter 4 to the UK construction industry. This is part of a wider investigation into the scope of activities undertaken by UK construction firms. Quality control over subcontracted work is shown to be a major strategic issue in the construction industry, affecting not only the extent of backward integration by the firm, but also the form of contracts of employment in the industry. A number of inefficiencies are detected in contemporary managerial strategies in the industry. It is suggested that the firms which are the quickest to rationalize their activities along the lines presented by theory will prove most successful in the long run.

The shipping industry, which is the subject of chapter 7, employs a wide range of sophisticated arm's length contractual arrangements which have evolved over many centuries of international operation. The development of highly organized arm's length markets can be explained by a combination of special factors which make shipping a unique industry. Internalization theory predicts that only a few sectors of the shipping industry will exhibit high levels of integrated operation, and this is in fact the case. The few instances where widespread integration does occur are successfully predicted by the theory.

Many early policy debates on the MNE focused upon the consequences of the integration of separate activities into the same firm. A wave of divestments in the past decade, however, has focused attention on the consequences of disintegration – i.e. the splitting up of integrated structures into separate parts. Divestment can take several forms, including management buy-out, closure, sale to another firm of a going concern, and so on. In some cases it may involve the reintegration of the divested activity into the operations of another firm. The precise form that divestment takes is often crucial for policy purposes. Chapter 8 examines how far the determinants of the different forms of divestment can be explained by internalization theory. The main points are illustrated using a case study from the international motor industry.

The extensions of the theory presented in this book go only part of the way towards the ultimate objective of a comprehensive theory in which the MNE appears as a special configuration of contractual arrangements over space. Some of the further steps required are charted in chapter 9, which also speculates upon the form that this 'ultimate theory' might take.

Acknowledgements

Although this book is, to some extent, a compilation of separate papers, there is an underlying theoretical unity and progressive development of ideas within it. The papers have all been revised with the requirements of coherence and continuity of argument in mind.

Chapter 1 is a revised version of a contribution to R. Clarke and A. McGuinness (eds) *Economics of the Firm*, Oxford: Blackwell, 1986. Chapter 2 is a completely rewritten version of a paper presented to the European Science Foundation Conference on *Multinationals: Theory and History* in Florence, September 1983, and published in a book of the same title edited by G. Jones and P. Hertner (Farnborough: Gower Press, 1986). Chapters 3 and 4 are specially written for this volume. Chapter 5 arose from an informal seminar held at the Business History Unit, London, at which I was a discussant. A longer version of this chapter is to appear in *Business History*, and I am grateful to the editors and the referees for their encouraging comments. Chapter 6 is a preliminary version of a paper prepared for the Science and Engineering Research Council project on Management Strategies of British Contracting Firms; a subsequent version will appear in a book edited by Pat Hillebrandt and scheduled for publication in 1988. Chapter 7 is republished with permission from the *Journal of Transport Economics and Policy*, 20(1), pp. 7–29. Chapter 8 is a rewritten version of a chapter contributed to J. Coyne and M. Wright (eds) *Divestment and Strategic Change*, Deddington, Oxon: Philip Allan, and also incorporates material from a report prepared for the International Labour Office, Geneva. Chapter 9 is based upon a compilation of material abstracted from earlier versions of several of the articles mentioned above.

Needless to say, numerous people have contributed comments at various stages of the preparation of this material. I am particularly grateful to Howard Archer, David Barry, Wilson Brown, Peter Buckley, Jean

Boddewyn, Jacquie Cannon, John Cantwell, Roger Clarke, Tony Corley, Richard Davenport-Hines, John Dunning, D. Dyster, Ford of Europe, Bernard Gardner, Sidney Gilman, Richard Goss, Monty Graham, Z. Hakam, Leslie Hannah, Pat Hillebrandt, Denis Horner, Neil Hood, Steven Jaffee, Geoffrey Jones, Charles Kindleberger, Tony McGuinness, Robert Read, Garel Rhys, Alan Rugman, Howard Seymour, John Stopford, Charles Sutcliffe, Talbot Motors, Danny Van Den Bulcke, Mike Utton, Mike Wright, Tony Woods and Stephen Young. Three anonymous publishers' readers also supplied extremely useful comments.

Sandra Winter showed considerable forbearance in typing and amending the various drafts, and I am grateful for her efforts in helping to meet the numerous deadlines for book and journal publications. Andrew Connolly provided excellent computing assistance. My wife, Janet, once again supplied trenchant criticisms, and also helped to make the book at least partially intelligible to the non-specialist reader.

1

The Economic Theory of the Multinational Enterprise: Its Contribution to the Theory of the Firm

1.1 INTRODUCTION

The economic theory of the multinational enterprise (MNE) lies at the interface of three separate specialisms: the theory of the firm, international trade theory, and international finance. Unfortunately, it is difficult to integrate these three branches of theory. As they are conventionally formulated, some of the assumptions made by each are inconsistent with those made by the others. Writers on the MNE have tackled this problem by reformulating the constituent theories – notably the theory of the firm. The result is a theory which deals simultaneously with both the spatial and organizational aspects of the firm. The modern theory of the MNE has the potential to become a general theory of the enterprise in space, and as such, to embrace theories of the multi-regional and multi-plant firm. The theory of the uninational single plant firm under perfect competition – a theory which used to be known quite simply as 'the theory of the firm' – turns out to be a quite trivial special case.

The study of the MNE is also valuable because it emphasizes a couple of points which have been rather neglected in the past. First, it demonstrates that the internal workings of large firms are a subject of intrinsic interest to the economist. When the value added by one of the world's largest multinationals can exceed the gross national product (GNP) of a small country, the idiosyncrasies of decision making within the enterprise are clearly important for the global allocation of resources. It can be misleading,

BOX 1.1   Some stylized facts about MNEs

1   HISTORICAL PATTERN OF GROWTH

MNE control of world manufacturing production grew very rapidly during the 1950s and 1960s, but has levelled off since then. In the 1920s and 1930s international cartels controlled some of the industries (e.g. chemicals) which MNEs now dominate. To some extent, therefore, there has been a substitution of one form of international control of production for another. Substitution along similar lines is evident in the marketing field, where many companies have replaced independent overseas sales agents with wholly owned foreign sales subsidiaries.

2   COUNTRY OF ORIGIN AND THE STRUCTURE OF INTERNATIONAL PRODUCTION

Three main types of MNE can be distinguished: (a) the US-based MNE which grew rapidly in the 1950s and early 1960s, and undertakes import-substituting investments in other developed countries (notably in Europe); (b) European-based MNEs which undertook backward integration into agriculture and minerals in the colonial territories in the 1920s and 1930s; and (c) Japanese MNEs which have invested in off-shore 'export platform' investments in the low-wage newly industrializing countries of SE Asia in the 1970s. There are plenty of hybrids, though: US MNEs which have invested in agriculture and minerals in Latin America, European MNEs that have cross-invested in Europe and in the US, and Japanese MNEs which have recently begun to undertake import-substituting investments in Europe and the US.

3   INDUSTRY CHARACTERISTICS

US MNEs predominate in industries with high research and development (R and D) to sales ratios and high advertising expenditure to sales ratios (as indicated by data relating to the US economy); also in industries with high ratios of salaried to weekly paid staff, and of administrative staff to production workers, and with high five-firm concentration ratios in the host country.

4   FIRM CHARACTERISTICS

Within an industry, MNEs appear to have the characteristics typical of the industry – as noted above – *only more so*. They undertake more R and D, have a relatively high proportion of administrative staff, and so on. They

continued

Box 1.1 continued

also offer higher wages, use different systems of wage negotiation – preferring to deal with fewer unions – and tend to export a higher proportion of their output than their indigenous competitors. Case study evidence suggests that many MNEs enjoy privileged access to either technology, reputable brand names, or managerial techniques (usually – though not invariably – techniques that are specific to the industry). Enterprises that produce in a very large number of countries tend to concentrate on a narrow range of products, whilst those that produce in very few countries tend to produce a wider range of products.

5 CONTRACTUAL ALTERNATIVES TO THE MNE

Licensing, franchising, subcontracting and joint ventures (as well as cartels) are all alternatives to the MNE so far as the international control of production is concerned. Licensing appears to be most common in industries such as float-glass, where process technology is easy to patent, and in publishing, where copyright protection is relatively secure. Franchising is common in food and in certain service industries, such as hotels. Subcontracting is widespread in many industries, whilst joint ventures are common in heavy chemicals and in component manufacture for mass assembly, where there are significant economies of scale. These alternatives to the MNE have been used more frequently during the last ten years than they were in the early post-war period.

6 VERTICAL INTEGRATION BETWEEN PRIMARY AND MANUFACTURING INDUSTRIES

Backward integration into minerals is much more common in some industries than others. It is common, for example, in aluminium and copper, but not in tin. Within the energy sector, it is common in oil but not in coal. Likewise, backward integration into agriculture is common in bananas, but not in cocoa, grain or cotton.

Sources: Buckley (1985b), Buckley and Enderwick (1984), Casson and associates (1986), Dunning (1981; 1983), Dunning and McQueen (1982), Hennart (1982), Pearce (1983), Stuckey (1983), Wilkins (1970; 1974), Wolf (1977).

therefore, to talk of a 'representative firm' when analysing an MNE, and to attempt to explain its behaviour as though it were a 'black box'.

The second point concerns the importance of stylized facts as a stimulus to theoretical development. Empirical study of MNEs has yielded an intriguing set of stylized facts, some of which are summarized in box 1.1

and the modern theory of the MNE successfully explains them. The need to explain facts has guided the development of the theory throughout, and this has conferred on the theory its major strength relative to other branches of economics, namely its immediate practical relevance.

The economic theory of the MNE can be viewed as an application of certain broad theoretical insights to the specific problems of co-ordinating economic activity over space. In each case, however, the theory of the MNE gives a special 'twist' to the theory in the course of the application.

The concept of 'principals' and 'agents', for example, is widely used to examine relations between the owners and managers of a firm (Jensen and Meckling, 1976). The same concept is used in the theory of the MNE to analyse relations between the overall management of a production process and the management of an individual operation (cf. Strong and Waterson, 1987). It is argued, for example, that under certain conditions agency problems are less acute when each of the individual operations involved in the process belongs to the same ownership unit. Common ownership gives the high level manager the right of access to information utilized by the lower level managers and so reduces their scope for strategic or deceitful use of the information at their disposal. The advantage of reducing information asymmetry through common ownership explains why high level managers of a firm may prefer to control an overseas production activity directly rather than subcontract the activity to an indigenous firm.

Strategic behaviour, in general, has a key role in the economic theory of the MNE. But while writers on the 'new industrial economics' emphasize the strategic issues created by scale economies (Eaton and Lipsey, 1978; Spence, 1977; Baumol, Panzar and Willig, 1982) the issue that dominates the economic theory of the MNE is the exploitation of proprietary knowledge. In one sense, the difference of emphasis is only superficial, for knowledge itself exhibits a kind of economy of scale. This is because the costs of discovering knowledge are fixed costs which are shared by all applications of the knowledge. The marginal cost of putting knowledge to an additional use is therefore well below the average cost. In another sense, however, the difference of emphasis is crucial, for scale economies in manufacturing production encourage the concentration of global production on just a few locations, and therefore discourage multinational operations. Since, on the other hand, knowledge is an internationally transferable asset, possession of proprietary knowledge positively encourages multinational operations.

Transaction cost theory also has a prominent role in the economic theory of the MNE. Writers on the MNE have, however, evolved their own traditions in applying transaction costs to the theory of the firm. One reason for this is their preoccupation with transaction costs in the market for knowledge. Another reason is a purely historical one – the first application of the Coasian concept of internalization to the MNE by McManus (1972) antedates Williamson's formulation of 'markets and hierarchies' theory (Williamson, 1975) and its application to the MNE by Teece (1982). Literature on the MNE is therefore refreshingly free from the jargon which is so conspicuous a feature of conventional 'markets and hierarchies' theory. Moreover, during the past decade, writers on the MNE have had far greater success in deriving testable propositions from transaction cost theory than have writers outside this field, as the following pages show.

1.2 THE EVOLUTION OF THE THEORY

The pioneering work in the modern theory of the MNE is Hymer's doctoral dissertation, written under Kindleberger's supervision at MIT and submitted in 1960 (Hymer, 1976). This work, however, remained unpublished until 1976, and much of what was known of it came from the summary of Hymer's argument in Kindleberger (1969). Unfortunately, Kindleberger's book, being based upon public lectures, revealed only some of Hymer's analytical insights. By the time of its publication Hymer had become a publicly committed Marxist and had modified his views of the MNE quite considerably as a result. Hymer's theory was not, therefore, properly disseminated until the late 1970s, by which time a considerable amount of independent work had been done along similar lines.

Hymer's contribution to the theory of the MNE has recently become a matter of some controversy (see Dunning and Rugman, 1985; Kindleberger, 1984a; Teece, 1985) and the following remarks are intended, in part, to clarify some of the issues in this controversy.

At the time of writing his thesis, Hymer's stance reflected the general concern of anti-trust economists in Canada and Western Europe over the growing impact of US foreign investment on their national economies (Rowthorn, 1979). But in order to analyse their national impact, it was necessary to understand what the MNEs were doing abroad in the first place. Hymer's basic premise was that the first-time foreign investor incurs costs of acclimatizing to the business environment abroad. How then, was it possible for US firms to produce abroad so successfully in competition with indigenous firms? Hymer argued that US foreign investors possessed various advantages over their US rivals. Drawing explicitly on Bain (1956), Hymer showed that many of these advantages were of a monopolistic or monopsonistic type. He supported his argument by empirical evidence drawn from various sources, particularly Dunning's study of US investment in Britain, which showed that US firms possessed superior technology and management skills (Dunning, 1958).

Another question considered by Hymer was why US managers did not attempt to have the 'best of both worlds' – transferring their technology, whilst avoiding the costs of doing business abroad – by licensing their technology to indigenous firms. Hymer's answer was essentially that the market for knowledge is not perfectly competitive. Hymer did not, however, clearly distinguish between two types of market imperfection. The first type is associated with market structure – in the sense of the concentration of buying and selling power, and the related phenomenon of strategic interdependence between oligopolistic firms. The second is associated with transaction costs incurred in connection with defining property rights and negotiating, monitoring and enforcing contracts.

The two types of imperfection are logically quite distinct. They are related, though, because market structure can influence transaction costs, and conversely the level of transaction costs can affect market structure. When the market structure is one of bilateral monopoly, for example, the costs of negotiating a price are liable to be very high. Conversely, when transaction costs are high because information on price and quality is difficult to obtain, the volume of trade will be low and monopoly is liable to prevail.

Hymer's failure to distinguish clearly between market structure and transaction costs meant that when analysing licensing he tended to argue directly from market structure, rather than from market structure to transaction costs, and from transaction costs to licensing. Although he mentions uncertainty and some other factors which affect transaction costs, he failed to relate his discussion explicitly to the work of Coase (1937). This crucial step was taken, largely independently, by a number of writers including McManus (1972), Buckley and Casson (1976), Brown (1976), Swedenborg (1979) and Hennart (1982). These writers look to institutional economics and the theory of property rights for an answer to the question 'Why are plants in different countries brought under common ownership and control?' The answer is 'Because the transaction costs incurred in intermediate products markets can be reduced by internalizing these markets within the firm'. The internalization approach is therefore much more general than Hymer's, because the concept of intermediate product it employs can embrace all the different types of good or service that are transferred between one activity and another within the production process.

Once the licensing decision was perceived as a special case of this more general issue, a number of other matters began to fall into place. The investments of European firms in colonial mining ventures could also be explained by internalization. The raw materials and semi-processed products traded within the European-owned mining firms were one type of intermediate product, while the know-how traded between the research division and the manufacturing division of the US high-technology firm was just another type of intermediate product. The fact that in the second case the intermediate product – knowledge – has some of the characteristics of a 'public good' (Johnson, 1970) explains why the high technology firm is not only 'vertically integrated' between research and manufacturing, but 'horizontally integrated' within manufacturing too.

The transaction cost approach can be used to tackle another issue raised by Hymer, namely the importance of collusion in explaining horizontal integration by MNEs. Hymer emphasized that global profits in an industry can be enhanced by collusion between producers in different localities, and he perceived that the MNE was a vehicle through which such collusion can be organized. But collusion can be effected through alternative arrangements – notably a cartel – and without a theory of transaction costs Hymer could not explain why, in certain industries and at certain times, an MNE prevails and, in other industries and at other times, an international cartel. The role of collusion in international operations is examined in section 1.3.

A theory of collusion is, in fact, implicit in modern analysis of the licensing decision. Because of the 'public good' character of knowledge, the proceeds of the competitive exploitation of knowledge are normally insufficient to defray the costs of research. If the research is privately financed, therefore, monopoly rents must be earned, and this in turn implies that when several plants exploit the same knowledge, they must normally collude. The role of collusion in the commercial exploitation of knowledge is considered in section 1.4.

Hymer's emphasis on knowledge-based monopolistic advantages has tended to obscure the important role of vertical integration (VI) in the operations of many MNEs. It is shown in section 1.5 that there are specifically multinational costs and benefits of VI. The benefits accrue from transfer pricing, whilst the costs are associated with the risks of nationalization or expropriation of foreign assets.

The emphasis on knowledge – and on the internalization of the market for knowledge in particular – means that the theory of the MNE is well adapted to handling dynamic issues concerned with innovation and the growth of the firm. Unfortunately, the full potential of the theory has yet to be realized in this respect. Section 1.6 shows how internalization theory can be used to develop a simple model of the growth of the firm. According to the model, the firm can choose between alternative strategies for promoting market growth, and the strategy mix it chooses will reflect the aptitudes of its researchers. Some firms will opt for strategies that rapidly turn them into multi-nationals, whilst others will not. The conclusions are summarized in section 1.7.

1.3   HORIZONTAL INTEGRATION AS INTERPLANT COLLUSION

The standard model of the horizontally-integrated MNE is due to Horst (1971; 1974). A more sophisticated version of the model is presented by Batra and Ramachandran (1980), but only a highly simplified version is used here. The model is used to illustrate Hymer's insight that an MNE may be formed in order to profit from collusion. The basic approach is similar to that of Fellner's joint profit maximizing theory of collusive oligopoly (Fellner, 1949) which was probably known to Hymer; the details are different, though, because of the spatial disaggregation of the product market which arises in the case of the MNE.

Consider an industry producing a homogeneous product in which there is initially a single-plant monopoly in each of two countries. There are no barriers to trade. Initially each monopolist charges a uniform price which he sets independently of the other firm's price, and sells only to customers in his home country. Figure 1.1 shows the demand curves D_1, D_2 in each country, the corresponding marginal revenue curves MR_1, MR_2, and the marginal cost curves for each plant MC_1, MC_2. Independent profit maximization by the monopolists generates equilibrium prices P_1, P_2 and equilibrium outputs Q_1, Q_2.

This equilibrium is unstable, however, unless the costs of international transport are prohibitively high. Since the price is higher in country 2 than in country 1, $P_2 > P_1$, there is an incentive for independent arbitrageurs to buy in country 1 for export to country 2. Secondly, there is an incentive for each monopolist to invade the other's market. This is because the price in country 2 exceeds the marginal cost in country 1, $P_2 > C_1$, and conversely the price in country 1 exceeds the marginal cost in country 2, $P_1 > C_2$. Finally, even if both independent arbitrage and mutual invasion could somehow be avoided, it would be efficient for the monopolists to switch some production from country 1 to country 2. This is because the marginal cost of production in country 1 exceeds the marginal cost of production in country 2, $C_1 > C_2$.

The joint profits of the monopolists are maximized when they agree

1 to sell, if possible, only to final consumers in each market, and so protect one another's markets by denying supplies to independent arbitrageurs;
2 not to invade each other's markets; and
3 to concentrate production on the lowest cost plant, and export the surplus for sale by the other monopolist.

Formally, the joint profits of the monopolists are maximized when the prices can be set independently in each market according to the local

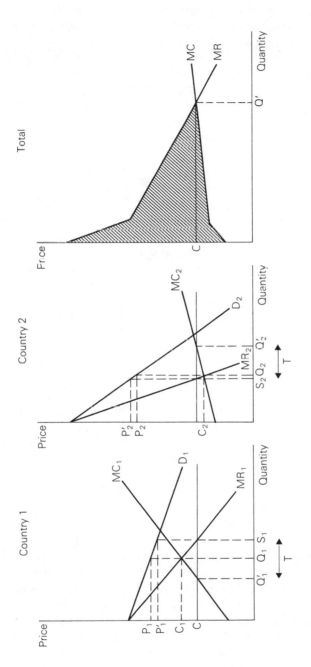

FIGURE 1.1 Horizontal integration

elasticity of demand, when the marginal costs of production are equalized across countries, and when the marginal revenue in each country is equal to the common level of marginal cost. (A fourth possibility, that the monopolists could discriminate between consumers within each market, is ignored.) These conditions assume zero transport costs; if transport costs are incurred then the conditions are modified slightly.

The determination of the joint-profit maximizing equilibrium is illustrated in the right-hand quadrant of the figure. The curve MR is the horizontal summation of the curves MR_1 and MR_2, and MC is the horizontal summation of MC_1 and MC_2. (Note that because of intermarket price discrimination, it is meaningless to sum the two demand curves.) The international equilibrium level of marginal cost is C, and total international output is Q'. Q_1' is produced in country 1, and S_1 is sold, with $T = S_1 - Q_1'$ being imported from country 2. Correspondingly, Q_2' is produced is country 2, and S_2 is sold, with $T = Q_2' - S_2$ being exported to country 1. The prices in the two countries are P_1' and P_2' respectively. The joint profit is measured by the shaded area in the right-hand quadrant.

There are three main institutional mechanisms by which this joint-profit maximizing equilibrium could be achieved. The first is for the two monopolists to negotiate an agreement prohibiting sales to arbitrageurs and outlawing market invasion, and then to bargain jointly over the level of arm's length trade between them. The second is for them to organize a cartel. The third is for them to merge to form an MNE.

The relative advantages of these arrangements have been examined by Casson (1985), drawing on earlier work by Robinson (1941) and Williamson (1975, ch. 12). The cartel is more effective than an arm's length agreement in the long term because it allows a sales syndicate to be set up to organize trade between the companies. By offering to buy unlimited quantities from the companies at the parametric price C, the syndicate can ensure that both plants will incur similar levels of marginal cost. By marking up the price C by a factor related to the elasticity of demand in each market, the syndicate can fix prices which equate marginal revenue in each country to marginal cost. The profits of the syndicate are then distributed between the two firms. In this way the monopolists can collude whilst retaining control of their own outputs. Production is rationalized without the producers having to divulge their costs to each other. If market conditions change then the syndicate simply announces a new parametric buying price, and the producers adjust their output accordingly. Once the syndicate has been established, therefore, there is no need to renegotiate 'from scratch' arm's length contractual arrangements between the firms. The sales syndicate is, in fact, only one of several systems that cartels can use, and the system that is preferred will reflect technical and market conditions in the industry concerned.

The main weakness of a cartel is that there is normally an incentive for members to cheat – particularly by secretly invading one another's markets. A common form of cheating is to offer special discounts to large customers who can be supplied direct from the factory rather than through normal sales outlets. Complete financial consolidation of the monopolies not only improves the ability to monitor price cutting but practically eliminates at source the incentive to cheat. When plants are located in different countries, financial consolidation leads to the creation of an MNE. The main obstacle to financial consolidation is the attitude of governments, who are often opposed to foreign control of industries of strategic importance. Strategic industries such as shipping and aviation, and the mining of key raw materials, therefore tend to be dominated by international cartels rather than by MNEs. More generally, whenever the international political climate worsens, and the owners of MNEs begin to fear expropriation of their foreign assets, there is an incentive to split up MNEs and form a cartel instead. Conversely, when the political climate improves – as it did in postwar Europe – there will be a tendency to abandon cartels and establish MNEs in their place.

Other considerations include the heterogeneity of the product, and in particular the pace of new product innovation. It is far more difficult to control non-price competition than to control price competition, and this means that a cartel is liable to disintegrate under the pressure of administrative work when products are varied and changing. Progressive conditions favour the MNE over the cartel.

It is also difficult for a cartel to rationalize production in an industry that affords substantial economies of scale, since this may involve closing down members' plants and preventing the plants from being sold off cheaply to potential entrants. The MNE is therefore more effective than a cartel in industries characterized by economies of scale. Several other, more minor, considerations are considered in Casson (1985).

1.4   THE ROLE OF COLLUSION IN THE EXPLOITATION OF PROPRIETARY KNOWLEDGE

In the discussion of horizontal integration it was implicitly assumed that in each country there was some barrier to entry which afforded each domestic producer a degree of long-run monopoly power. In the theory of the MNE, analytical developments have focused upon one particular type of barrier to entry, namely possession by the firm of exclusive knowledge.

In the theory of the MNE, the concept of knowledge is a very broad one. To begin with, it includes at least three distinct types of know-how:

1 technical know-how, i.e. technological expertise in producing goods and services;
2 marketing know-how, i.e. expertise in selling things, and in purchasing them too; and
3 managerial know-how, i.e. expertise in administration, delegation, and all aspects of decision making not included in 1 or 2.

Know-how depends in turn on 'know-that' and 'know-who', and upon being 'known-of'. Know-that is the factual knowledge that underpins all successful problem-solving. Know-who is the knowledge of who is able to supply missing information and, more generally, of who is willing to buy or sell a resource that is not regularly traded on an organized market. Being known of means having a reputation that makes other people willing to offer information and, more generally, to become a trading partner. A reputation for product quality is invaluable in marketing a product, whilst a reputation for integrity and sound judgement is crucial in procuring finance for its production.

Since knowledge has a value there is, in principle, a market for it. In practice, the market for knowledge is a quite peculiar one. It has a number of features which, though they are not unique when considered separately, are not found all together in any other case:

1 there is considerable uncertainty about the quality of the product;
2 the product is indivisible, but the capacity of any one unit to generate services is theoretically infinite; this means that the supply of just one unit is normally sufficient to satiate the buyer's needs;
3 the supply of the product is irreversible; this means that it is not normally feasible to supply it 'on approval';
4 property rights to the product may be ill-defined and, where they exist, are costly to enforce;
5 the product may have multiple uses; and
6 the first unit is normally expensive to produce, but thereafter any one unit can normally reproduce itself fairly easily; this means that the marginal cost of supply is very low compared to the average cost; it also means that each customer becomes a potential competitor of the seller from whom he bought the product.

The problem of quality-uncertainty mentioned under 1 above has deep philosophical roots. All human knowledge is provisional. It is quite conceivable that a new discovery could be made tomorrow which would radically change the way that people look at things, or that the world itself could change so that some scientific law was superseded and became of only historical significance. The value we place upon what we 'know' therefore reflects, essentially, the strength of our belief that it will not shortly become obsolete. We cannot estimate the risk of obsolescence objectively, and so we can never be sure just how provisional our knowledge is. There is also a risk that past observations have been in error, or that previous interpretations of available evidence have been misguided, so that what we believe we 'know' is actually false. Different people may assess the risk of error differently. Given the same evidence, for example, one person who was naturally confident might infer the truth of a proposition that a more cautious person would be unwilling to accept.

What is sold in the knowledge market, therefore, is not a certainty, but a claim which may be either true or false. In the absence of a decisive test for truth, opinions may differ about the veracity of the claim. The seller may be sure of it, but the buyer will normally be sceptical, either because he distrusts the seller's judgement, or because he believes him to be deliberately concealing relevant evidence. Business ethics normally allow a seller to remain silent about factors which would diminish the value of the product, provided that in the seller's judgement the buyer is still being offered a reasonable deal (Nider, 1468). Most sellers, though, would probably go further than this in concealing relevant information.

This is a special case of a more general problem of quality uncertainty which affects nearly all markets. In the case of knowledge, the paramount quality of the product is its truth, although *provided that it is true*, other qualities are important as well, such as its relevance to commercial operations.

A common response to quality uncertainty is for the supplier to offer a small sample of the product to the buyer. In the case of knowledge, the only sample that can usually be offered is the knowledge itself, and once the buyer has acquainted himself with it he has no need to make a purchase. It is pointless for the seller to insist that the sample be 'returned' to him because the buyer can memorize the details. Indeed, once the buyer has memorized the details he is in a position to set up in competition with the seller to supply the knowledge to third parties.

In principle, it is possible to establish a system of property rights which separates the right to use or exploit knowledge from the right merely to gain access to it for purposes of assessment. In practice, though, it is difficult to define such rights precisely. Advertising such rights for sale, by drawing attention to the knowledge, may merely serve to increase the risk of illegal exploitation, and involve the seller in heavy litigation costs. The international patent system provides only limited protection in this respect, since its scope is limited both geographically, and by the type of knowledge and the uses to which it is put. Most knowledge can not only be put to immediate use but can be used in research to generate further knowledge. This new knowledge may open up new fields of application far more valuable that the original one, or may generate further developments in the same field which render the original knowledge obsolete. The patent system provides negligible protection against the use of knowledge in further research. As a result, there is a strong incentive for firms which have developed path-breaking innovations to keep them secret. The incentive is even stronger if the immediate application cannot be patented either.

The problem of marketing knowledge described above is known as the 'buyer uncertainty' problem (Buckley and Casson, 1976; Casson, 1979). Some writers on the MNE, notably Vaitsos (1974) have, however, used the term in an unfortunate way. They suggest that buyer uncertainty leads buyers to pay too much for their knowledge, whereas the theory actually suggests that the reverse will be the case. Typically, it is alleged that 'buyer uncertainty' leads government officials and private licensees in developing countries to pay too much for advanced technology obtained from Western enterprises. The argument rests upon the implicit assumption that the buyers are stupid enough to believe uncritically all of the claims made for the new technology, and that they fail to 'shop around' amongst alternative suppliers of technology before concluding a deal. In fact, the buyer uncertainty argument suggests that the seller of knowledge will normally have to compensate the buyer for suspicions about its quality which the seller, for strategic reasons, cannot afford to allay. The buyer may, of course, occasionally make a mistaken purchase. But because of the greater risks he perceives he will, on average, demand a higher return on imported technology, and this means that the price offered to the seller will be low. The low price explains, in turn, why corporations are reluctant to license and prefer, were possible, to undertake foreign investment instead.

The problem of buyer uncertainty is also an element in what Magee (1977) calls the 'appropriability problem' and Rugman (1981) calls the 'dissipation problem'. These terms are not, however, very specific, and might well apply to another problem which is logically quite distinct from buyer uncertainty, though often occurs along with it. This is the problem of efficiently decentralizing the exploitation of proprietary knowledge amongst a group of licensees.

Consider a firm which is licensing technical know-how to other producers in the same industry. It has invested heavily in developing the technology and, in the long run, cannot remain in the innovation business unless the rents accruing from the exploitation of technology cover the costs of its development. But because the marginal cost of utilizing technology is very low, unrestricted competition in the exploitation of the technology will eliminate practically all producer rent. A firm that has developed a new technology can therefore only recover its costs through the exercise of monopoly power.

Suppose that the firm nominates one licensee in each country. If the product cannot be traded, because of prohibitively high transport costs or tariffs, say, then each licensee has a national monopoly and in order to extract a monopoly rent the licensor can simply charge each licensee a lump sum annual fee equal to his expected supernormal profit. If the product can be traded then the licensor has a problem. He must prevent the licensees from invading one another's markets by bidding down prices, for in this way they will dissipate rents that could be appropriated by the licensor. The licensor can choose between two main strategies. One is to provide each licensee with an exclusive sales area, and to prohibit each licensee from selling outside this area. This restores the national monopoly situation described above. It is a simple concept in principle, but the export restrictions may be difficult to enforce in practice – particularly as such restrictions are illegal in many countries.

The second strategy is to structure the schedule of licence fees so that it discourages price cutting by raising the marginal costs of licensees. This is normally an inadequate substitute for export prohibition, but there is one case in which it is fully effective (Casson, 1979, ch. 2). This is where there are no barriers to trade in the product, so that all the licensees are competing in a single integrated market. In this case the licensor can appropriate the entire monopoly rent in the industry by levying a royalty on each unit produced that is equal to the mark-up of the industry-wide monopoly price on the licensee's minimum average cost of production. By basing the royalty on the minimum average cost of the most efficient licensee, the licensor can ensure that only the lowest cost producers in the industry remain in business.

The situation is illustrated in Figure 1.2. In the left-hand quadrant the curves MC and AC represent the cost structure of a least-cost licensee,

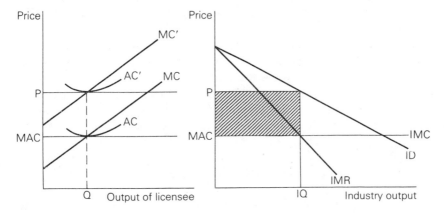

FIGURE 1.2 Licensing in a competitive industry

and they determine the minimum average cost MAC and its associated level of output Q. Equilibrium in the industry as a whole is illustrated in the right-hand quadrant. It is assumed that adjustments to industry output are effected by the entry and exit of least-cost licensees, and not by the adjustment of the licensees' outputs. Thus, if the indivisibility of firms is ignored, the industry marginal cost curve IMC is horizontal at a level MAC. The industry marginal revenue curve IMR is derived from the industry demand curve ID in the usual way. The intersection of IMR and IMC indicates that industry-wide profit is maximized with a price P and industry output IQ. This determines the equilibrium royalty rate P-MAC. The costs of the licensee, inclusive of royalty, are indicated by the curves MC' and AC'. It can be seen that a profit-maximizing licensee can just break even by continuing to produce an output Q. The full monopoly rent, measured by the area of the shaded rectangle in the right-hand quadrant, is appropriated by the licensor.

When transport costs are high but not prohibitive, and export restrictions are difficult to enforce, it is hard for a licensor to devise a structure of royalty fees which provides suitable incentives for licensees. To maximize monopoly rents in this situation it is normally necessary for the owner of the know-how to retain overall control of marketing. Instead of licensing production, it is better to subcontract it. The subcontractor, in this case, is an independent producer who, like a licensee, uses the client's technology to produce his output. But under subcontracting the output is sold back to the client and not directly to final consumers. The client can avoid the subcontractor appropriating some of the monopoly rents by offering the subcontractor a package deal in which the price is tailored to the average cost of producing a stipulated quantity of output. If the client does not know the structure of the subcontractor's costs then a similar result can be obtained by eliciting competitive tenders for various quantities of output. The economics of subcontracting are considered further in the next section.

The discussion suggests that the MNE is particularly effective as a vehicle for the commercial exploitation of knowledge when the knowledge is difficult to patent, and when the global market is difficult to segment because transport costs are low, export restrictions are illegal, etc. Conversely, licensing is a viable alternative to the MNE when patent protection is effective and market segmentation is easy.

1.5   VERTICAL INTEGRATION

The theory of VI applies the general insights of internalization theory to the specific question of the co-ordination of an upstream activity and a downstream activity within a production sequence. To fix ideas, it is assumed that the two activities are linked by a single intermediate product flow and that the intermediate product does not have any of the characteristics of a public good. It is useful to distinguish four main groups of factors which influence the decision to integrate: technical factors, market power factors, dynamic factors and fiscal factors.

Technical factors. The technical aspect of production gives rise to two distinct issues. The first is the inability of arm's length contracts to cope with rigidities and irreversibilities in the production process. The second is their tendency to distort substitution decisions concerning those parts of the process that are flexible.

A major instance of a rigidity in production is a fixed cost: i.e. a cost that has to be incurred for any positive level of production independently of how much output is actually produced. Consider a pair of independent producers trading an intermediate product in a competitive market. When one of the stages of production incurs high fixed costs, the intermediate product market may break down. The competitive price may distribute, to one of the producers, insufficient quasi-rent to cover his fixed costs of production. The other producer, however, may be making sufficient profit to compensate the first producer in full for his losses. Because of complementarities between the two stages, subsidization is necessary for efficiency. But a private subsidy may be difficult to negotiate and enforce, and the government may be reluctant to intervene. The natural solution is for the two producers to merge. The intermediate product market is internalized and the allocation problem is solved by a notional transfer of accounting profit between the two divisions of the consolidated firm.

The fixed cost problem becomes more serious when producers cannot recover the costs once they are committed to them. This is exemplified by investment in highly specific equipment which cannot be converted to alternative uses and has no scrap value. The committed firm becomes vulnerable to threats by its major customers to pull out from purchasing output derived from this equipment unless contracts are renegotiated on more favourable terms. Further problems arise when three or more parties become involved in multilateral bargaining: two or more parties may attempt to collude against the others, and if there are sufficient permutations of collusion, bargaining may become practically impossible because of the problem that game theorists describe as 'the empty core'. The natural solution in this case is for the firms to merge before any of them becomes committed to non-recoverable costs.

Another rigidity in production arises from the use of continuous flow technology, because the 'spill-over' effects of disruption at any stage are potentially great. To minimize the risk of disruption, it is important to secure the supply of inputs before the production run is set up. One solution is to hold sufficient inventory at the start to meet all foreseeable requirements, but this is very expensive in storage space and interest costs. It is more efficient to make forward purchases of inputs, but unfortunately contracts of this kind are difficult to enforce. The only way to achieve security is to take over the suppliers of the inputs through backward integration.

The rigidity of continuous flow technologies stems from the fact that the intermediate products created and annihilated within a continuous process cannot be stored. In many cases this is because the intermediate products are inherently perishable. The classic examples of this are processes relying on heat transfer and thermodynamic equilibrium. Perishability, however, may also be a quite independent source of rigidity. For example, the perishability of certain agricultural products – e.g. tropical fruits – means that their picking, boxing, transport and distribution must be planned carefully in advance. In principle, forward markets could do this. But in practice, it is precisely when products are perishable that forward markets tend to be least developed. The natural solution to the perishability problem is therefore VI.

Perishability is in turn related to another issue, namely uncertainty about the quality of the intermediate product. Perishable products are of uncertain quality to buyers who have not had the chance to inspect them prior to use: utilizing a perished product can be not only unproductive but hazardous as well. This is a special case of a more general problem. Sellers usually have a reasonable opportunity to inspect their product and so know more about its quality than do buyers. This understandably makes buyers suspicious about quality, particularly when the seller is likely to hold the best items back. Honest sellers may offer guarantees, but these are subject to abuse on both sides. Internalization of the intermediate product market gives the buyer unrestricted access to the seller's premises and thereby eliminates the asymmetry of information; it also removes the incentive to deceive the buyer in the first place.

Now consider substitution possibilities within the production process. In the absence of monopoly and monopsony power, and of externalities involving third parties, there is no reason to believe that arm's length pricing of intermediate products will distort producers' decisions with respect to input and output proportions. It may, however, distort their decisions regarding substitution over time and space.

Consider, for example, a sudden unforeseen increase in demand for downstream output, due to a major customer urgently bringing forward his order. The logical response, given sufficient flexibility, is to switch workers away from the upstream stage to the downstream stage, where they are able to increase the speed with which the intermediate product is finished off. It is difficult to see how, in practice, an arrangement of this kind could be operated by two independent producers relying upon simple arm's length contracts. If such situations recur frequently, there is a strong incentive to bring both stages of production under common control.

A similar argument applies if production at one of the stages is distributed over space, and the supply or the demand for the intermediate product is liable to fluctuate across locations. Precautionary inventories need to be held in order to smooth out the fluctuations. It is possible to economize on inventories if consignments of the intermediate product can be redirected at short notice, but this calls for very substantial information linkages between locations. It is much easier to meet the information requirements through a centralized organization that through a set of arm's length markets.

Technical factors are also associated with potential *diseconomies* of VI. The first diseconomy arises when internal markets are closed, so that the integrated enterprise is entirely self-sufficient in intermediate products: upstream plants do not sell to independent downstream plants, and downstream plants do not purchase from independent upstream plants. If plants at different stages operate most efficiently at different scales then to keep all plants at all stages operating efficiently it is necessary that the scale of the operation of the enterprise as a whole must be equal to the lowest common multiple (LCM) of the efficient scales at each stage. The LCM is usually so large that it exceeds the total market size and, even if it does not, the problem of generating sufficient investor confidence to finance an operation of this scale would be immense.

VI increases the diversity of the operations brought under a single management unit. This can impose enormous demands on decision makers responsible for overall corporate strategy. Two technical factors contribute to diversity: a multiplicity of joint inputs and joint outputs, which forces managers to buy and sell in many diverse markets; and economies of scope in the utilization of an indivisible asset, which involve the firm in the processing of a wide variety of products. Both of these factors therefore discourage VI.

Market power factors. The second group of factors is concerned with the distortion of intermediate product prices arising from the exercise of monopoly power. The exercise of monopoly power does not invariably lead to price distortion: a monopolist who levies a fixed charge for the right to purchase his product and then prices individual units at marginal cost encourages efficient use. But in practice few monopolists can achieve this level of sophistication; instead, they levy no fixed charge and exploit their power by pricing all units at a mark-up on marginal cost. This leads to wasteful substitution against the monopolized product at the downstream stage of production. If the downstream purchaser is also a monopolist (in the market for his own output) then the monopolistic price distortion will be further aggravated by a second mark-up on cost when the downstream ouput is sold to final buyers. The monopolist can avoid these distortions by integrating forward into the activities which utilize his intermediate product. The intermediate product is transferred between divisions of the integrated firm at a 'shadow price' which is equal to the marginal cost of upstream production: this shadow price is associated with a production plan that maximizes the joint profits of the integrated activities. A producer with monopsony buying power can avoid an analogous problem by integrating backwards into the production of the intermediate product he uses.

A monopolist seeking to reinforce barriers to entry may attempt to deter entry at adjacent stages. By refusing to buy intermediate inputs from independent producers, or to sell intermediate outputs to them, he forces new entrants to increase the scope of their operations to make themselves self-sufficient in intermediate products. This increases the scale of their investment, magnifies the risks, and raises their cost of capital. This strategy works only if the internal market is closed. It has already been noted, however, that when the internal market is closed, there is a problem of operating all the stages of production at the LCM of their efficient scales. The operation of a closed market, therefore, faces the firm with a trade-off between higher barriers to entry and higher costs of production. So far as final buyers are concerned, of course, the closed market, with its combination of high costs and high barriers to entry, represents the worst possible outcome.

Dynamic factors. The main dynamic factor governing VI is the novelty of the division of labour. The innovation of a new technology often modifies the division of labour and creates a new set of intermediate products. Because the various products are complementary, the producers must synchronize their investments to get all the plants on stream at the same time. It is difficult to achieve this using price incentives, since prices for intermediate products that have not yet been produced do not exist. It would be necessary to set up forward markets before the corresponding spot markets had begun operation. It is administratively simpler to use centralized planning, which normally involves starting up all stages of production under common ownership.

The influence of novelty on the level of VI is reinforced by some of the other factors already mentioned above. The entrepreneur who innovates a new division of labour may have a temporary monopoly of it, and he may be anxious to avoid the distortions associated with arm's length exploitation of monopoly power. If the new division of labour cannot be patented then he may also be reluctant to subcontract production in case the subcontractors steal his ideas, or make further improvements in their own name that he himself would have hoped to make. Novelty means that producers are inexperienced in the technology, and therefore poses serious problems of quality control – problems that would be exacerbated by subcontracting. In a novel division of labour it is unlikely that any of the intermediate products will have a close substitute. When production incurs substantial set-up costs, this makes it easy for one producer to hold the rest of the system to ransom by threatening to pull out at the last moment unless his contract is renegotiated on more favourable terms.

Fiscal factors. Of the fiscal factors influencing VI, the best known are the incentives for transfer pricing. Transfer pricing occurs when the accounting price at which intra-firm transactions take place differs from the price that would prevail in an arm's length market. Opportunities for transfer pricing arise when customs authorities are lax in checking the prices of intra-firm exports and imports, or when the intermediate products are so specific that there is no arm's length price to check against. The incentives to transfer pricing stem from the opportunity it provides to reduce the firm's global tax liability by transferring accounting profits to low-tax countries. It is also possible to reduce *ad valorem* tariff payments by understating the value of imports, and to avoid exchange controls by disguising capital transfers as expenditure flows.

Statutory intervention in intermediate product markets – e.g. through price regulation – also provides an incentive to VI, although the relevance of this factor in international trade is rather limited. Finally, host country restrictions on foreign direct investment, coupled with the risk of expropriation, provide a powerful disincentive to VI, especially where the plants that would be integrated are located in politically hostile countries.

1.6 THE GROWTH OF THE FIRM

The theory of internalization provides a useful basis for a theory of the growth of the firm. Consider the three functions of production, marketing and R and D. Each is linked to the others by flows of information, as indicated in Figure 1.3. The very high transaction costs associated with knowledge suggest that these activities will all be carried on within the same enterprise. The internalization of knowledge has important implications for growth. The firm's production division, for example, becomes committed to exploiting all the knowledge generated by its R and D division. If a steady level of expenditure on R and D generates a continuous flow of new knowledge then the consequent improvements to technology, product quality, etc., will steadily increase the firm's potential market (assuming a stable environment). This generates an 'acceleration'

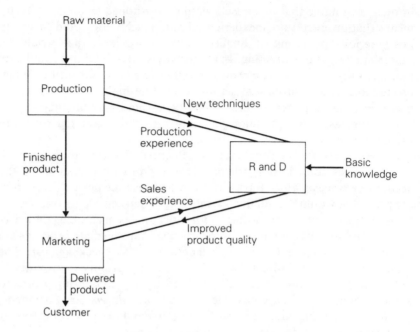

FIGURE 1.3   Integration of production, marketing and R and D
Source: Adapted from Buckley and Casson (1976, figure 2.1); see also Hymer (1979, figure 1)

mechanism by which the *level* of R and D activity governs the *rate of growth* of production.

The original objective of Buckley and Casson (1976) was, in fact, to use the concept of internalization to develop a model of the growth of the MNE. This objective has largely been abandoned by later writers on the MNE, who have taken the technological capability and the marketing and management skills of the firm as given (see Buckley, 1983b). An extension of the Buckley and Casson model is presented below.

It is assumed that the firm grows either by entering new markets or by increasing its penetration of existing ones. At any time $t > 0$, the firm produces a range of $N(t)$ different products, each of which is sold in $M(t)$ national markets. Each market is serviced by local production, so that $M(t)$ is also an index of the multinationality of the firm's operations. Each product has to be adapted, to some extent, to local conditions (though the adaptation may be quite superficial, and concerned only with packaging and branding to suit national tastes). The average quality of the firm's products, as perceived by consumers in a representative country, is measured somehow by an index $Q(t)$. It is assumed that $Q(t)$ is reflected in the extent of the typical product's penetration of a national market.

The technology of production is constant over time, as are factor prices. Production and marketing take place under constant returns to scale, so that the marginal cost of output is a constant, c, which is independent of time.

In each national market, the demand for each product is a function solely of its own price, all other relevant factors being assumed to be constant. It is assumed that the size of the market and the price dependence of demand is the same for all products and in all countries, and that the firm sets the same price, p, for all products everywhere. In the light of the other assumptions made about cost of production and demand, the optimizing strategy for the firm is in fact to maintain a constant price. It simplifies the presentation of the model, however, if this property of the solution is included amongst the assumptions. World-wide demand for the firm's output, $X(t)$, may thus be expressed in the form

$$X(t) = A(t) \, D(p) \tag{1.1}$$

where $D(p)$ satisfies the usual conditions of differentiability and negative slope. The factor $A(t)$ measures the scale of demand, as governed by the number of products, the number of national markets and the quality of the product

$$A(t) = M(t) \, N(t) \, Q(t) \tag{1.2}$$

R and D activity can be channelled in three main directions. First, it can be used to develop new products: a constant level of R and D activity directed in this way generates a constant logarithmic rate of change in the number of products, n. Secondly, it can be used to adapt existing products to the requirements of new national markets: a steady application of R and D in this direction generates a constant logarithmic rate of change in the number of national markets that are served, m. Finally, it can be directed to an overall improvement in the quality of products in the range. This increases the firm's penetration of each of the markets in which it operates; a steady application of R and D in this direction generates a constant logarithmic rate of change in the quality index, q. It follows that a constant level of R and D is associated with exponential growth in M, N and Q

$$M(t) = M_0 e^{mt} \tag{1.3a}$$
$$N(t) = N_0 e^{nt} \tag{1.3b}$$
$$Q(t) = Q_0 e^{qt} \tag{1.3c}$$

whence the firm's global output also grows exponentially

$$X(t) = A_0 D(p) e^{zt} \tag{1.4}$$

where

$$A_0 = M_0 N_0 Q_0 \qquad (1.5)$$

and

$$z = m + n + q \qquad (1.6)$$

As already noted, production and marketing costs, $C_1(t)$, vary directly with global production

$$C_1(t) = cX(t) \qquad (1.7)$$

The cost of R and D, C_2, is maintained constant over time, and so too are the rates of progress m, n, q. R and D takes place under decreasing returns to scale, and exhibits diminishing marginal rates of substitution as one line of research is pursued at the expense of the others. The costs of research are governed by a parameter, v, which is specific to the firm, and describes the particular aptitude of the research team for one kind of research rather than another. The cost function for R and D, therefore, is of the form

$$C_2 = C_2(m, n, q, v) \qquad (1.8)$$

The owners of the firm, it is assumed, can borrow and lend in a perfect capital market at a parametric rate of interest, r. This assumption is, of course, difficult to defend given the emphasis of this chapter on transaction costs. It may be taken, however, as a reasonable assumption for a company where management has an outstanding reputation in the capital market. The managers maximize the value of the firm, as measured by the present value, V, of the profit stream $\Pi(t)$, where

$$V = \int_0^\infty e^{-rt} \Pi(t) dt \qquad (1.9)$$

and

$$\Pi(t) = pX(t) - C_1(t) - C_2 \qquad (1.10)$$

To solve for the optimizing behaviour of the firm, it is convenient to form the Lagrangian which can be expressed, using 1.1–1.10 in the form

$$L = A_0(p - c) D(p)/(r - z) - C_2(m, n, q, v)/r + \lambda(m + n + q - z) \qquad (1.11)$$

The first-order condition with respect to p gives the familiar formula for the equilibrium monopoly price

$$p^* = (\eta/(\eta - 1))c \qquad (1.12)$$

where $\eta = -(dD/dp)/(p/D)$ is the own price elasticity of demand.

The first-order conditions with respect to m, n, q and λ determine the rates with which research progresses in each direction and the marginal cost of research, as functions of the desired rate of overall market growth and the parameter of research aptitudes. The marginal conditions reduce to

$$\partial C_2 / \partial m = \partial C_2 / \partial n = \partial C_2 / \partial q = \lambda \qquad (1.13)$$

and the solutions are

$$m = m(z, v) \qquad (1.14a)$$
$$n = n(z, v) \qquad (1.14b)$$
$$q = q(z, v) \qquad (1.14c)$$
$$\lambda = \lambda(z, v) \qquad (1.14d)$$

The determination of the direction of research strategy conditional upon the rate of overall market growth is illustrated in figure 1.4. The iso-cost surface ABC represents the various technically-efficient options for channelling R and D in different directions. It is concave to the origin, indicating that there are diminishing marginal rates of technical substitution

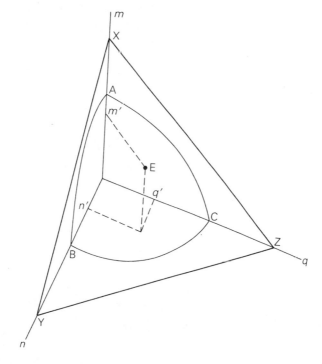

FIGURE 1.4   Determination of optimal research strategy conditional upon target rate of overall market growth

between different directions of research. The iso-z plane XYZ represents the different combinations of research progress which generate the target rate of overall market growth. The point of tangency, E, between ABC and XYZ indicates the optimizing research strategy, conditional upon z. The strategy m', n', q', represented by E achieves the target rate of overall market growth at minimum cost. This optimizing strategy may vary from firm to firm, according to the research aptitudes, as reflected in the shape and positioning of the iso-cost surface. A special case of this trade-off between directions of research has been noted by Wolf (1977), who has emphasized that the development of new products (i.e. an n-intensive strategy) and the transfer of existing products to new national markets (i.e. an m-intensive strategy) are alternative methods of achieving corporate growth. Pearce (1983) has tested this approach on a sample of the world's largest firms, and has obtained promising results.

   The optimizing rate of overall market growth is determined by the first-order condition with respect to z

$$A_0(p^* - c)\,D(p^*)/(r-z)^2 - \lambda(z,v) = 0 \qquad (1.15)$$

The solution of this equation is illustrated graphically in figure 1.5. Note that the marginal valuation of additional market growth, MV, approaches infinity as market growth, z, approaches the rate of interest, r, so that for an economically meaningful solution it is necessary that the marginal cost of market growth, MC, rises from below the marginal valuation to

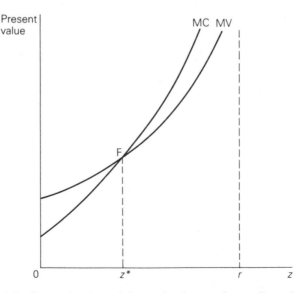

FIGURE 1.5   Determination of the optimal rate of overall market growth

above before z has reached r. The intersection F determines the equilibrium rate of overall market growth, z^*, and by back-substitution into (1.14) this gives the optimal research strategy m^*, n^*, q^*. The full solution is then of the form

$$p^* = p^*(c) \qquad (1.16a)$$
$$m^* = m^*(A_0, c, v) \qquad (1.16b)$$
$$n^* = n^*(A_0, c, v) \qquad (1.16c)$$
$$q^* = q^*(A_0, c, v) \qquad (1.16d)$$
$$z^* = z^*(A_0, c, v) \qquad (1.16e)$$

The model shows, therefore, how the initial size of the world market, A_0, the cost of production and marketing, c, and the research aptitudes of the firm's R and D division, v, simultaneously determine the firm's research strategy and its overall rate of market growth. The research strategy induces a constant proportional rate of growth in the firm's product range, the multinationality of its operations, and its overall product quality, as reflected in its average penetration of the markets which it supplies. Different firms, however, will pursue different strategies which reflect the different aptitudes of their researchers. Some firms will develop highly multinational operations based upon a narrow product range; others will develop a wide product range which is confined mainly to the home market, whilst still others will concentrate on further deepening their penetration of an existing market niche.

1.7   CONCLUSION

Judged by criteria of simplicity, elegance and mathematical sophistication, the theory of the MNE does not perform well. But judged by the criterion of relevance, it is highly successful. Indeed, the lack of elegance in the theory is to some extent a reflection of the complexity of the issues with which it deals – and the fact that it does full justice to them. The theory is not devoid of aesthetic appeal, however. At a conceptual level there are underlying themes which give an overall coherence to the theory. The subjectivity of knowledge, the universality of transaction costs, the assumptions that purposeful human action encourages the minimization of overall transaction costs, are all very general insights which can be applied to other fields as well. To apply them successfully, however, they need to be combined with specific assumptions about transaction costs, and the appropriate assumptions vary from case to case.

The theory also has a definite logical structure. The direction taken by R and D depends upon the aptitude of the firm's research team, and this determines the strategic issues of organizational form that arise in exploiting the knowledge generated by R and D. For knowledge which is difficult to patent, commercial exploitation requires its deployment to be administered by 'vertical' integration between production and R and D, whilst maximizing monopoly returns calls for horizontal integration amongst producers at different locations. However, the incentive to integrate does not arise solely from proprietary knowledge; it may also be due to more general problems, such as the desire to provide quality assurance through ownership of upstream production facilities.

This framework generates a range of specific models, rather than just a single one. Each of the models is based upon essentially plausible assumptions. Taken together, moreover, the specific models collectively explain all of the stylized facts that were summarized in box 1.1. The relevant explanations are tabulated in box 1.2. Thus – strange as it may seem to many economists – the theory of the MNE is an example of an economic theory which is not merely plausible, but actually 'works'. There still remain gaps in the theory, but by rigorous analysis of special topics these gaps may be filled in due course.

BOX 1.2   Explanations of the stylized facts presented in box 1.1

---

1   HISTORICAL PATTERN OF GROWTH

MNEs have replaced cartels in the post-war period because (a) greater political stability in Europe has reduced the expropriation risk of foreign direct investment, (b) improvements in communications and management techniques have facilitated tighter control of international operations, and (c) cartel arrangements are ill-suited to the growing number of progressive industries in which there is a proliferation of new and/or differentiated products. Similar changes explain the switch from sales agencies to wholly-owned sales subsidiaries.

2   COUNTRY OF ORIGIN AND THE STRUCTURE OF INTERNATIONAL PRODUCTION

US-based MNEs exploit mass production technologies, harnessed to mass-market sales methods, originally developed in the large multi-ethnic US market, and therefore well adapted to other large markets in developed countries – notably the European Community market. European-based MNEs processed the raw materials obtained from colonies, and integrated backwards to secure further supplies against pre-emption by rivals. In the 1950s and 1960s they learnt mass production methods from US enterprises, and during the early 1970s developed a temporary technological leadership

continued

Box 1.2 continued

of their own in a few industries. The Japanese MNEs have taken mass production methods one stage further than US firms. They have evolved new methods of managing a complex inter-industry division of labour through tight inventory management and quality control. They have split up production processes within an industry so that different stages can be carried out at different locations. Unskilled labour-intensive operations have been concentrated upon low-wage newly industrializing countries.

3 INDUSTRY CHARACTERISTICS

These charateristics reflect the fact that technological progress derives from R and D and that successful product innovation (and differentiation) relies heavily on advertising. Mass production methods make intensive use of supervisory staff and economize on manual labour. The high set-up costs associated with the dedicated production line generate economies of scale, which are reflected in high industrial concentration. The high fixed costs of R and D, and the prevalence of patents and trade secrets also create barriers to entry. While the market is expanding, rivalry between the firms behind the barrier generates innovation. (If the market is static in future, however, inter-firm collusion may result.)

4 FIRM CHARACTERISTICS

Because knowledge has the characteristics of a 'public good', the firm with privileged knowledge tends to become multinational. Thus the multinationality of the firm discriminates, within a progressive industry, between the firms that have privileged knowledge, and those that do not. The MNEs, therefore, are the firms that highlight the characteristics of a progressive industry. Firms that are skilful in differentiating products to local conditions will tend to concentrate on this to the exclusion of new product development. Conversely, firms that are skilful in product development will tend to hand over their products, through licensing or profit-sharing arrangements, to firms that are good at local adaptation. Thus specialization according to corporate comparative advantage, in the field of R and D, generates an inverse relationship, in a cross-section of firms, between the multinationality of the firm and the range of its products.

5 CONTRACTUAL ALTERNATIVES TO THE MNE

Licensing is easiest when patent protection is secure, and when the global market is easily segmented. Patent protection is fairly secure for process

continued

Box 1.2 continued

technologies and the printed word, and segmentation is easy for services since they are difficult to transport. Joint ventures are a useful method of rationalizing production in an oligopoly, or sharing risks under bilateral monopoly, when there are significant economies of sale. Political opposition to foreign control of production – particularly in developing countries – has recently encouraged the exploitation of these alternative contractual arrangements.

6   VERTICAL INTEGRATION

There are economies of scale in smelting aluminium, copper and tin, but the supplies of ores are more concentrated for aluminium and copper than they are for tin. The resolution of bilateral monopoly conflict encourages integration in the first two cases, therefore, but not in the third. Economies of continuous flow, and the hazards of transportation, are more significant in oil than in coal, so that centralized control of the sequential stages is more important. Integration is therefore more common in oil. Bananas pose serious problems of quality control which can be resolved through skilled plantation management and the integration of growing, shipping and ripening. In the case of other agricultural products, the problems are not so acute. Agribusiness operations by vertically integrated MNEs are therefore confined mainly to bananas (though a few other instances are known).

2

General Theories of the Multinational Enterprise: A Critical Examination

2.1 INTRODUCTION

The previous chapter has demonstrated some of the strengths of the economic theory of the MNE. It has been shown that the theory forms the basis for a general analysis of how firms co-ordinate activities over space. To realize its full potential, however, much further work needs to be done. The success of future developments depends upon their being built upon secure foundations. These foundations are constituted by the current literature on the subject.

The main object of this chapter is to alert future researchers to certain weaknesses in recent work on the MNE, and to suggest ways of remedying them. Three sources of weakness can be identified. First, too much is claimed for the theory in its existing state of development. The limitations of the theory do not seem to be fully appreciated by those who are most zealous in expounding it. This is particularly conspicuous in the case of recent writers who claim to have produced new general theories of the MNE. There are several rival contenders for the title of the most general theory. Dunning's 'eclectic theory' (Dunning, 1977; 1981) vies with Rugman's generalized internationalization theory (Rugman, 1981) and Teece's multinational version of Williamson's 'markets and hierarchies' theory (Teece, 1982; Williamson, 1975; 1981). Kojima's macroeconomic theory of foreign direct investment is more specifically concerned with the differences between Japanese and Western MNEs (Kojima, 1973; 1978) and as it has already been critically examined elsewhere (Buckley, 1983a; 1985c) only passing reference is made to it here. Another contender is the synthesis between internalization theory and neoclassical location theory originally proposed by Buckley and Casson (1976) and elaborated by Casson (1979). This last approach has never really claimed to be general, however, which is just as well given the very restrictive assumptions upon which it is based.

The second weakness is a superficial one, and is shared by many other branches of modern economic theory. It is that some of the authors direct too much effort into artificially differentiating their theories from others, and spend too little time on original analytical developments. The same concept appears in different guises in different theories, so that the essential simplicity and parsimony of the conceptual framework is lost in the proliferation of rival jargon.

By far the most serious weakness, however, is that logical errors remain undetected in some versions of the theory. These errors persist in spite of the abundance of literature reviews – Buckley (1981; 1983b), Calvet (1981), Caves (1982), Hennart (1982), Rugman (1982; 1986) – to name just a few. Even the existence of a 'second generation' literature reviewing the reviewers (Kay, 1983) has not ironed out all the problems. The length of time for which errors persist undetected is one indication of the general standard of theorizing, and in this respect the theory of the MNE does not perform very well.

The first part of this chapter develops in detail these criticisms of existing theory, while the second part adopts a more constructive posture, and indicates the kind of developments which are needed if the claims for generality that have already been made are to be fully justified. The developments outlined in the second half of this chapter constitute the impetus for the work reported in the remainder of this book.

2.2   THE CONCEPT OF OWNERSHIP ADVANTAGE

Dunning's eclectic theory asserts that three different types of advantage are necessary to explain the existence of MNEs: ownership advantage, internalization advantage and location advantage. Other writers, such as Buckley and Casson, and Rugman, deny that ownership advantage is necessary.

This conflict arises because of the unconventional way in which Dunning attempts to synthesize the Hymer–Kindleberger and internalization theories. Recall from chapter 1 that the Hymer–Kindleberger theory began as an attempt to explain post-war US corporate investment in Western European manufacturing industry. Initially, two main questions were posed:

1 Why do the investing firms produce in Europe rather than in the US?
2 How can they compete with indigenous producers, given the additional costs of doing business abroad?

The answer to the first question is that the investments were import substituting. Sourcing the foreign market by local production was made profitable by the avoidance of transport costs and tariffs. In some cases it also provided access to cheaper labour. Although labour productivity may have been lower in Europe – due partly to the lower scale of production – labour was still relatively cheap because the combination of the dollar shortage and nominal wage stickiness in the US (Gordon, 1982) made the US own-product wage very high. In Dunning's terminology, Europe enjoyed a location advantage relative to the US. The answer to the second question lies in the technology gap: the cost to US firms of doing business abroad was offset by better product design and lower costs arising from superior technology and management. In Dunning's terminology, the US firms possessed ownership advantages relative to their European rivals.

These answers lead naturally to a third question, posed by Hymer but neglected by Kindleberger, namely:

3 Why do US firms not license their ownership advantages to European firms?

Dunning invokes internalization theory to answer this question. Following other writers, he identifies various disincentives to licensing, which are associated with 'imperfections' in the market for knowledge. The benefits of avoiding these imperfections confer 'internalization advantage' on the firm.

This argument demonstrates that the three advantages identified by Dunning are *sufficient* to explain multinational operations, but it does not demonstrate their necessity. Ownership advantage is not necessary because a combination of internalization and location advantage is itself sufficient to explain multinational activities. For example, the theory of vertical integration summarized in section 1.5 shows that when profit tax rates are not harmonized between two countries, firms in an industry whose product is mined in one country and processed in another have an incentive to merge in order to minimize joint tax liabilities through transfer pricing. In this case, transfer pricing coupled with locational factors predicts that a multinational can compete successfully with independent indigenous firms.

Dunning's error arises because he underestimates the power of internalization theory. He does not realize that internalization liberates the theory of the MNE from dependence on the postulates of the Hymer–Kindleberger theory. Dunning implicitly retains the assumption that the MNE incurs additional costs of doing business abroad. But this assumption is no longer crucial because these costs are simply one component of the overall cost of integrating activities in different countries, and it is only the overall cost that is crucial to the theory. Likewise it is unnecessary to retain the postulate that an MNE possesses an ownership advantage such as a superior technology because the benefits of internalization are themselves sufficient, in principle, to outweigh the costs of internalization and so make integrated operations profitable.

The necessity of the ownership advantage can be salvaged if the term is redefined so that ownership advantage includes the advantage derived from internalization itself. Dunning has chosen to adopt this strategy, though the fact that he has done so does not seem to have been appreciated by many of those who have discussed his views. This strategy has the disadvantage that it reduces the necessity of ownership advantage to a mere tautology. But its effect is, in practice, worse than this, because it fudges a distinction between two different kinds of advantage.

Both Hymer (1976) and Caves (1971) emphasized the monopolistic nature of the ownership advantage, Hymer pointing to privileged access to proprietary technology, and Caves to special skills in the design and marketing of differentiated products. Other writers emphasized non-monopolistic advantages, for example Aliber (1970) who argued that stockholder preferences for strong-currency assets gave an advantage to all firms whose parent company was based in a strong currency area. In this context, internalization must be treated as a non-monopolistic advantage, since internalization is, in principle, available to any firm.

The distinction between monopolistic and non-monopolistic advantages is crucial in the interpretation of the theory. 'Advantage' is a relative concept – someone always has an advantage *relative* to someone else – and it is important to specify who that someone else is. When a foreign firm enjoys a monopolistic advantage, such as a proprietary technology, it enjoys an advantage not only over indigenous firms but over all firms everywhere. On the other hand, a foreign firm which enjoys a non-monopolistic advantage may enjoy an advantage only over indigenous firms. This means, for example, that in an industry where there are no indigenous firms, none of the foreign firms need have any kind of advantage relative to the other firms actually operating in the industry. In applied work on multinationals, therefore, it is incorrect to assume that each multinational in the industry must have some kind of advantage relative to the others. This is true if the advantages are monopolistic, but untrue if they are not.

The interpretation of internalization as a source of non-monopolistic advantage leads to some tortuous semantics when Dunning discusses the place of vertical integration in his theory. For the question arises whether a vertical integration advantage has itself to be internalized when it is exploited. Dunning's answer appears to be in the affirmative, simply on the grounds that it is self-evidently true. It is one of the anomalies of Dunning's theory that he uses internalization theory to answer the question 'Why does a firm with the ability to vertically integrate not license the advantage to another firm?'. By focusing upon this almost meaningless question, he diverts attention from the substantial issue, which concerns the nature of the factors which generate economies of vertical integration in the first place.

To summarize, Dunning's eclectic theory implicitly denies the original powerful insight of Coase, which is that internalization is the *raison d'être* of the firm. Dunning thus uses Coasian theory in a thoroughly non-Coasian way. Dunning is only one of several writers to do this, however. Many writers employ internalization merely to explain why a company may avoid licensing a monopolistic advantage. They often speak of 'internalizing an advantage' as though internalization had its everyday connotation of 'keeping to oneself'. They fail to recognize that in the theory of the firm it is markets that are internalized and not the advantages themselves.

Nevertheless a paradox arises here. Empirical work on the MNE regularly points to the importance of ownership advantages – even in pre-war investments, where vertical integration was an important factor too. The evidence also suggests that managers rarely perceive licensing as a crucial issue – the advantages of internalizing the market for know-how are usually believed to be heavily outweighed by the costs. The resolution of this paradox may lie in identifying a rather different question, namely:

4 Why is it that certain firms are persistently successful and grow large while other firms are only short-lived or always remain small?

Dunning is on firmer ground when he argues that the *success* of MNEs *vis-à-vis* non-MNEs rests on their possession of ownership advantages. His analysis of internalization advantages may be reinterpreted as a statement of the fact that managerial skills in organizing internal markets contribute to the profitability of the enterprise. In this context, however, it is the superiority of the firm's management skills over those of its rivals that is crucial, rather than the superiority of management over markets in general. This brings the analysis almost full cycle, back to Hymer's original analysis. It suggests that, after all, it is the monopolistic advantage of superior management rather than non-monopolistic advantage that is crucial in explaining success. It identifies Dunning's contribution as pointing out that superior management as well as superior technology is a factor in the long-term success of the enterprise.

This interpretation of Dunning is supported by a reconsideration of the two questions posed at the beginning of this section. It is worth noting that while question 1 concerns managerial choice between two alternative strategies of sourcing a foreign market, question 2 is not directly concerned with managerial choice, but with the ability of the firm to survive in a foreign market environment. The fact that question 2 is concerned specifically with competition from indigenous producers does not alter the fact that the basic issue is the survival of the firm. Questions of managerial choice and questions of survival are logically quite distinct. Internalization theory represents an extension of the theory of choice to encompass the choice, within each market, of the appropriate contractual arrangement. Ownership advantage, however, is not concerned with choice, but with the performance of the firm once managerial choices have been made. Its proper place is not within the subdivision of the theory that deals with choice, but within the subdivision that deals with the success, and the consequent growth, of the firm.

2.3   THE CONCEPT OF INTERNALIZATION

It might appear that our critique of the ownership advantage concept indicates support for Rugman's view that internalization alone constitutes the general theory of the MNE (Rugman, 1981; 1982). Rugman's work is notable for its lively and readable presentation of the major analytical concepts. Unfortunately, however, Rugman's use of the internalization concept is not always consistent. Internalization has different connotations in different branches of economics. *Internalization of a market* refers to the replacement of an arm's length contractual relationship (i.e. the external market) by managerial co-ordination within the firm (i.e. the internal market). Internalization of an externality, however, refers to an improvement in social efficiency achieved by removing a defect or distortion in the price system.

The first concept of internalization is used in industrial organization theory and the second in the economics of welfare. Writers who discuss the welfare implications of alternative forms of industrial organization need always to keep the distinction between these two concepts in mind. Rugman, unfortunately, confuses them at crucial points in his analysis.

In 'textbook' welfare economics, the internalization of an externality is often illustrated by the creation of a market for some hitherto unpriced good (or unpriced bad, in the case of pollutants, etc). It is now widely recognized, however, that it is usually because of the high costs of defining and enforcing property rights, and administering transactions in these rights, that a market price did not exist in the first place. This suggests that, in more general terms, an externality is internalized by replacing a set of institutional arrangements with high transaction costs by a new set of arrangements with lower transaction costs. The creation of an entirely new market then becomes a special case in which the original transaction costs were so high that they prohibited any trade. It can then be shown, quite generally, that if all other markets function perfectly, a reduction of transaction costs will improve social efficiency.

There is some disagreement in the welfare literature as to whether the internalization of an externality involves a reduction in transaction costs of *any* kind (as suggested by Mishan, 1976, ch. 16) or whether it involves a reduction in transaction costs specifically through the unification of ownership (as suggested by Ng, 1983, p. 175). If the former interpretation is used then the internalization of an externality does not imply the creation of an internal market, whereas if the latter interpretation is used then it does. The first interpretation will be used below.

The internalization of a market does not, in general, internalize an externality. Consider, for example, the internalization of a market in collusive agreements. If two firms wish to restrict output in an industry, an arm's length agreement may be easy to cheat on, and so internalization of collusion through horizontal integration may serve to reduce transaction costs (see section 1.3). If the implementation of collusion helps to encourage R and D in the industry, then social welfare may, on balance, be improved, but if the two firms are simply taking advantage of barriers to entry created by statutory intervention or high transport costs borne by imported products then social welfare is likely to fall. In such cases, therefore, internalization of collusion may significantly reduce social welfare.

An example of Rugman's misuse of internalization is in his discussion of tariffs. He argues that the distortion of international relative prices by tariffs creates an externality which can be 'internalized' by 'internalizing' international markets within the firm. Notice here how the use of the same term in two different ways can be used to give plausibility to the argument. If the argument is placed on a more rigorous footing, it can be seen that under certain conditions the argument is indeed correct, but it is not universally correct as Rugman appears to suggest. Because many tariffs on intermediate products are levied on an *ad valorem* basis, internalization of intermediate product trade allows the firm to minimize the distorting effect of tariffs through transfer pricing. But the tariffs themselves may be already correcting for distortions elsewhere in the system. Moreover, the ability of some firms to benefit from transfer pricing, whilst others cannot, may lead to trade being diverted to firms which are actually less efficient, in a technical sense, than those which are able to benefit from transfer pricing. Transfer pricing also encourages firms to invest heavily in accounting systems which minimize tax and tariff liabilities rather than systems which provide management with accurate information on opportunity costs. Under certain conditions, therefore, the internalization of international markets may well reduce social efficiency.

Although Rugman is seeking a general theory, he is actually very restrictive in his interpretation of internalization. He often assumes, for example, that the external alternative to the internal market is missing altogether. He asserts, for example, that 'the MNE is in the business of bypassing externalities by creating an internal market to replace *missing* external markets' (Rugman, 1981, p. 27, my italics) but in his defence, however, it may be said that Rugman's recent empirical work includes studies of the oil and drugs industries (Rugman, 1983a; 1983b) where he shows that the crucial markets internalized within the firm do indeed appear to be missing altogether outside it. This is an empirical issue on which further research must be done before Rugman's restrictive view of internalization can be fully supported.

Rugman also identifies internalization of a market with centralization of control. He fails to recognize that when ownership is unified, control can still be decentralized using shadow prices or other kinds of flexible budgetary control within the ownership unit. He also claims that R and D activity must be centralized within the MNE, a claim that seems contrary to his emphasis elsewhere upon the benefits of the international division of labour within the MNE.

2.4   THE SYNTHESIS OF INTERNALIZATION AND THE ORTHODOX THEORY OF TRADE

The current economic theory of the MNE has developed independently of orthodox trade theory. Attempts by trade theorists to develop a theory of the MNE by grafting capital movements onto the Heckscher–Ohlin–Stolper–Samuelson (HOSS) model have signally failed. This is because the HOSS model stands firmly in the neoclassical tradition. There are no transaction costs in the HOSS model, and so there are no grounds for distinguishing between direct and indirect investment. This is a point altogether ignored by Kojima (1973; 1978). Yet it is clearly unsatisfactory for the theory of the MNE to remain divorced from mainstream trade theory, and a number of efforts have been made to integrate them.

The simplest way to integrate internalization theory with the HOSS model is to recognize that the case for multinational operations rests upon the relative and not the absolute costs of transacting (Casson, 1979).

Suppose that, apart from transaction costs, the HOSS assumptions apply. If it is assumed that, although certain institutional arrangements may be costly, the cheapest method of transacting is always a costless one, then the HOSS approach to the location of production remains valid. So long as the MNE plans efficiently, it will mimic the location of production that would prevail under arm's length contracts, as described by HOSS. (This result is analogous to the theoretical equivalence between competitive general equilibrium and idealized central planning that was discovered in the 1930s.)

The result is, of course, of limited interest because of the strong assumptions upon which it is based. It becomes more interesting when the HOSS model is modified to allow for technology gaps and for intermediate product trade. With these modifications, the basic insight of the HOSS model – that trade in final products can substitute for factor movements – is augmented by two further insights:

1 Technology transfer can substitute either for trade in final products or for factor movements.
2 Intermediate product trade can substitute for trade in final products and also for technology transfer and factor movements.

Insight 1 encompasses the case where the export of technology through foreign direct investment substitutes for the export of high-technology products, as occurs in the 'maturing product' phase of the product cycle (Vernon, 1966). In this way the modified HOSS model can shed light on the global implications of import-substituting high technology investment, as discussed in section 2.2.

Insight 2 encompasses the case of internationally rationalized production, exemplified by an assembly line supplied with components from a number of different locations. The potential for rationalized production in manufacturing has existed since the development of mass production and interchangeable parts in the early part of the century, but because of political instability and obstacles to trade in the inter-war period, it was not until the creation of customs unions and free trade areas in the 1960s and 1970s that the potential has been fully exploited.

It is not difficult to integrate the modified HOSS model with the modern theory of international finance. Both theories, being neoclassical, emphasize that markets facilitate functional specialization. Each new market that is created permits a further separation of functions. The introduction of an international market in risk capital and an international market in loanable funds demonstrates that the provision of risk bearing and the provision of 'abstinence' or 'waiting' can be separated from the organization of production and trade (Casson, 1982b). This result has two important consequences.

First, it demonstrates that a firm can obtain a controlling equity stake in a foreign plant merely by exchanging its debenture debt for equity debt in the foreign country. As a result, what is called foreign direct investment may involve no international movement of capital at all. Foreign direct investment may occur simply at the expense of foreign indirect investment, leaving the total stock of foreign investment completely unchanged.

Secondly, it means that when financial markets are globally integrated, a firm may produce in one set of countries, be funded by debenture-holders in another set of countries, and have its risks borne by equity-holders in yet another set of countries. This has serious implications for people who wish to talk of 'US' multinationals or 'British' multinationals, since an important element in multinationality is that ownership, funding and production operations can each have quite distinct patterns of multinationality.

The main problem with the attempted synthesis of transaction costs and neoclassical theory is that the synthesis concedes too much to the neoclassical position. The focus in neoclassical theory is upon markets, and upon the functional specialization that markets permit: the firm is of no intrinsic interest. All the theory requires is a representative firm that can be regarded as a 'black box'. The 'black box' must have an upward sloping long-run supply curve of output and downward sloping long-run derived demand curves for factors, and that is all.

The synthesis achieved with transaction cost theory makes it possible to predict, in principle, the institutional arrangement that will prevail within the black box, but only at the expense of assuming that the institutional arrangement will be one in which the management function is totally trivial. The triviality of management follows both from the fact that the institutional arrangement is by assumption costless, and also from the fact that since the firm's environment is purely neoclassical, all relevant information about the environment is encapsulated in freely available market prices (or a fully known demand curve in the case of product monopoly). In the neoclassical world, the invisible hand of the market does practically all the managing that is required. One cannot have an economic theory of the MNE that includes both the neoclassical theory of location and a realistic theory of management.

2.5 MARKETS AND HIERARCHIES THEORY

Williamson's markets and hierarchies theory is genuinely differentiated from the other theories reviewed in this chapter by the fact that it integrates internalization theory, not with theories of trade and market structure, but with other quite distinctive strands of economic thought. Bounded rationality, for example, which has been successfully used by Simon (1982; 1983) to interpret managerial behaviour in public and private bureaucracies, is used to explain the kind of organizational structure that is appropriate for the administration of internal markets. Williamson also develops the traditions of American institutional economies, and in particular Commons's contractual analysis of labour unions and industrial relations (Commons, 1934). This allows him to follow Coase in using internalization to analyse not only vertical and horizontal integration but also the nature of the employment contract.

Apart from his somewhat tortuous terminology, the main problem with Williamson's presentation is the lack of any formal model which specifies precisely the technical structure of the production process and the nature of the market environment which is assumed. This is important because these factors govern the logic of the decisions that managers must make. If, for example, a firm faces the same duopolistic rival in many different national markets for its product then interdependence between marketing decisions will be far greater than if the firm faces many quite separate rivals in each market (see chapter 3). This suggests that, so far as the geographical decentralization of marketing decisions is concerned, a unitary configuration, which centralizes marketing decisions, will more often be preferred to a multi-divisional configuration when rivalry stems from a single duopolist than when it does not. The absence of formal modelling inhibits the deduction of testable hypotheses of this kind, and so restricts the explanatory power of the theory. (For further information on the organizational structure of MNEs, see Caves, 1982, ch. 3.)

In terms of theoretical generality, it is obvious that a theory of the multinational enterprise must in principle be more general than a theory of the uninational enterprise, because the concept of the multinational enterprise embraces the concept of the uninational enterprise as a special case. Williamson, however, seems to be unaware of the pitfalls of generalizing from a special case. In outlining the application of his theory to the MNE, he fails to emphasize sufficiently the special problems, and peculiar opportunities, of managing across different legal jurisdictions and different fiscal systems – a most unfortunate omission, in view of the emphasis he places elsewhere on the firm as a unit of governance, and the parallel this suggests between the firm and the nation state.

When discussing the MNE, Williamson follows other writers in focusing almost exclusively on the role of transferable proprietary know-how, with the result that he often simply articulates earlier results in less familiar jargon. Indeed, he appears to be quite unaware of the earlier literature. As recently as 1985, Williamson has reiterated the view that 'transaction cost economising and organisational form issues have been relatively neglected in efforts to assess MNE activity' (Williamson, 1985, p. 290).

This approach is, in fact, the cornerstone of the theory which has evolved since Hymer's work in 1960 (Hymer, 1976), and is summarized in chapter 1.

Williamson's work does, in fact, complement quite nicely the synthesis of neoclassical location theory and internalization theory presented in the previous section. His approach is strongest where the other is weakest, and vice versa. For example, neoclassical location theory provides a formal model which describes the nature of the location decisions that managers must make. Williamson's theory, on the other hand, provides a model of how managers make decisions, but lacks the model that describes the environment in which the decisions must be made. Putting the two together should provide new insights into locational decision making within the MNE.

The moral, therefore, is fairly clear. Rivalrous theorizing, in which each theorist claims to treat all aspects of the MNE, has discouraged the synthesis of the insights afforded by the different theories. Further work which seeks to develop such a synthesis should pay substantial dividends. Some particularly promising avenues of research of this kind are outlined in the remaining sections of this chapter.

2.6   MARKET STRUCTURE:
OLIGOPOLY AND BILATERAL MONOPOLY

It is evident that recent theoretical work has been preoccupied with the internal organization of the MNE. External market structure has not been ignored, but assumptions about it have tended to be rather naïve. For example, it is typically assumed that in each country the firm operates in a competitive labour market and enjoys monopoly power in the product market.

Neither of these assumptions is accurate. To begin with, many MNEs are involved in oligopolistic product markets in which they act upon, and react to, the competitive strategies of rival firms. In some cases the product of each oligopolist is differentiated from those of the others, whereas in other cases it is not. The extent of differentiation typically declines as the product moves through its lifecycle (Vernon, 1966; 1974; 1979). Entry barriers into the industry may also decline as the product matures. In industries with constant or decreasing returns to scale this means that the market will tend to become atomistically competitive, whereas with increasing returns, but low sunk costs, it may merely become more contestable (Baumol, Panzar and Willig, 1982). Although previous writers have discussed in general terms the effects of the maturing of the product on market structure, and hence on MNE behaviour, comprehensive models of this process have not yet been developed.

A crucial aspect of MNE rivalry has already been alluded to, and that is that the firm is liable to encounter the same oligopolistic rivals in each national market. Thus oligopolistic rivalry proceeds simultaneously on several fronts. This provides the firm with an opportunity for linking its strategies in different markets to outwit a rival which is pursuing independent strategies in each market. It also allows a firm to learn from its encounter with a rival in one market in order to modify its behaviour towards that rival in another market (Porter, 1981; 1985). Global rivalry of this kind may lead managers to develop a special strategic skill – in Dunning's terminology, an ownership advantage which is specific to the successful oligopolistic MNE. Theoretical developments along these lines are explored in chapter 3.

In the context of the labour market, some MNEs may be such large employers in a locality that they enjoy considerable monopsony power – particularly when they demand certain special skills much more intensively than do other firms. In many cases, however, the MNE must recruit unionized labour, and this can lead to a bilateral monopoly situation in the locality. Few unions are organized on an international basis, however, and so it is difficult for labour to pursue a co-ordinated international bargaining strategy against the MNE. The MNE can therefore play off a labour union in one locality against a labour union in another locality without fearing that the two unions will collude by refusing to accept work that has been switched from one locality to the other. It has been argued that the ability of the MNE to co-ordinate bargaining across localities is a major source of monopsony profit (Sugden, 1983). Further research is necessary, however, in order to formulate the argument in a comprehensive and rigorous way.

2.7 MARKETING STRATEGY AND VERTICAL INTEGRATION

Internalization theory rightly emphasizes the role of transaction costs in intermediate product markets, but it must be recognized that transaction costs arise in both factor markets and final product markets too. Because firms trade with *households* in factor and final product markets, rather than with other firms – as in intermediate product markets – opportunities for internalization are more limited (though they are present to some degree). It is still possible, however, for firms to make a contribution to reducing transaction costs in these markets. There are certain measures which, when undertaken by a firm, reduce household transaction costs by more than they raise the firm's transaction costs. In a final product market, for example, mass media advertising may reduce consumer's search costs by more than the cost of advertising incurred by the firm. In such cases the firm can take the initiative in minimizing *overall* transaction costs by increasing the proportion of the transaction costs which it bears itself.

Social efficiency requires that the firm incurs transaction costs up to the margin where the additional cost to the firm is just equal to the savings achieved by the households. Social efficiency will only be achieved, however, if the firm can appropriate the savings it affords to the households in the form of a lower wage or a higher product price. It must appropriate at least enough of these savings to cover its own costs.

The costs incurred by the firm in reducing household transaction costs are not necessarily confined to the market in which the household is involved. They may also be incurred in markets in which the firm alone is involved, and even in markets which are completely internal to the firm. This is particularly significant in connection with the firm's marketing activity.

An important aspect of marketing is the reduction of household transaction costs in final product markets. Two strategies in particular contribute to reducing household transaction costs:

1   the provision of a reliable product, which does not require to be returned regularly for servicing or replacement, and
2   the specialization of responsibility for product reliability upon a single reputable individual or organization, to whom all complaints and claims can be directed.

The spill-over from the final product market to other markets arises because the reliability of the product depends on, amongst other things, the quality of the inputs. Thus the quality of the inputs, as well as the quality of the output, is of direct concern to the firm that assures the reliability of the product.

The relevant inputs include not only labour but also components and semi-processed materials generated at earlier stages of production. The quality of these inputs depends, in turn, upon the quality of the labour employed at these earlier stages. Transaction costs incurred in the screening of job applicants and the supervision of workers may therefore have to be increased in order to improve product quality and so allow the transaction costs of consumers to be reduced. Likewise transaction costs incurred in respect of quality control may have to be increased at upstream stages of production in order to reduce transaction costs downstream at the retail stage. The logic of the process drives the firm to minimize the overall transaction costs associated with the entire sequence of production and distribution, but in doing so transaction costs may have to be increased at some stages so that they can be reduced elsewhere.

The firm that guarantees quality may be identified with the 'channel leader' described in the marketing literature. One of the strategic decisions that has to be taken by the channel leader is whether vertical integration within the production and distribution sequence is necessary in order to 'internalize' the externalities between the transaction costs incurred at different stages.

So far, the literature on the MNE has not pursued the analysis of transaction costs to this length. The theory of vertical integration has, in practice, been confined to a single intermediate product market, and has not considered in detail an entire system of markets embracing factors of production and final products as well. While it has been recognized that marketing skill is one of the ownership advantages that a firm may possess (Caves, 1971), it is usually treated as if it were exactly analogous to a technological advantage, and as if the major strategic issue facing management were how this marketing advantage can be sold.

There are, however, a few isolated contributions which analyse in some detail the marketing activities of MNEs. The transaction cost approach to marketing outlined above is based upon Casson (1982a, ch. 9) and is applied to the MNE in Casson (1982b; 1985). A synthesis of the transaction cost approach and conventional marketing theory has been developed by Brown (1984) in a very interesting paper which also considers applications to the MNE. Nicholas (1983) has studied the marketing strategies of the MNE from a historical standpoint, drawing widely on business history case studies, and charting the movement of forward integration in which the overseas sales agency is replaced by the wholly-owned foreign sales subsidiary. A first step towards developing a system-wide view of marketing and vertical integration, based upon quality control considerations, is presented in chapter 4. Some of the links between product quality and contractual arrangements for the supervision of labour are considered in chapter 6.

2.8 CAPITAL CONSTRAINTS AND THE GROWTH OF THE FIRM

Buckley and Casson, and Rugman, assume that the firm can borrow unlimited funds at the market rate of interest. Hymer, Kindleberger and Dunning, on the other hand, identify privileged access to capital as a potential ownership advantage. They do not, however, consider in detail the consequences of the capital market 'imperfections' which underlie this phenomenon.

A firm which has a reputation for good management may be able to borrow more cheaply than others because lenders subjectively associate lower risks with its operations. But no firm's reputation extends equally to all potential investors, so that even a reputable firm must come to a point where further borrowing forces it to approach investors who are less optimistic about its prospects, and who therefore demand a higher return to compensate for the greater risk. Thus as a firm's scale of borrowing increases relative to its reputation, management will become increasingly aware of a capital constraint.

Some firms function subject to a self-imposed capital constraint. A small firm, for example, may refuse bank credit because the owner-manager fears losing control to the bank's nominees in the event of temporary difficulties with repayment. A family-controlled firm may avoid diluting control by refraining from issuing new equity. Whatever the reason, the capital constraint can influence strategic decisions. It not only influences the scale of the firm's operations, but also the scope of its operations. It may, for example, discourage the firm from vertical integration because ownership of a production facility ties up more capital than does purchasing materials from a subcontractor or selling know-how to a licensee.

The influence of capital constraints on vertical integration was ignored in section 1.5, since conventional literature has paid little attention to this point. It is argued in Chapter 5, however, that capital constraints have a crucial role in influencing the choice of contractual arrangements for international business operations. The interpretation of historical case-study evidence is consistent with the view that capital constraints carry a weight three times that of any other factor in describing the form of overseas involvement adopted by British MNEs.

A firm that faces a totally inelastic capital constraint may well find that it must divest one activity before it can take another on. To take advantage of a new opportunity it may be necessary to sell off an existing project. Thus *dis*integration involving one activity may be the price of the integration of another activity into the firm's operations. This view of integration as an aspect of corporate restructuring under conditions of capital rationing is characteristic of the management strategy literature (Coyne and Wright, 1986).

A totally inelastic capital constraint is more likely to be encountered when the firm is in financial difficulties and has lost the confidence of the capital market. In such cases the firm may even have to dispose of activities for cash to pay off creditors. If a cash crisis occurs at short notice, then the transaction costs incurred in finding buyers may differ very considerably between activities. Activities which are only loosely integrated into the firm's operations may appeal most to outside buyers, since the disruption caused to the activity when it is 'spun off' will be minimal. Activities which are highly profitable will also tend to have low transaction costs, since outsiders will not expect to find hidden problems with them. Unprofitable activities, on the other hand, may be suspected of having problems far more serious than even their current financial performance suggests, so that they can only be disposed of after allowing buyers time to investigate them fully. Because profitable activities enjoy greater 'liquidity' than unprofitable ones, the firm may have to sell off its most profitable activities in order to keep its less profitable ones going. Short-run expediency – aimed at financial survival – may therefore dictate a policy that is contrary to the long-run interests of the firm.

When divestment occurs under crisis conditions, it is easy for the parties involved to lose sight of the long-run factors in the situation. The inability of the divesting firm to borrow reflects external perceptions of the limited capabilities of its management team. This in turn suggests that the fundamental constraint may lie, not in the capital market itself, but in the availability of management skills to the firm. The divestment is, in effect, a method of supplying additional management skills to the divested resources. Changing the ownership of the resources is a means of avoiding a bottleneck in the supply of management skills. This long-run approach to the analysis of divestment is supported by the case study presented in chapter 8. Even large MNEs can get into financial difficulties. In the Chrysler case, the cash crisis which precipitated the disposal of its European operations can be traced back to a long-run managerial failure. While the immediate cause of the divestment was the illiquidity of the parent company, the underlying cause was mainly the failure to rationalize the scope of the firm's operations much earlier on.

An important aspect of transaction costs in any market is that a significant component is a fixed cost, independent of the size of the transaction. Transaction costs in the capital market are no exception to this. This means that to economize on transaction costs, a divesting firm may dispose of activities, not singly, but as a group. Since transaction costs tend to be highest when divestment is undertaken at short notice, as explained above, the 'lumpiness' of the divested package is likely to be greatest in this case. The acquiring company, however, because it is in a stronger financial position, may be able to dispose at leisure of individual activities within the group that do not fit in with its other operations. Because it can allow more time, the transaction costs it faces are lower than those faced by the original divestor. The small-scale divestments made by the second company therefore represent the knock-on effects of an earlier larger scale divestment by another company.

In some cases the transaction costs involved in disposing of a small-scale activity may be sufficiently large, whatever the time allowed, that the acquiring firm decides to retain them even though they do not fit in with its main operations. There is some evidence that the perception of the transaction costs involved in such disposals varies between firms. Firms with 'managerial inertia' may perceive relatively high transaction costs, and so retain peripheral activities that have been acquired as part of a larger group. The evidence presented in chapter 6 suggests that inertia of this kind is endemic in medium-sized firms in the UK construction industry. These firms do not appear to have a clearly defined long-run strategy regarding the scope of their operations. It seems likely that the scope of their activities is explained by a pattern of opportunistic acquisitions in the past, which have not subsequently been rationalized by the disposal of peripheral activities.

It seems, therefore, that the explanatory power of the economic theory of the MNE has in the past been restricted by the failure to appreciate the full significance of capital market constraints. The reputation of the firm sets an effective limit to the scale of funding available, and forces different avenues of integration to be assessed as alternative to one another. The main writers to have taken this perspective seriously so far are Wolf (1977) and Pearce (1983). Capital market constraints also force the firm to evaluate investment and divestment decisions simultaneously. Investments and divestments need to be 'paired up' in order to restructure the firm's operations. The presence of fixed transaction costs affects the way this policy is implemented. It suggests, in particular, that restructuring will often proceed in two stages, with activities being divested as a group in the first stage, and then rationalized individually on a smaller scale later. When the second stage does not occur, however, the scope of the firm's activities remains unrationalized, and comes to reflect the legacy of previous acquisition decisions.

2.9   COLLABORATIVE ARRANGEMENTS

Further development of the theory is also needed to take account of the growing variety of international contractual arrangements which are neither purely firm-like nor purely market-like. These intermediate arrangements, which include joint ventures and industrial collaboration agreements, involve the sharing of ownership and control. Although these arrangements have attracted considerable attention from policy makers, and have been the subject of some analysis (Buckley, 1985a), there is no doubt that much more theoretical work needs to be done. The implications of existing theory for 'collaborative arrangements' are considered in chapter 5. What is really needed, however, is a synthesis between conventional theory and the theories of 'implicit contracts' and 'relational contracting' (Okun, 1981; Williamson, 1985) that have been developed in slightly different contexts. Particular attention needs to be paid to collaborative arrangements which involve a public body from one country and a private enterprise from another.

2.10   SUMMARY

This chapter has considered a number of weaknesses of the existing theory of the MNE, and has indicated the kind of theoretical developments that are needed to remedy them. Some of these developments are linked to the analysis presented in the subsequent chapters of this book.

It has been argued that the theory of internalization is essentially a branch of the theory of choice, where the objects of choice are alternative institutional arrangements. The concept of ownership, however, is related to the survival power of the firm, which in turn depends upon the strength of the competition within the market environment. This is reflected in the fact that ownership advantage must always be measured relative to the capabilities of other firms. Ownership advantage, therefore, is primarily relevant, not to the analysis of choice, but to the analysis of the process of selection and survival within the system as a whole.

It has been pointed out that there is ambiguity in the way that the term 'internalization' is used in economics, and that this has caused confusion in analysing the welfare consequences of MNE operations. Criticism has also been levelled at the naïve interpretation of market structure and of marketing skills, and at the restrictive nature of the models used to analyse vertical integration. The neglect of capital constraints, it has been argued, has further restricted the explanatory power of the theory.

Some further limitations of the theory, which are endemic to other branches of economics too, are set forth in chapter 9. That chapter also places the future developments called for above within the wider context of future developments within economic theory as a whole.

3

Foreign Investment and Economic Warfare: Internalizing the Implementation of Threats

3.1 INTRODUCTION

This chapter attempts to rectify two of the main weaknesses of the conventional theory of the MNE reviewed in chapter 2, namely:

1 there is too much emphasis on the exploitation of a transferable ownership advantage as a motive for foreign investment, and
2 there is too little modelling of inter-firm rivalry between MNEs.

It is, in fact, easy to rectify these problems by drawing upon a rather different strand of MNE theory which was influential in the early 1970s but has since been partially eclipsed by the kind of theory reviewed in the two preceding chapters. This theory is strongly influenced by the work of Hymer and Rowthorn (1970), Knickerbocker (1973) and Vernon (1974) on oligopolistic rivalry between MNEs. It has continued to be reflected in the work of writers associated with the Harvard Business School (for recent examples see Stopford and Turner, 1985; Vernon, 1983).

The particular aspect of the theory with which this chapter is concerned is Graham's thesis that foreign direct investment represents an exchange of threats between oligopolistic firms (Graham, 1974; 1978). In Graham's original formulation, inter-firm rivalry creates an environment of great uncertainty for the firm. As a result, firms are motivated by a desire to minimize risk rather than to maximize profits. Uncertainty is so pervasive that optimizing investment strategies cannot be calculated with any precision and so, to minimize risk, firms fall back upon a simple behavioural rule – namely, to imitate each move that their rivals make. Exchange of threats is thus presented as a special case of imitative behaviour, and imitative behaviour is proposed as a general principle by which foreign direct investment can be explained.

Subsequent writers have inferred, quite reasonably, that Graham's theory represents an alternative to, rather than an application of, the Coasian theory of the multinational enterprise (MNE) described in chapter 1. This inference is unwarranted, however. As Graham himself has recognized, the prevalence of uncertainty, and the disposition to imitate one's rivals, are superfluous to the underlying logic of the argument; they are rather refinements to an argument whose logic is really very simple. This chapter shows how Graham's theory can be simply reformulated as a theory of profit-maximizing behaviour in which the implementation of threats is internalized by the firm. It can then be shown that exchange of threats will occur if and only if certain crucial conditions are satisfied. It can also be seen that Graham's theory has much closer affinities with conventional duopoly theory than is commonly realized. In fact, the precise relation between Graham's theory and conventional duopoly theory turns out to be an interesting subject in its own right.

The essence of the model formulated below is that a profit-maximizing oligopolist invests abroad merely to threaten a rival firm. A technologically advantaged firm in a global industry confronts a technologically weak firm. Although disadvantaged, the weak firm is not entirely without power, however, because it can 'spoil' the strong firm's home market. The weak firm defends itself, therefore, not in its own home market where it is under attack, but through counter-attack in the strong firm's home market. It does this because it believes that the strong firm has more to lose in its own home market than it has to gain by aggression overseas.

Now it cannot be a 'first best' strategy for two firms to engage in rivalry in which one spoils the market for the other. But the first best arrangement may well involve a sophisticated rationalization agreement between the firms which it is prohibitively costly for them to enforce. Thus it is a failure to agree on rationalization that leads to the exchange of threats.

If a mere verbal threat to spoil the market is effective then the weaker firm need not actually bother to invest abroad. But to make the threat more credible, and to indicate that it 'means business', the firm may prepare to implement it. Although it could, in principle, subcontract the 'spoiling' activity to another firm – which would dump its output in the rival's market in return for a subsidy paid by the weaker firm – such an arrangement would be difficult to enforce. It is therefore natural for the weaker firm to internalize the implementation of the threat by investing in production overseas.

It should be noted that in this case it is technological weakness rather than technological strength that is the driving force in the decision to invest overseas. While the investing firm may have some advantage relative to other indigenous competitors in the home market where it holds large market share, it is actually disadvantaged *vis-à-vis* the foreign firm. It is this disadvantage which is the crucial influence on its behaviour. Its threat to spoil the foreign firm's market is first and foremost a device to compensate for this disadvantage.

3.2   THE CREDIBILITY OF THREATS

Recent research has emphasized that threats must be credible if they are to influence a rival's behaviour. A threat which is self-damaging is unlikely to be credible because, when it comes to the point, it is not in the threatener's interests to actually implement it (Vickers, 1985). Therefore, it has been argued, self-damaging threats cannot influence behaviour, and must be excluded from the analysis of conflict, on the grounds that they are irrelevant. If correct, this conclusion would seriously undermine the theory that follows; for the kind of threat discussed in this chapter is definitely self-damaging, in the sense that it involves the firm in spoiling the market not only for its rival but also for itself.

There is, however, a flaw in the final stage of the argument above. It arises from a failure to distinguish properly between the situation that prevails before the threat has been made and the situation that prevails afterwards. The issuing of a threat creates an irreversible change in the incentive structure facing the threatener. This is because, by issuing a threat, the threatener places his reputation for doing what he says he will do 'on the line'. Prior to making the threat, the announcement of a self-damaging threat is rational if the threatener believes that the threat will have the desired effect on the rival, because then the threat will not need to be implemented. After the threat has been issued, it may become self-damaging *not* to implement it, because otherwise a valuable reputation will be damaged. If the intended victim is aware of this, then the threat becomes credible. The threat, therefore, stands a good chance of being successful, and so the original decision to make it is validated.

Another way of putting this is to say that a rational manager will allow for reputation effects when evaluating the strategic options in a sub-game, and that when reputation effects are allowed for, implementation of the threat may no longer appear to be self-damaging.

This line of reasoning hinges crucially on the assumption that the threatener enjoys a reputation which is sufficiently valuable, and sufficiently vulnerable, that the loss associated with failure to implement the threat more than outweighs any potential short-term gains. The value of the reputation arises from the prospect that the threatener will be involved in future encounters with the same party, or with other parties who have observed, or heard at second hand, about the encounter. If the threat is not implemented in the present case, it is assumed, the other parties will infer (rightly or wrongly) that threats will not be implemented in future either. They may also infer, more generally, that since the threatener has not stuck to his announced intention in this particular instance, he will not stick to his commitments in other respects either, so that his general reputation for integrity is damaged as well.

It could, of course, be argued that failure to implement a self-damaging threat would be excused by other parties anyway, on the grounds that it was never really credible in the first place. Thus, reputation would not be seriously jeopardized. This leads, however, to the view that the only reputation that matters is a reputation for doing what it is in your own interests to do anyway. This moves the argument on to a rather different plane, for it raises the question of whether, in repeated encounters between two parties, a reputation for integrity in honouring, without exception, *all* threats and commitments is valuable. The theory of transaction costs and internalization indicates unambiguously that such integrity is necessary if transaction costs are to be minimized. So, within the context of the approach adopted in this book, a reputation for doing what one says one will do, irrespective of short-term interest, is indeed of major value.

When analysing rivalrous encounters between oligopolistic MNEs, it is quite realistic to assume that a reputation for integrity in respect of threats and commitments is very important. This is because the typical MNE has a long life expectancy, and is engaged in ever-changing situations of conflict with the same small number of rival firms. A large MNE is in conflict with its rivals simultaneously on many different fronts – namely the different national markets for its major product. Failure to implement a threat will not only damage the firm in respect of future encounters on the same front, but in respect of encounters on all other fronts as well. Thus, it is reasonable to assume, in the context of the model below that a threat to spoil the market, although self-damaging, is still credible because, once it has been made, the firm has much to lose in terms of reputation by not implementing it.

It is important, however, not to go to the other extreme and assume that any threat, however extreme, is credible. A threat which, if implemented, would oblige the firm to operate in perpetuity at a loss is not credible (unless it could be established that the rival would quickly go out of business, and would have to leave the industry first). A more interesting case arises when the threatener has only a modest reputation, so that what the firm stands to lose by failing to implement the threat may be fairly marginal compared with what it stands to gain. It is in such cases that the acquisition of a foreign subsidiary by the threatening firm is particularly useful.

By sinking costs into the acquisition, the threatener reduces the subsequent administrative costs of spoiling the market. This signals to the rival that the short-term losses incurred through implementing the threat are now lower than they would otherwise have been, so that the margin in favour of implementing the threat has been increased. This reduces the probability that the rival will instigate warfare, and so reduces the probability that the threat will have to be implemented. It is cases of this kind that are the focus of the model below.

3.3   PLAN OF THE CHAPTER

The model introduced in section 3.4 below is confined to a duopoly involving two firms which have similar marginal costs in each market. The firms differ, however, in their fixed costs. Unlike conventional duopoly theory, which assumes that firms make conjectural variations about how their rivals will respond to changes in their own output, it is assumed, in this chapter, that each firm has a constant market share. Market shares change only when firms enter or leave the market. It is assumed that there are two main forms of market conduct. When both firms are present in the market, there is normally tacit collusion in which both firms set a price which maximizes industry profit. The alternative to tacit collusion is price warfare, in which one of the firms attempts to drive the other out of the market. It is argued in section 3.4 that these assumptions are on the whole more realistic than those of conventional duopoly theory.

Section 3.5 applies the theory to a single market. It is shown that the relative strength of a firm depends upon whether the price at which its operations just break even is above or below that of its rival. The lower the break-even price relative to that of its rival, the stronger is the firm. The strength of the firm, measured in this way, is governed by two factors: its technological advantage – as reflected in its level of fixed costs – and its market share. The lower its fixed costs, and the larger its market share, the more difficult it is for its rival to drive the firm out of the market through price competition. In this respect, the theory accords with the view, widely held amongst businessmen, that *relative market share* is a crucial factor in inter-firm rivalry.

A firm is most likely to benefit from driving its rival out of the market when it has only a small market share. The small market share means that the firm has relatively little to gain from the alternative strategy of collusion, while it may be able to appropriate the large market share of its rival through price warfare. Thus a reduction in costs effected by new technology may well lead a firm with a large market share to innovate without driving out its rivals, whereas a firm with a small market share will behave much more aggressively. A diagrammatic illustration of this is given in section 3.6.

Section 3.7 extends the analysis to a two-country world. To counter aggression by a firm with a small market share, the rival may decide to price aggressively in the market where the aggressor has a greater market share. By threatening to hit the aggressor 'where it hurts', the aggressor may be discouraged from expanding in the market where its share is small. As a result, theory predicts that in a two-country world, defensive foreign investments are most likely to occur in industries where each duopolist has a large share of one market and a small share of the other. The application of this idea to foreign investment is examined in section 3.8.

Theory also predicts that aggressive investment and defensive investment will take place at about the same time, so that there is cross-investment within the industry. Each firm starts up production in the country where its market share is smallest and that of its rival is greatest. This is very similar to the pattern of cross-investment between Europe and the US in the 1970s, where, in a number of industries, technologically unsophisticated European firms appear to have invested in the US for defensive reasons.

In general, however, exchange of threat investments do not have to be undertaken by firms of different nationalities. Thus a US firm without European operations that faced rivals which were well entrenched in Europe – for example, Chrysler in the early 1960s – might invest defensively in Europe to counter aggressive activity in the US market by its US rivals – for example, Ford and General Motors.

This observation clarifies the link between the 'exchange of threats' motive and the 'follow my leader' type of investment discussed by Knickerbocker. In certain cases, follow my leader investment may be an attempt to prevent a rival from developing a monopolistic base overseas that would be immune to counter-threat should the rival later attack the home market. The likelihood of aggression by the rival is greatest when the rival has a small initial share of the home market and its operations overseas are likely to generate technical improvements which can be fed back into domestic production.

The theory also has close affinities with recent analyses of predatory pricing (Salop, 1981; Utton, 1985). Rivalry between MNEs selling the same product in several national markets in analogous to rivalry between domestic conglomerates selling several products in the same national market – in the first case the market is defined geographically, and in the second case by the nature of the product involved. The analogy becomes particularly clear when cross-subsidization is involved. In both cases, a threat of cross-subsidization is viable when the rival firm cannot counter with cross-subsidization of its own, but involves considerable risks when the rival itself can cross-subsidize, since the rival may then be able to eliminate the profits which are the source of the subsidy.

It should be noted that defensive investments are unlikely to achieve the same degree of long-term success as aggressive investments – they are, after all, a symptom of weakness rather than strength. Because they are likely to be short-term investments undertaken for a specific strategic purpose, they may be designed to be quickly implemented and easily sold off later. This suggests that foreign acquisitions of going concerns, which remain only loosely integrated with other operations, are likely to be characteristic of defensive investments, in comparison with carefully planned green field investments integrated in world-wide operations, which will be more characteristic of aggressive investments (Dubin, 1975; Wilson, 1980).

Section 3.9 extends the analysis to the case where there is competition between the foreign firm and the domestic firm for the acquisition of a local rival of the domestic firm, whilst 3.10 considers the strategic consequences of cross-subsidization.

Recent case study evidence on defensive investment is examined in section 3.11, where it is shown that the strategic behaviour of a number of firms can be explained in terms of the theory. The wider implications of the theory are discussed in section 3.12.

3.4   DUOPOLY WITH FIXED MARKET SHARES

Duopolies may be either potential or actual. A potential duopoly is one in which an established monopolist faces competition from a single potential entrant. An actual duopoly is one in which both firms are in production. In industrial organization theory, actual duopoly is often analysed using a variant of the Cournot assumption, in which firms conjecture quantity-adjusting reactions by their rivals, whilst potential duopoly is analysed using concepts relating to strategic entry-deterrence. The model outlined below analyses both potential and actual duopoly simultaneously, using a third approach, which is to assume that each duopolist has a *fixed potential market share*.

The thinking behind this approach is that in a potential duopoly, the established firm always has a certain proportion of dissatisfied customers who will switch to a new entrant whenever one appears. Once an actual duopoly has been established, price matching by the two firms will maintain their market shares stable. In practice, of course, long-run changes in market share will occur because of advertising etc., though the actual effects may be small if advertising by one firm is normally matched by advertising by the other. Such changes are not considered in this chapter: in the model below, market shares change only when firms enter or leave the market.

It is assumed that both firms produce under increasing returns to scale. Each firm incurs a recurrent fixed cost of production at each location, and thereafter output is generated at a constant marginal cost which is the same for both firms but varies between locations. This seems to be a reasonable description of the cost structure in many mass production manufacturing industries. Relaxing these assumptions for the sake of greater realism complicates the analysis quite considerably.

Because there are economies of scale, neither firm can survive if competition drives down price to marginal cost. It is assumed that both firms recognize this, and normally tacitly collude in fixing the market price.

Another consequence of economies of scale is that duplication of production facilities within the same market is wasteful. A programme of rationalization which shuts down one of the plants in each market would reduce the total cost of producing a given level of industry output. To maximize industry profit, the firm with the higher fixed cost should close down. But the firm with the higher fixed cost is not necessarily the weaker one, for the high cost firm may have by far the larger market share. In the absence of transaction costs, the higher cost firm would potentially benefit most by closing its own production down, but in practice the difficulties of enforcing the rationalization agreement may persuade it to induce the other firm, by threats, to close down instead.

In the model below, it is assumed that the costs of monitoring and enforcing an agreement to close down one of the plants are prohibitive. Thus tacit collusion rather than rationalized collusion is the normal state of affairs in the industry. This seems to be a realistic description of the situation in many oligopolistic industries (see Fellner, 1949; Shubik, 1959; Shubik with Levitan, 1980).

3.5 COLLUSION VERSUS WARFARE

This section deduces the conditions under which either collusion or warfare will prevail when the firms make no attempt to co-ordinate their strategies across markets. It is also assumed that no trade can take place between the markets. From the strategic point of view, therefore, each market is isolated from the other, and the behaviour of the firms can be determined by analysing each market separately.

The two markets are interpreted as national markets, although they could also represent continental, regional or metropolitan markets, say.

The jth firm has a constant share of the ith market, m_{ij} ($0 \leqslant m_{ij} \leqslant 1$) so long as both firms remain in production:

$$\sum_{j=1}^{2} m_{ij} = 1 \qquad (i = 1,2) \qquad (3.1)$$

Each firm matches the other's price, so that it is never undersold. The indirect demand curve in the ith market is

$$p_i = a_i - b_i q_i \qquad (i = 1,2) \qquad (3.2)$$

where p_i is the price, q_i is the quantity demanded and a_i, $b_i > 0$ are fixed parameters. Let q_{ij} be the quantity supplied to the ith market by the jth firm. Then

$$q_i = \sum_{j=1}^{2} q_{ij} \qquad (i = 1,2) \qquad (3.3)$$

Both firms have the same marginal costs, c_i ($0 < c_i < a_i$) although their fixed costs $d_{ij} > 0$ may vary. The fixed cost is a recurrent cost which is avoided if the firm shuts down production. Although firms outside the market cannot enter, either of the firms within the market can leave if production becomes unprofitable. There are no barriers to exit and no barriers to re-entry. Thus a firm that has left the market remains a competitive threat to the other firm because it can always re-enter with no set-up cost. These are very strong assumptions and the consequences of relaxing them are considered later.

Let π_{ij} be the profit of the jth firm in the ith market. Then

$$\pi_{ij} = p_i q_{ij} - c_i q_{ij} - d_{ij} \qquad (i,j = 1,2) \qquad (3.4)$$

Industry profit is

$$\pi_i = \sum_{j=1}^{2} \pi_{ij} \qquad (j = 1,2) \qquad (3.5)$$

Each firm in the ith market has two strategic options:

1 to set the monopoly price which maximizes industry profit (and hope the other firm will follow); and
2 to drive the price down to a level at which one of the firms must leave the market.

The outcome of the interplay of strategies is illustrated in table 3.1. Strategy 1 leads to tacit collusion (outcome A) if the other firm also chooses strategy 1. Under tacit collusion both firms supply the market at the monopoly price which maximizes their joint profits. Strategy 2 leads to warfare (outcome B) whether the other firm sets a monopoly price or not, because once the monopoly price has been undercut the other firm must cut its price as well.

TABLE 3.1   Outcomes of the interplay of strategies in
an isolated market

		Firm 2's strategy	
		1	2
Firm 1's strategy	1	A	B
	2	B	B[a]

[a] It is never the case that both firms prefer strategy 2, as the
following analysis shows.

Outcome A: Tacit Collusion

The two firms tacitly agree to set industry price to maximize industry profit.
Translating from industry price to industry output using the demand curve
(3.2) gives the first-order condition

$$d\pi_i/dq_i = 0 \qquad\qquad (i=1,2) \qquad\qquad (3.6)$$

Substituting equations (3.1)–(3.4) into (3.5) and solving (3.6) gives

$$p_i^A = (a_i + c_i)/2 \qquad\qquad (i=1,2) \qquad\qquad (3.7)$$

$$q_i^A = (a_i - c_i)/2b_i \qquad\qquad (i=1,2) \qquad\qquad (3.8)$$

$$q_{ij}^A = (a_i - c_i)m_{ij}/2b_i \qquad\qquad (i,j=1,2) \qquad\qquad (3.9)$$

$$\pi_{ij}^A = d_{ij}((m_{ij}/\bar{m}_{ij}) - 1) \qquad\qquad (i,j=1,2) \qquad\qquad (3.10)$$

where

$$\bar{m}_{ij} = 4b_i d_{ij}/(a_i - c_i)^2 \qquad\qquad (i,j=1,2) \qquad\qquad (3.11)$$

and where the superscript A indicates the collusive equilibrium.
   In the light of earlier assumptions, the break-even market share is
positive, $\bar{m}_{ij} > 0$. It is also assumed that both firms can at least break
even under tacit collusion, so that from the inequality

$$\pi_{ij}^A \geqslant 0 \qquad\qquad (i,j=1,2) \qquad\qquad (3.12)$$

and equation (3.10) we have

$$m_{ij} \geqslant \bar{m}_{ij} \qquad\qquad (i,j=1,2) \qquad\qquad (3.13)$$

Applying equation (3.1) to equation (3.13) shows that

$$0 < \bar{m}_{1j}, \bar{m}_{2j}, \bar{m}_{1j} + \bar{m}_{2j} \leqslant 1 \qquad\qquad (j=1,2) \qquad\qquad (3.14)$$

Note that the break-even market share $\bar{m}_{ij}$ is directly proportional to the fixed cost of production, d_{ij}, and the price insensitivity of demand, b_i. It is inversely related to the intensity of demand, a_i, and directly related to the marginal cost of production, c_i. Thus, as one would expect, the break-even market share is greater the higher is the fixed cost of production and the lower is the intensity of demand.

Outcome B: Warfare

Consider first the limit pricing strategy pursued by firm 1 in order to drive firm 2 out of the market. In the light of the earlier assumptions, it is assumed that a firm leaves a market whenever its profits fall to below zero. Dynamic strategies, in which the firm 'hangs on' in the market in the hope of somehow securing future profit, are ignored. Using equations (3.1), (3.3) and (3.6), and setting

$$\pi_{i2} = 0 \qquad\qquad (i = 1,2) \qquad (3.15)$$

gives a quadratic equation in q_{i2}. This equation has real roots whenever the inequality (3.12) is satisfied for $j = 2$. Only the larger root of the equation is relevant, since the larger quantity is generated by the lower of the two prices that equate firm 2's profits to zero. Firm 2 could counter the higher price by price cutting, but it cannot counter the lower price without going into loss. Using this larger root and making back substitutions gives the break-even price for firm 2. This is the limit price for firm 1 to drive firm 2 out of the ith market:

$$\bar{p}_{i2} = [(a_i + c_i) - (a_i - c_i)(1 - (\bar{m}_{i2}/m_{i2}))^{\frac{1}{2}}]/2 \qquad (i = 1,2) \qquad (3.16a)$$

A similar argument establishes that the limit price for firm 2 to drive out firm 1 is

$$\bar{p}_{i1} = [(a_i + c_i) - (a_i - c_i)(1 - (\bar{m}_{i1}/m_{i1}))^{\frac{1}{2}}]/2 \qquad (i = 1,2) \qquad (3.16b)$$

When one firm introduces price cuts it forces the other firm into retaliatory action. The price is driven down until the higher of the two break-even prices is reached. (In the special case where the break-even prices are equal, both firms drive out each other at the same price, in which case the quantity supplied by each firm is indeterminate.)

Equations (3.16) show that the break-even price for the jth firm is higher, the larger is the break-even market share $\bar{m}_{ij}$ relative to the actual market share m_{ij} ($j = 1,2$). Using equation (3.11) as well, it is possible to prove the intuitively obvious point that for each firm the break-even price increases with the ratio of the actual market share to the fixed cost of production. Thus

$$\bar{p}_{i1} \gtreqless \bar{p}_{i2} \quad \text{as} \quad \bar{m}_{i1}/m_{i1} \gtreqless \bar{m}_{i2}/m_{i2} \quad \text{as} \quad d_{i1}/m_{i1} \gtreqless d_{i2}/m_{i2} \quad (i=1,2) \quad (3.17)$$

Note that if one firm prefers warfare, the other will always prefer collusion. Only the firm with the lower break-even price will prefer warfare, for the firm with the higher limit price will earn zero profit under warfare but a positive profit under collusion.

Choice of Options by the Stronger Firm

Since the initial labelling of the firms is arbitrary, we may use the convention that firm 1 has a lower break-even price that firm 2:

$$\bar{p}_{i1} < \bar{p}_{i2} \tag{3.18}$$

This means that using limit pricing, firm 1 can drive out firm 2 but firm 2 cannot drive out firm 1.

With firm 1 the stronger, the warfare outcome is

$$p_{i1}^B = \bar{p}_{i2} = [(a_i + c_i) - (a_i - c_i)(1 \quad (\bar{m}_{i2}/m_{i2}))^{1/2}]/2 \tag{3.19}$$

$$q_i^B = (a_i - c_i)[1 + (1 - (\bar{m}_{i2}/m_{i2})^{1/2}]/2b_i \tag{3.20}$$

$$q_{i1}^B = q_i^B \tag{3.21}$$

$$q_{i2}^B = 0 \tag{3.22}$$

$$\pi_{i1}^B = d_{i1}((\bar{m}_{i2}/\bar{m}_{i1} m_{i2}) - 1) \tag{3.23}$$

$$\pi_{i2}^B = 0 \tag{3.24}$$

$$\pi_i^B = \pi_{i1}^B \tag{3.25}$$

Comparing equations (3.10) and (3.23) using (3.1) shows that

$$\pi_{i1}^B - \pi_{i1}^A = (d_{i2}/\bar{m}_{i2} m_{i2})(m_{i2}^2 - m_{i2} + \bar{m}_{i2}) \tag{3.26}$$

Equation (3.26) has real roots only for $\bar{m}_{i2} \leqslant 0.25$. These roots are

$$m_{i2}^* = \frac{1}{2} - \frac{1}{2}(1 - 4\bar{m}_{i2})^{1/2} \tag{3.27a}$$

$$m_{i2}^{**} = \frac{1}{2} + \frac{1}{2}(1 - 4\bar{m}_{i2})^{1/2} \tag{3.27b}$$

where $\bar{m}_{i2} \leqslant m_{i2}^* \leqslant m_{i2}^{**} \leqslant 1$. Thus firm 1 prefers

$$\left.\begin{array}{l} \text{warfare if } \textit{either } \bar{m}_{i2} > 0.25 \\ \qquad \text{or} \quad \bar{m}_{i2} \leqslant 0.25 \text{ and } \textit{either } m_{i2} \leqslant m_{i2}^* \\ \qquad\qquad\qquad \text{or} \quad m_{i2} \geqslant m_{i2}^{**} \\ \text{tacit collusion if } \bar{m}_{i2} \leqslant 0.25 \text{ and } m_{i2}^* \leqslant m_{i2} \leqslant m_{i2}^{**} \end{array}\right\} \tag{3.28}$$

These results are summarized in figure 3.1. Firm 1's decision is illustrated in the bottom half of the figure and firm 2's decision in the top half. Firm 1's market share is measured along the top horizontal axis from the origin O_1 in the upper right-hand corner, and firm 2's market share along the

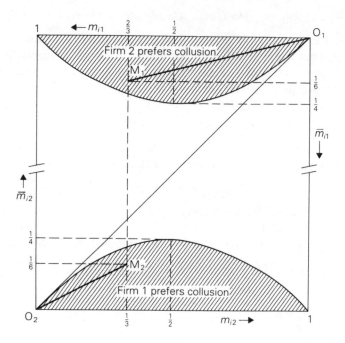

FIGURE 3.1   The choice between tacit collusion and warfare

bottom axis from the origin O_2 in the lower left-hand corner. Each point on the top axis corresponds to the same division of the market as the point directly below it on the bottom axis. The combinations of actual market share and break-even market share for firm 2 that encourage firm 1 to opt for collusion when it is the stronger are represented by the points in the lower of the shaded areas. The combinations of actual market share and break-even market share for firm 1 that encourage firm 2 to opt for collusion when it is the stronger are represented by the points in the higher of the shaded areas. If the actual and break-even market shares are plotted in the figure, and a ray is drawn from each point to the corresponding origin, then the ray with the smaller slope identifies the stronger firm.

Suppose, for example, that both firms have a break-even market share of one-sixth, and that firm 1 holds two-thirds of the market. Firm 1 is represented by the point M_1 and firm 2 by the point M_2. The ray OM_1 subtends a smaller angle with the horizontal axis than does the ray OM_2, so that firm 1 is the stronger firm. The point M_2 lies within the lower shaded region, so that firm 1 prefers collusion to warfare, and since firm 1 is the stronger firm, collusion will prevail.

The 45-degree line O_1O_2 indicates the critical condition for each firm where the actual market share is equal to its break-even value. Points lying between the 45-degree line and the relevant shaded area indicate the situation under which warfare is preferred to collusion. The figure illustrates the fact that warfare is normally preferred only when the rival firm's actual market share is reasonably close to its break-even level. The main exception is when the rival's market share is very large, in which case the potential gains from eliminating it are so high that warfare is preferred whatever the rival's break-even market share.

An important consequence of equations (3.28) is that the stronger firm's decision between tacit collusion and warfare depends only upon the weaker firm's actual and break-even market share. This means that no change in the stronger firm's own fixed costs can influence its decision so long as it remains the stronger firm. Only a change which turns it into a weaker firm can affect its attitude. Likewise, no change in the weaker firm's fixed costs can alter its preference for tacit collusion so long as it remains the weaker firm. The only way that a change in its *own* fixed costs can influence a firm's attitudes is if *either* the fixed costs of a weaker firm fall to the point where it becomes the stronger firm and wishes to force its rival out, *or* the fixed costs of the stronger firm rise to the point where it becomes the weaker firm and wishes to collude instead. This result has important consequences for the sequential analysis presented in section 3.8.

3.6 A DIAGRAMMATIC ANALYSIS OF THE CHOICE BETWEEN COLLUSION AND WARFARE

Some readers may be interested to know how the preceding analysis relates to conventional duopoly theory. The connection is illustrated in figure 3.2. Readers who are not interested in this connection can proceed directly to section 3.7.

In the top quadrant of figure 3.2, firm 1's output is measured along the horizontal axis and firm 2's output along the vertical axis. The industry output that maximizes joint profit, conditional upon both firms being in production, is measured by $OK_1 = OK_2$ (this is derived in the lower quadrant – see below). The various ways in which this output can be allocated between the two firms are shown by the 45-degree line $K_1 K_2$. The ratio of firm 2's market share to firm 1's market share – i.e. firm 2's *relative* market share – is measured by the slope of the ray OC'. The intersection of OC' with $K_1 K_2$ determines the collusive equilibrium A.

To ascertain whether production at A is profitable, zero-profit loci are drawn for the two firms. The zero-profit locus for firm 1 is $F_1 NQG_1$ and the zero-profit locus for firm 2 is $F_2 NQG_2$. The intersection M_1 of $F_1 NQG_1$ with $K_1 K_2$ indicates the allocation of collusive output at which firm 1 just breaks even. Likewise the intersection M_2 of $F_2 NQG_2$ with

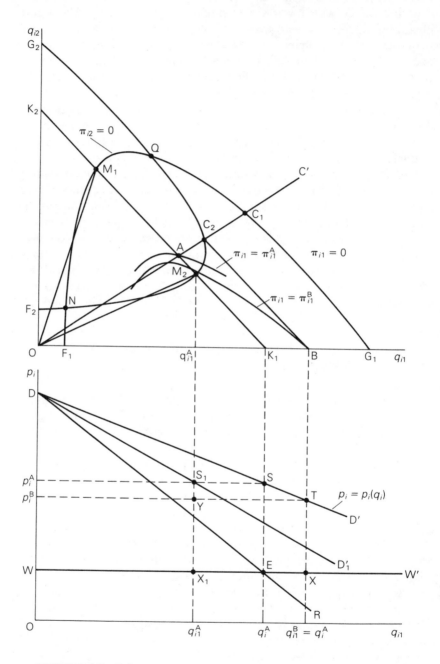

FIGURE 3.2   Prices and quantities under tacit collusion and warfare

$K_1 K_2$ represents the allocation of output at which firm 2 just breaks even. The slope of the ray OM_1 *with respect to the vertical axis* measures firm 1's break-even relative market share, whilst the slope of the ray OM_2 with respect to the horizontal axis measures firm 2's break-even relative market share.

It is well known that each zero-profit locus is just one element of a set of iso-profit lines which can be constructed for each firm; and the closer is an iso-profit locus to the axis which it intersects, the higher is the level of profit to which it corresponds. The interior of $NM_1 QM_2$ indicates the combinations of outputs at which both firms are profitable. Given the specified market shares, the point A lies in the interior of $NM_1 QM_2$, so that tacit collusion allows both firms to make a profit.

If firm 1 is to drive firm 2 out of the market, it needs to move production levels out along the ray OC' to the point C_2 where the ray intersects firm 2's zero-profit locus. This corresponds to an industry output OB. This is effected by reducing price. Firm 1 is the stronger, because the intersection C_2 with firm 2's zero-profit locus lies below the intersection C_1 with firm 1's zero-profit locus. When production has been moved to C_2 and firm 2 has left the market, firm 1 enjoys a monopoly and so the final outcome under warfare is at B. Firm 1's iso-profit locus passing through B lies below its iso-profit locus passing through A, and so warfare is more profitable than collusion. Firm 1 therefore opts for driving firm 2 out of the market.

Visual inspection of the figure suggests that firm 1 prefers warfare to collusion because point C_2 is close to point A. C_2 is close to A because A is in turn close to M_2, which implies that firm 2 can be driven out of the market by only a small increase in industry output. If, on the other hand, A were much further from M_2, C_2 would be further from A, the distance OB would be larger, and warfare would be unprofitable for firm 1. The discrepancy between A and M_2 measures the extent to which firm 2's relative market share exceeds its break-even level. This shows that the closer is firm 2's relative market share to its break-even level, the more likely it is that firm 1 will drive firm 2 out of the market.

Another view of the same phenomenon is presented in the lower quadrant of the figure. Price is now on the vertical axis. The industry demand curve is DD', and with both firms in production firm 1's demand curve is DD_1'. The reason why firm 1 and not firm 2 has been selected for portrayal in the lower quadrant is that the analysis in the upper quadrant has identified it as the stronger firm. The collusive equilibrium is at E, where the industry marginal revenue curve DR intersects the industry marginal cost curve WW'. This equilibrium is associated with point S on the industry demand curve and with point S_1 on firm 1's demand curve. If price is driven down from p_i^A to p_i^B then the new outcome is represented by point T on the demand curve. Since firm 1 monopolizes the market, this is the equilibrium for both firm and industry.

The profit earned by firm 1 under warfare is measured by the area of the rectangle $p_i^B TXW$, and the profit earned under collusion by the area of the rectangle $p_i^A S_1 X_1 W$. The net profit to warfare is therefore measured by the excess of the area $YTXX_1$ over the area $p_i^A S_1 Y p_i^B$.

3.7   GLOBAL STRATEGY

In the preceding analysis, both firms pursued quite separate strategies in the two markets. This meant that a weak firm in either market had no sanction it could bring against the stronger firm. If, however, a firm integrates its strategies in the two markets then it can acquire threat power. This arises because the firm that threatens it with warfare in one market may prefer tacit collusion in the other market. Either firm, however, can initiate warfare, and so the threatened firm can announce that if its rival initiates warfare in one market it will initiate warfare itself in the other market. This means, effectively, that each firm can deny the other the option of warfare in one market and collusion in the other. Thus a firm that, given a free choice, would choose warfare in one market and collusion in the other, may choose collusion in both if the only other option is warfare in both. In this way the weaker firm may induce the stronger firm not to opt for warfare.

The seriousness of the threat that one firm can make to another depends upon whether it is willing to subsidize price cutting in one market out of profits made in the other. At one extreme, the firm may decide that operations in *each* market must at least break even, so that there is no internal cross-subsidization of losses. At the other extreme, the firm may allow cross-subsidization up to the point where all the profits in one market are used to make good the losses in the other market. In this second case the constraint on warfare is not that operations must break even in each market, but only that the global operations as a whole must break even instead.

The analysis below assumes that cross-subsidization does not occur. The rationale for this assumption could be that management policy does not permit subsidiaries to run at a loss, or that there are fiscal barriers to the international transfer of funds. The consequences of allowing cross-subsidization are considered briefly in section 3.10.

The outcome of the interplay of the various options is illustrated in table 3.2. In the absence of threats, each firm has a choice of four strategies, generated by permuting the collusion and warfare options over

TABLE 3.2   Outcomes of the interplay of strategies in a two-country world

		Firm 2's strategy			
		11	12	21	22
	11	AA	AB[1]	BA[1]	BB
Firm 1's strategy	12	AB[2]	AB[0]	BB[1,2]	BB[0]
	21	BA[2]	BB[1,2]	BA[0]	BB[0]
	22	BB	BB[0]	BB[0]	BB

See text for notes to this table.

the two markets. The interplay of these four strategies leads to four possible global outcomes, also based upon permutations of collusion and warfare over the two markets. Thus in the second row and third column of the table, firm 1's choice (1,2) of collusion in the first market and warfare in the second, interacts with firm 2's choice (2,1) of warfare in the first market and collusion in the second, to generate the outcome (B,B) of warfare in both markets.

It has already been established that, in the absence of threats, only the stronger firm in a market ever prefers warfare and the weaker firm always prefers collusion. This means that if one firm prefers warfare in a given market, the other necessarily prefers collusion. As a result, the outcomes superscripted 0 in the table will not be observed. Threats issued by firm 1 deny the possibility of outcomes superscripted 1 in the table, whilst threats by firm 2 deny the possibility of the outcomes superscripted 2. The combined effect of the threats, therefore, is to eliminate all of the outcomes superscripted either 1 or 2 (or both) in the table. Given also the impossibility of the outcomes superscripted 0, there are only two possible outcomes under threats: either global collusion (A,A) or global warfare (B,B).

Suppose now that firm 2 faces a situation where firm 1 would like to drive it out of one of the markets (say market 2) whilst firm 2 itself would rather collude in both. In the absence of a threat, firm 1 could choose strategy (1,2) and realize the outcome (A,B). It is firm 2's threat that denies it this possibility. Firm 2's threat is effective if firm 1's profitability under (A,B) exceeds that under both (A,A) and (B,B), and at the same time firm 1's profitability under (A,A) exceeds that under (B,B). By permuting the identity of the markets and the identities of the firms, this can be shown to be typical of all the cases superscripted singly, either 1 or 2, in the table.

Formally, the conditions for an effective threat in this case are

$$\pi_{11}^{A} > \pi_{11}^{B} \tag{3.29}$$

$$\pi_{21}^{B} > \pi_{21}^{A} \tag{3.30}$$

$$\pi_{11}^{A} + \pi_{21}^{A} > \pi_{11}^{B} + \pi_{21}^{B} \tag{3.31}$$

Rearranging terms gives the single condition

$$\pi_{11}^{A} - \pi_{11}^{B} > \pi_{21}^{A} - \pi_{21}^{B} > 0 \tag{3.32}$$

From equation (3.26), this condition is satisfied if and only if

$$\sum_{i=1}^{2}(d_{i2}/\bar{m}_{i2}m_{i2})(m_{i2}^{2} - m_{i2} + \bar{m}_{i2}) < 0 \tag{3.33}$$

The condition for firm 2 which corresponds to (3.32) is

$$\pi_{12}^{A} + \pi_{22}^{A} > \pi_{12}^{B} + \pi_{22}^{B} \tag{3.34}$$

and since, from earlier arguments

$$\pi_{12}^{A}, \pi_{22}^{A} > 0, \quad \pi_{12}^{B} = \pi_{22}^{B} = 0 \tag{3.35}$$

the condition (3.34) is always satisfied.

In the case of the doubly superscripted entries, threats will be effective only if both firms prefer global collusion (A,A) to global warfare (B,B). Suppose, for example, that firm 1 would like to drive firm 2 out of market 2 and collude in market 1 – strategy (1,2) – whilst firm 2 would like to drive firm 1 out of market 1 and collude in market 2 – strategy (2,1). Firm 2's threat persuades firm 1 that the only possible outcomes are either (A,A) or (B,B). The only way firm 1 can achieve (A,A) is if it chooses strategy (1,1). If (A,A) is preferred to (B,B) it has nothing to lose by choosing this strategy, since the worst possible outcome is (B,B) which is what it would certainly get if it chose (2,2). Likewise firm 1's threat will persuade firm 2 to choose (1,1) if firm 2 prefers (A,A) to (B,B), and (2,2) otherwise. If both firms prefer (A,A) to (B,B), then both will choose (1,1) and (A,A) will be obtained. If either prefers (B,B) to (A,A) then (B,B) will be obtained. Thus if firm 1 prefers (A,B) to (A,A,) to (B,B,), and firm 2 prefers (B,A) to (A,A) to (B,B), then threats produce the outcome (A,A) rather than (B,B). Permuting the identities of the firms shows that this case represents both the doubly superscripted entries in the table.

Formally, the conditions in this case for effective threats are

$$\pi_{11}^{A} > \pi_{11}^{B}; \quad \pi_{12}^{B} > \pi_{12}^{A} \tag{3.36}$$

$$\pi_{21}^{B} > \pi_{21}^{A}; \quad \pi_{22}^{A} > \pi_{22}^{B} \tag{3.37}$$

$$\pi_{1j}^{A} + \pi_{2j}^{A} > \pi_{1j}^{B} + \pi_{2j}^{B} \quad\quad (j = 1,2) \tag{3.38}$$

Since from earlier arguments,

$$\pi_{11}^B = \pi_{22}^B = 0 \tag{3.39}$$

the conditions (3.36)–(3.38) reduce to

$$\pi_{11}^A > \pi_{21}^B - \pi_{21}^A > 0 \tag{3.40}$$

$$\pi_{22}^A > \pi_{12}^B - \pi_{12}^A > 0 \tag{3.41}$$

Using equations (3.10) and (3.26), the conditions (3.40) and (3.41) may be expressed respectively in the form

$$d_{11}((m_{11}/\bar{m}_{11}) - 1) > (d_{22}/\bar{m}_{22} m_{22})(m_{22}^2 - m_{22} + \bar{m}_{22}) \tag{3.42a}$$

$$d_{22}((m_{22}/\bar{m}_{22}) - 1) > (d_{11}/\bar{m}_{11} m_{11})(m_{11}^2 - m_{11} + \bar{m}_{11}) \tag{3.42b}$$

The common factor in both these cases is that both firms prefer (A,A) to (B,B), but one or both of them prefers either (A,B) or (B,A) to (A,A). In the absence of threats the outcome could be either (A,B), (B,A) or (B,B), whereas with threats the outcome is (A,A).

Comparative static analysis can be applied to the conditions (3.33) and (3.42) to examine the effects of various changes, including the growth of a market, as measured by an increase in the intensity of demand, a_i, and a fall in fixed costs, as measured by a reduction in the value of d_{ij} $(i,j = 1,2)$. Other exercises can be performed, involving reductions in a_i, increases in d_{ij}, changes in the price insensitivity of demand, b_i, changes in marginal costs, c_i, and various combinations of these. The remainder of this chapter focuses upon changes which have a direct bearing on the question of rivalistic foreign investments.

3.8 FOREIGN INVESTMENT AS AN INSTRUMENT OF RIVALRY: A SEQUENTIAL ANALYSIS

Suppose that one of the duopolists – say firm 1 – develops a new technology which is initially so idiosyncratic that it is prohibitively costly to transfer abroad. As a result, firm 1 produces only in market 1. As the technology matures, however, it becomes increasingly easy to transfer abroad (Vernon, 1966; 1979). Initially, firm 1 invests abroad but is willing to collude with its foreign rival, firm 2. Eventually, however, firm 1 becomes so strong that it threatens to drive firm 2 out of its domestic market, and at this stage firm 2 responds with a counter-threat to spoil firm 1's home market.

This process can be modelled through a sequence of comparative exercises in which at each stage in the sequence the costs of firm 1 are reduced. It is normally assumed that technical progress influences both the fixed costs and the variable costs of production. In the model presented here it influences only the fixed costs of production. This postulate is not quite so implausible as it may seem, however. First, it should be noted that the fixed costs in this model are recurrent costs that are avoidable by shut-down; they do not, therefore, correspond to the sunk costs associated with the introduction of the technology. Second, it should be noted that a high proportion of costs in many industries are independent of output, so that technical progress must of necessity reduce recurrent fixed costs in many cases if it is to be of any significance. Thirdly, it should be noted that technical advances in organizational design and administrative practices, which reduce X-inefficiency in the corporate bureaucracy, may reduce fixed costs while leaving variable costs quite unchanged. Finally, the results derived by focusing exclusively upon fixed cost reductions are intuitively reasonable and appear to be fairly robust to minor variations in the specification of the model.

It is assumed that the technical advance effected by firm 1 cannot be licensed to firm 2 because of the difficulties of devising, monitoring and enforcing the licensing contract.

The sequential analysis is illustrated by the numerical example shown in table 3.3. Firm 1 enjoys a substantial share of its home market – market 1 – whilst firm 2 dominates market 2. Firm 1 has fixed costs which are initially low in market 1 and very high in market 2. Firm 2's operations in market 1 have fairly modest fixed costs, but due to bureaucratic inefficiency its operations in its home market incur fairly high fixed costs.

In each market the intensity of demand $a_i = 12$, the price insensitivity of demand $b_i = 2$, and the marginal cost of production $c_i = 4$ $(i = 1,2)$. Equation (3.11) implies that under these conditions the break-even market share in each country is one-eighth of the fixed cost of production. In market 1 firm 1's break-even market share is 0.0312, below the corresponding value 0.0625 for firm 2. In country 2, on the other hand, firm 1's break-even market share is 0.5, well above the corresponding value 0.25 for firm 2 (see line 1 of the table).

Firm 1 has a 0.75 share of market 1 and (potentially) a 0.25 share of market 2. Firm 1 is the stronger firm in market 1, since the ratio of its break-even market share to its actual market share is lower, at 0.041, than the corresponding value 0.25 for firm 2. This means that firm 1 can set a lower limit price than firm 2 and can therefore, if it wishes, drive firm 2 out of the market. Firm 2, however, is stronger than firm 1 in market 2. This is because firm 1 is very weak rather than because firm 2 is particularly strong. Indeed, firm 1's break-even market share exceeds its actual market share, so that it cannot produce at all in market 2.

In market 1 firm 1 can earn a profit of 5.75 units from collusion with firm 2, but only 1.75 units from warfare. Firm 1 therefore opts for

TABLE 3.3 Sequential analysis of a switch from monopoly to tacit collusion to warfare in a duopoly

Line no.	a_1	b_1	c_1	a_2	b_2	c_2	m_{11}	m_{12}	m_{21}	m_{22}	d_{11}	d_{12}	d_{21}	d_{22}
1	12	2	4	12	2	4	0.75	0.25	0.25	0.75	0.25	0.5	4	2
2	12	2	4	12	2	4	0.75	0.25	0.25	0.75	0.25	0.5	1	2
3	12	2	4	12	2	4	0.75	0.25	0.25	0.75	0.25	0.5	0.25	2
4	12	2	4	12	2	4	0.75	0.25	0.25	0.75	0.5	0.1	0.25	2

Line no.	$\bar{m}_{11}$	$\bar{m}_{12}$	$\bar{m}_{21}$	$\bar{m}_{22}$	$\bar{m}_{11}/m_{11}$	$\bar{m}_{12}/m_{12}$	$\bar{m}_{12}/m_{21}$	$\bar{m}_{22}/m_{22}$	Stronger firm in market	
									1	2
1	0.031	0.062	0.5	0.25	0.041	0.25	2	0.33	1	2
2	0.031	0.062	0.125	0.25	0.041	0.25	0.5	0.33	1	2
3	0.031	0.062	0.312	0.25	0.041	0.25	0.125	0.33	1	1
4	0.062	0.012	0.312	0.25	0.083	0.25	0.125	0.33	2	1

Line no.	π^A_{11}	π^B_{11}	π^A_{12}	π^B_{12}	π^A_{21}	π^B_{21}	π^A_{22}	π^B_{22}	(A,A)		(A,B)		(B,A)		(B,B)	
									π^1	π^2	π^1	π^2	π^1	π^2	π^1	π^2
1	5.75[1]	1.75	1.5	0	0	0	4[1]	2	6.75	5.5	5.75	3.5	2.75	4	1.75	2
2	5.75[1]	1.75	1.5	0	1	0	4	0	7.5	5.5	10.33[2]	1.5[2]	3.5	4	6.33	0
3	5.75	1.75	1.5	0	1.75	4.58[1]	4	0	7.25	5.9	10.08[2]	1.9[2]	1.75	4.57	4.58	0.57
4	5.5	0	1.9[1]	0.57	1.75	4.58[1]	4	0								

[1]Indicates the profit earned by the stronger firm in the market.
[2]Indicates an outcome prohibited by threat.

collusion, providing firm 2 with a share of industry profit equal to 1.5 units. In market 2 firm 2 earns a monopoly profit of 6 units.

Firm 1's technology now matures and firm 1's fixed costs in market 2 fall to below those of firm 2. Firm 1's fixed costs in market 2 still remain above its fixed costs in market 1, however (see line 2 of the table). The fall in fixed costs reduces firm 1's break-even market share in market 2 from 0.5 to 0.125. Since firm 1's potential market share is 0.25, it is now profitable for it to tacitly collude with firm 2. Firm 2 is still the stronger, though, in market 2, but not strong enough to wish to drive firm 1 out of the market. Firm 2 can earn 4 units of profit from tacit collusion in market 2, but only 2 units from warfare. Firm 2 therefore allows firm 1 into market 2, permitting firm 1 to earn 1 unit of profit. Firm 1 prefers this to warfare, since under warfare firm 1, being the weaker firm, would earn no profit at all.

It should be noted that at this stage firm 2 has nothing to gain from attempting to co-ordinate its strategy towards firm 1 in the two markets. Its optimal strategy is to collude with firm 1 in both markets, and collusion is the optimal strategy in each market considered separately. Firm 2's profits in market 1, therefore, are the same as they would be were firm 1's rival in market 2 an entirely independent firm. Likewise firm 2's profits in market 2 are the same as they would be if its operations in market 1 were actually owned and controlled by an independent firm.

Firm 1's technology now matures to the point where it is completely standardized and can be transferred abroad at no cost. Firm 1's fixed costs in market 2 are now the same as in market 1, and so firm 1 has lower fixed costs than firm 2 in both markets (see line 3 of the table). Firm 1 also becomes the stronger firm in market 2; its ratio of break-even market share to actual market share falls to 0.125, well below the corresponding ratio 0.33 for firm 2. Moreover it is now profitable for firm 1 to drive firm 2 out of its home market. Firm 1's profit from warfare in market 2 rises to 4.58 units, compared to 1.75 units from collusion. In market 1, on the other hand, firm 1, although also the leader, still prefers to collude with firm 2. Nothing has changed in market 1, and so firm 1 would stand to lose 4 units of profit, as before, from an outbreak of warfare.

It now becomes advantageous for firm 2 to co-ordinate its strategies across markets. Firm 2 would stand to gain 4 units if firm 1 would abandon its warfare strategy in market 2. Firm 1 would lose 2.83 units of profit in market 1 by doing this. But firm 2 can inflict a loss of 4 units on firm 1 if it instigates warfare in market 1. Thus if firm 2 can make a credible threat to instigate warfare in market 1 unless firm 1 agrees to collude in market 2, firm 1 will make a net gain of 1.17 units by complying with firm 2's wishes. Although firm 2 would lose 4 units of profit if it had to actually implement its threat, this loss will not be sustained so long as the threat is successful.

Because firm 2 needs to co-ordinate its strategies, it is essential that its operations in both countries are under common ownership and control. For reasons already given, it would be unsatisfactory to co-ordinate strategies through an arm's length contractual arrangement. An objection to this argument might be that since the threat, if successful, need not be implemented, the costs of monitoring and enforcing the contract may not actually be incurred. Firm 1's perception of the credibility of the threat, however, will almost certainly be affected, and if firm 1 believes that the threat could not be effectively implemented then there is no need for it to modify its behaviour.

The effectiveness of the threat strategy may be affected by which is the stronger firm in market 1. Suppose that firm 2 and not firm 1 were the stronger in market 1. A case of this kind is illustrated in the bottom line of the table which shows firm 1 with fixed costs of 0.5 units in market 1, and firm 2 with fixed costs of only 0.1 units. Firm 2's ratio of break-even market share to actual market share is now only 0.05, below the corresponding figure 0.083 for firm 1. Firm 2's optimal strategy is to collude, generating a profit for itself of 1.9 units and for firm 1 of 5.5 units. All of firm 1's profit would be lost if firm 2 were to instigate warfare, and the loss to firm 2 would be only 1.33 units. Thus with firm 2 and not firm 1 the stronger firm in market 1, the threat power of firm 2 becomes even greater than before.

Following this sequence through, it can be seen that it is firm 1's decision to abandon the overseas exploitation of its technology by tacit collusion that triggers firm 2's threat. It is only when firm 2 needs to issue the threat that the international co-ordination of firm 2's operations become important. This implies that if firm 2 did not actually own the operation in market 1 that rivalled firm 1 then it would be advantageous at this stage for it to acquire it. In this way an overseas acquisition by firm 2 of an established rival to firm 1 may be a direct response to the aggressive exploitation of technology by firm 1.

Notice also that firm 2's threat is only effective because firm 1's operations are already international. If firm 2 had licensed a producer in market 2, and so no longer had control of pricing strategy in market 2, then a threat by firm 2 to spoil market 1 would be pointless, since there would be nothing that firm 1 could do about it. If the threat were then carried out, both firm 1 and firm 2 would be the losers. It is not, therefore, merely the possession of advanced technology that induces threats against firm 1, it is the combination of advanced technology, overseas exploitation through warfare, *and* the use of an equity rather than non-equity mode of transfer that is crucial.

3.9   OPPORTUNISM AND RIVALRY IN ACQUISITIONS

The discussion so far has ignored the possibility that firm 1 could forestall firm 2's foreign acquisition by acquiring its domestic rival itself. The management of firm 1 will know, before firm 2, about its own technological advance, and therefore has a 'head start' in considering the strategic consequences. Provided the owners of the domestic rival are unaware of its key position, firm 1 need pay no more than its rival's value as an independent going concern, and therefore cannot lose by the acquisition.

It is quite likely, however, that if the national government of country 1 has a strict competition policy of a conventional type – based upon restricting the market shares of the leading firms – then firm 1 will be prevented from acquiring its domestic rival on the grounds that the acquisition will increase seller concentration in the market. This in turn may allow in firm 2, and hence indirectly keep firm 1 from eliminating firm 2 from market 2. From the standpoint of conventional competition policy this consequence is an added bonus since with two producers in country 2 rather than just one, industrial concentration is reduced there too.

It is now widely appreciated that conventional competition policy takes too static a view of such situations. Although the symptoms of atomistic competition are more closely reproduced, the dynamics of the competitive process are inhibited. In the case above, the competition policy in country 1 stimulates tacit collusion in country 2. The new technology does not drive the old technology entirely out of market 2, so that market 2 is supplied at higher costs than necessary. Notice also, that because of the presence of economies of scale, wasteful replication of production units occurs in both markets.

Government intervention of a different kind could, however, work to firm 1's advantage. If the government of country 1 imposes restrictions on inward foreign investment then firm 2 may be unable to acquire the rival. Firm 1 then becomes immune to counter-threat, and therefore does not need to acquire the rival either. Hence the ban on inward foreign investment may help to preserve static competition in the domestic market.

This result seems rather strange, since the opposite case is often argued, namely that inward foreign investment promotes competition in domestic industry. The case for banning inward investment depends, however, upon the fact that the industry concerned is active in outward investment. If the industry is not aggressively investing overseas then there is no reason to protect domestic firms from counter-threat. In recent years the Japanese have made extensive use of the policy of promoting aggressive investment overseas whilst restricting counter-investments in Japan. As a result the Japanese have been able to take full advantage of the weaknesses of European competition policy, as outlined above.

In the absence of government interventions of any kind, it is quite possible that firms 1 and 2 may simultaneously arrive at an appreciation of the strategic significance of firm 1's domestic rival. If firms 1 and 2 bid competitively for the rival then the price of acquisition will rise to the point where one of the firms drops out. The maximum value of the rival to firm 1 is equal to its value under tacit collusion in market 1 *plus* the gain to firm 1 from being able to pursue warfare rather than collusion in market 2. The maximum value of the rival to firm 2 is equal to its value under tacit collusion in market 1 *plus* the gain to firm 2 from being able to avoid warfare in market 2. Thus if, in market 2, firm 1's gain from warfare exceeds firm 2's loss from warfare, firm 2 will drop out of the bidding first. Firm 1 will acquire the rival for a price equal to its maximum value to firm 2. Firm 2's threat will be nullified, and warfare will result in market 2. If, on the other hand, firm 2's loss from warfare exceeds firm 1's gain from warfare, then firm 1 will drop out of the bidding first. Firm 2 will acquire the rival at a price equal to its maximum value to firm 1. The threat will prevail, and collusion will occur in both markets.

In the case shown in line 3 of table 3.3, the gain to firm 1 from pursuing warfare rather than collusion in market 2 is only 2.83 units, whereas the gain to firm 2 from avoiding warfare in market 2 is 4 units. Thus firm 1 will drop out of the bidding first. Firm 2 will pay a total of $1.5 + 2.83 = 4.33$ units (suitably capitalized) for the rival. The threat will remain in force, and collusion will prevail in both markets. The net gain to firm 2 from avoiding warfare is $4 - 2.83 = 1.17$ units. The gain to firm 1 from producing overseas is a mere 1.75 units. The biggest gainers by far in this case are the owners of the rival firm, whose net gain is 2.83 units. This highlights the general point – already well known – that the innovation of a new technology can create substantial externalities, and that strategic behaviour by other firms can dissipate much of the innovator's potential reward (Kamien and Schwartz, 1982; Reingaum, 1981; 1985). What is interesting about this particular instance is that the major beneficiary of the innovation behaves entirely passively; it needs neither to innovate itself, nor to imitate the innovations of others. Neither does it benefit from initiating collusion; rather, it benefits because of the break-down of collusion between others.

3.10 CROSS-SUBSIDIZATION

In popular discussions of industrial policy, exchange of threats and cross-subsidization are often confused with one another (for a recent example see Hamel and Prahalad, 1985). This confusion is understandable, however, because of the complexity of the issues involved.

Economic principles suggest that it is inefficient for a profit-maximizing firm to cross-subsidize, except under very stringent conditions. The gist of the argument is that cross-subsidization can only be necessary to keep going an unprofitable activity, and unprofitable activities should be closed down. In applying this principle, though, it is important to recognize that accounting measures of cost may not always reflect true opportunity costs, particularly where there are complex interrelationships between individual activities. Thus cross-subsidization may be desirable in an accounting sense when accounting values and economic values have become out of line with each other, but only on the condition that when values are adjusted to an economic basis, the subsidy disappears.

This objection to cross-subsidization does not necessarily apply, however, to a *threat* of cross-subsidization which, if successful, will not have to be carried out. Neither does it always apply to actual cross-subsidization on a purely temporary basis, as explained later on.

The main advantage of cross-subsidization is that it increases the threat power of the firm. The firm's capacity to spoil a market is increased by its ability to switch profits earned elsewhere into underwriting losses in a spoiled market. There is a catch, however, and this is that cross-subsidization potentially increases the threat power of the rival too.

If the rival is somehow prevented from cross-subsidization then threatened cross-subsidization may well work unambiguously to the advantage of the firm. The rival, for example, may have no operations in other markets, or its other operations may generate no profit; alternatively the transfer of funds may be blocked by government or by management policy. Under these conditions, cross-subsidization can benefit a firm whether it is acting aggressively or defensively.

Consider to begin with a firm with an external source of profit that plans to enter a market dominated by an established firm which has no external source of profit. This is quite common in cases where an established MNE plans to enter a new national market which has hitherto been controlled by an indigenous monopolist. It is also quite common in cases of conglomerate diversification into a market for a different product. Suppose, however, that the entrant is the weaker firm, in the sense that, without a subsidy, the market price at which it breaks even is higher than that for the established firm. The entrant cannot therefore expect to drive out the established firm, but only to tacitly collude with it. Given the earlier assumption that re-entry is costless, it is not efficient for the firm to use a subsidy to drive out its rival, because the subsidy would have to be maintained on a permanent basis (see below). All it wishes to do is use the threat of a subsidy to persuade its rival to allow it to enter and collude.

Now under certain circumstances it may be more profitable for the established firm to deter entry by reducing price to the entrant's break-even level than to allow entry to occur. To counter such a move, the entrant may announce that it is willing to push the price down even further through cross-subsidization to a point at which tacit collusion becomes more profitable for its rival than continuing to resist entry. If this threat is credible then it will induce the established firm to tolerate entry on the basis of tacit collusion. Although the threat is self-damaging, it may still be credible on the basis that it is feasible to implement and that, once made, it is in the firm's long-run interests to ensure that it is carried out.

Cross-subsidization can also be used as a defensive strategy. Suppose for example that a potential entrant with no external source of profit plans to enter a market dominated by an established firm with an external source of profit. This is typical of the case of a small-scale entrant challenging an established MNE or conglomerate. Suppose, furthermore, that the entrant is the stronger firm and finds it profitable, in the absence of counter-threats, to drive the established firm out of the market. The established firm announces, however, that it will cross-subsidize price reductions in the market to the point where it would be more profitable for the entrant to tacitly collude than to take the whole of the market at the lower price. If the threat is credible, then the established firm will be able to survive with a diminished share of the market.

When both firms are able to cross-subsidize, matters become more complicated. Each firm can, in principle, use the threat of counter-cross-subsidization in an attempt to nullify cross-subsidization threatened by the other firm. This neutralizes any unilateral threat of cross-subsidization, and forces firms to choose, essentially, between tacit collusion and bilateral cross-subsidization. Under bilateral cross-subsidization, it is the overall strength of the firm that becomes crucial, rather than its strength in the particular market where the conflict occurs.

In the case where each firm draws its subsidy from a different market, which the other firm cannot penetrate, then the relative size of the profits generated in these markets becomes a key determinant of the relative strength of the two firms. It is possible, however, that both firms plan to draw their subsidies from the same market, in which case each firm must consider whether its planned source of subsidy will not itself be undermined by its rival's strategy. In the duopoly model discussed in the previous section, for example, firm 1 must consider, when threatening to cross-subsidize in market 2, whether firm 2 can in fact eliminate the planned source of profit by spoiling market 1. Likewise firm 2, in threatening to spoil market 1, must consider whether firm 1 can eliminate its planned source of profit by spoiling market 2.

This, in turn, raises the question of whether the threats exchanged between the two firms are mutually consistent, and what happens if an attempt is made to implement mutually inconsistent threats if tacit collusion breaks down. It is quite possible that the attempted implementation of inconsistent threats could bankrupt both firms. With the firms attempting to spoil both markets, neither may be able to break even, as each is denied the source of subsidy that it is depending on. In practice, the difficulty of determining whether threats are mutually consistent may discourage firms from threatening cross-subsidization in the first place. The devastating consequences of implementing inconsistent threats through error of judgement may create 'a balance of terror' in which mutual forbearance results. This in turn suggests that the assumption of no cross-subsidization made earlier may be much more plausible than at first it seems.

So far in the discussion, no role has been accorded to cross-subsidization in helping to drive a rival firm out of the market altogether. This is because it has been assumed, until now, that there are no barriers to the re-entry of a firm that has been driven out of a market. Given this assumption, a subsidy used to drive out a rival would have to be implemented on a permanent basis, and would therefore undermine the long-run profitability of the firm.

If, however, there is a barrier to re-entry then inter-firm rivalry may invoke cross-subsidization as a temporary expedient for forcing out a rival. Once the rival has been driven out, re-entry may be prohibitively costly, and so the successful firm enjoys permanent monopoly power. In determining which firm will be successful in driving out the other firm, the capital constraints facing the two firms have an important role (see chapter 2). The severity of the capital constraint determines how long the firm can sustain losses in the short run in order to 'see-off' its rival in the long run. The firm whose capital resources are most generous relative to the losses it stands to incur from the spoiling of markets is most likely to profit in the long run from initiating economic warfare. Cross-subsidization is useful to such a firm because it allows the capital constraint to be relaxed by temporarily drawing upon the profits earned in other markets. If, on the other hand, its rival stands to gain even more from cross-subsidization, then the dire prospect of mutual cross-subsidization may encourage the firm to seek tacit collusion instead. Even with barriers to re-entry, therefore, the risks of miscalculating the effects of cross-subsidization may deter firms from using the policy.

3.11   CASE STUDY EVIDENCE

Graham (1974) emphasizes that rivalistic foreign investment is not a new phenomenon. Of the historical cases he discusses, the most convincing support for his thesis is provided by the entry of Royal Dutch Shell into the US petroleum market between 1913 and 1930. This was in retaliation for Standard Oil's price-cutting tactics in Shell's major markets in Europe. In 1910 Standard Oil dumped excess kerosene in both Europe and the Far East, and at the same time cancelled contracts to buy Far Eastern petroleum from Shell. Sir Henri Deterding of Shell told his shareholders in 1911 that:

Although the price of crude oil was on the increase, our great competitor reduced the price of refined products on the market. This has been still more marked in the course of 1911, and has strengthened us in our conviction that the price reduction has no objective other than to hamper us as much as possible in the development of our business . . . A curious fact, which in our opinion is characteristic of the intentions of our competitors, is that the prices of kerosene were reduced most and quickest in the Netherlands Indies, whilst in Holland, where we sell no kerosene but only benzene, the benzene prices were reduced the most . . .

When our business grew to such international dimensions, we obviously had to dig ourselves in as traders on the American soil; otherwise, we would have lost our foothold everywhere else. Until we started trading in America, our American competitors controlled world prices, because . . . they could always charge up their losses in underselling us in other countries against business at home where they had a monopoly.

(Beaton, 1957, pp. 57–8, quoted in Graham, 1974, p. 30)

A well-known case, in which exchange of threats led to a market-sharing cartel agreement rather than cross-investment, concerns James Buchanan Duke's attempted acquisitions of British tobacco companies in 1901–2. Duke's American Tobacco Company held a virtual monopoly of the US market, and was protected from import competition by a high level of tariffs. His programme of acquisitions in Britain was halted by the creation of the Imperial Tobacco Company through a merger of British firms. Imperial decided that the best way of defending the British market was to mount an attack on Duke's monopoly of the US market, which was the major source of his financial strength.

The more strategically minded of Imperial's directors advocated a counter-attack by carrying the battle into the enemy's own territory. With suitable publicity, therefore, three members of Imperial arrived in the United States with the stated objective of acquiring a company that could be used to establish a bridgehead in the American market. Although these representatives failed in their immediate objective, they did decide on a suitable company and, in July, after they had returned to England negotiations for its acquisition were begun; and it is more than likely that Duke got to hear of these moves. A little later in the month, however, Imperial's directors were meeting at the Paddington Hotel when they received a visit from Mr. Ryan, one of Duke's closest business associates, and his right-hand man in England.

(Alford, 1973, p. 268)

Soon afterwards, a cartel agreement was signed. 'The American Tobacco Company agreed to withdraw from the UK and undertook not to re-enter it, and Imperial agreed not to invade the United States market. Each company acquired the trading rights in one another's brands and patents in its own home market, including the right to use respective trade marks' (p. 269). This agreement remained in force until 1911 when, following a US Supreme Court decree under the Anti-Trust Acts, the American Tobacco Company was split into four main companies – one of which retained the name American Tobacco Company – and some smaller units. A modified arrangement, however, continued in force until 1973 when a further agreement was reached along rather different lines.

Jones (1985a, p. 20) provides another example of a European company attempting to invest in the US to defend its home market against US competition. The example is taken from the motor tyre industry, which provides several examples of rivalistic behaviour.

Throughout the 1920s the Dunlop board never wavered from the belief that it was vital for the company to maintain a large manufacturing operation in the United States. A manufacturing company in the United States was seen as an important tool in the struggle against the major American tyre manufacturers. 'The big market of the world is the United States', the Dunlop board was reminded in 1928, 'and there our competitors are strong and we have not yet grown to the size we would like. There is always a danger so long as that situation lasts that we may be attacked in our strong market and very seriously damaged, whilst our competitors could carry the results of competition of that kind without suffering any appreciable set-back themselves'.

(Jones, 1985, p. 20)

The tyre industry witnessed in the 1970s a renewal of intense oligopolistic rivalry between European and US firms. In contrast to the previous case, however, the aggressor was a European firm and the defender was a US firm (Hamel and Prahalad, 1985). During the early 1970s consumer demand for radial tyres increased rapidly at the expense of cross-ply tyres. The technology of cross-ply manufacture was fairly mature, and in the US Goodyear was the market leader. In radial manufacture, however, Michelin had a significant technological lead over Goodyear. The conditions for threat and counter-threat deduced in section 3.4 were precisely satisfied. Michelin had a small share of the US market and a large share of the European market whilst Goodyear had a large share of the US market and a small share of the European market. Michelin undertook green field investment in the US and Goodyear countered with acquisition in Europe.

Goodyear's threat to cut prices in Europe did not deter Michelin from expansion in the US, and so its threat was actually implemented. Implementation of the threat did, however, slow up Michelin's expansion in the US, because it reduced the supply of funds for investment generated internally by Michelin's European operations. Both firms, however, suffered from the price war. They would both have been more profitable if Michelin had licensed its technology to Goodyear and the two firms had then colluded to maintain radial tyre prices in both the US and Europe. Consumers gained, of course, and so too did the owners of the facilities acquired by Goodyear in Europe.

Recent examples of cross investments can be found in other industries too (see, for example, Graham, 1985; Hennart, 1985). The phenomenon, however, is not a universal one, and it is probably of fairly limited significance compared to other motives for foreign investment such as backward integration to secure supplies of raw materials. Indeed, it cannot really be a complete theory of foreign investment, since technology transfer, or some other motive, is needed to explain the initial investment. For these reasons the theory is best viewed, not as an alternative to existing theories, but rather as an interesting extension of them.

3.12 IMPLICATIONS FOR FUTURE RESEARCH

The strategic issues that arise in the analysis of defensive investments have parallels in several other areas of economics. Indeed they have parallels in all the social sciences that deal with the role of threats in conflict escalation and conflict resolution. This suggests a very wide-ranging and lengthy agenda for future research.

There are, however, a number of more specific points which need to be taken up right away. It is important to relax a number of the restrictive assumptions on which the preceding model is based. It has been assumed, for example, that the two firms have similar marginal costs in each country. Linked to this is the assumption that technical progress reduces fixed costs but leaves variable costs unchanged. Relaxing these assumptions increases the complexity of the model, but should serve to increase its realism as well.

The model assumes only two countries. Generalizing the model to $m > 2$ countries appears to be fairly straightforward so long as all the other simplifying assumptions are maintained. In the m-country model the optimal counter-threat is to threaten warfare in all markets except the ones where the rival firm threatens aggression. Thus under appropriate conditions the *m*-country model becomes simply a 2-sector model in which each sector comprises several countries.

A more difficult project is to generalize the model to an oligopoly of $n > 2$ firms. In this case a number of different possibilities emerge, each requiring separate treatment. The crucial issue is how the entry or exit of a firm affects the distribution of each market between the remaining firms.

A particularly fruitful line of inquiry involves the introduction of international trade into the model. In this case the attitude of firms towards the protection of their home markets is crucial. Tariff lobbying at home is an effective defence against aggressive exporting by a rival. But to what extent is it also useful to an aggressive exporter which is seeking immunity from a counter-threat to its home market? If an aggressive firm employs both exporting and foreign investment to invade overseas markets, should it therefore lobby for both tariffs and restrictions on inward investment at home? To what extent can such strategic considerations explain the trade and investment strategy of Japan?

Another line of research is to relax the assumption that price cutting is the only threat available to the firm. Firms have other strategic weapons, such as advertising and counter-innovation. If price cutting is considered as an essentially short-run strategy, then advertising is a medium-run strategy, as it normally takes longer to prepare an advertising campaign than it does to announce a new price. Advertising, like price cutting, is a rivalistic phenomenon. Just as a reduction in price is likely to be matched by a rival, so an increase in advertising expenditure is also likely to be matched in order to maintain stability of the market shares.

It is also possible to distinguish between 'aggressive' and 'defensive' advertising. Aggressive advertising is a mechanism for launching a new or improved product. Defensive advertising is undertaken to counter aggressive advertising. The optimal response for a firm threatened by aggressive advertising by a rival may be to advertise defensively, not in the threatened market, but in another market elsewhere. The larger is a firm's existing market share, the greater is the probability that an advertiser using mass media is 'preaching to the converted' – i.e. advertising to existing customers. The smaller is his market share, therefore, the most cost effective his advertising is likely to be. This encourages firms to concentrate their advertising on markets where their share is small. Thus the optimal response for a firm whose home market is threatened by aggressive advertising may be to threaten the rival firm's home market rather than defend itself at home. As a result, 'cross-advertising' may be associated with 'cross-investment'.

In the long run, neither price cutting nor advertising removes the fundamental weakness of the firm whose costs are relatively high or whose product quality is relatively poor. The only really effective defence against innovation is some form of counter-innovation. This may involve merely imitating the rival's product. Imitation can be effected either with or without the consent of the aggressive firm. If the aggressor has patent protection then his consent is required, and if this is not forthcoming through a licensing contract, then the defensive strategy may involve heavy investment in R and D to develop an independent new technology or alternative product design. In this context, price cutting and defensive advertising may be used as 'holding operations' whilst the R and D programme is put into effect. A full analysis would therefore need to take account of how price cutting, advertising and R and D can be combined within the global strategies of both aggressive and defensive firms.

4

Quality Control and
Vertical Integration

4.1 THE RELEVANCE OF QUALITY CONTROL

Although product quality figures prominently in a number of recent discussions of market structure (Dixit and Stiglitz, 1977; Ireland, 1983; Lancaster, 1979) the mechanisms by which quality is assured have received little attention from economists. While quality has been recognized as an important element of non-price competition (Klein and Leffler, 1981; Shapiro, 1982), quality control itself has not been isolated from the rest of the production process to receive special study. One reason for this may be that a 'black box' approach to the production process persists among many economists, in spite of the pitfalls involved (Rosenberg, 1982). One major pitfall is the tendency to regard decisions taken within the black box as being of a purely technical nature. It is implicitly assumed that questions of statistical technique or engineering design do not involve economic considerations. As experts on these subjects are only too well aware, however, economic considerations are often paramount. This is apparent both in the literature on engineering production functions (Smith, 1961) and on statistical methods of quality control (Champernowne, 1953; Duncan, 1974; Wetherill, 1977). Where quality is concerned, ignoring economic factors leads to one of two extreme positions: either 'quality at any cost' or 'lowest cost whatever the quality'. Incorporating economic factors demonstrates that efficiency calls for the highest quality for a given cost, or equivalently, the lowest cost for a given quality. Efficiency considerations determine a frontier which trades off cost against quality, for a given quantity of output. Alternatively, quality and quantity can be traded off for a given cost. The optimal point on the trade-off is achieved when the benefit conferred by the marginal improvement in quality is just matched by the additional cost incurred.

One of the earliest writers to recognize the importance of quality control was the nineteenth-century English genius Charles Babbage. His interest in quality control arose partly from his attempts to construct a sophisticated mechanical computer for calculating mathematical and actuarial tables. These attempts were thwarted by the inability of London engineering firms to manufacture components to the requisite degree of precision. Babbage took a personal interest and through this developed a practical appreciation of the problems of quality control. In his book *On the Economy of Machinery and Manufacturers* (1832) he considered in detail methods of disciplining and rewarding workmen in order to improve workmanship and avoid wastage of materials in the factory. Regrettably, no writer since Babbage has presented such a comprehensive view of the place of quality control in the industrial system.

To appreciate the full significance of quality control it helps to follow Babbage and adopt a 'system view' of production. The division of labour within any economy means that most final products are generated by several stages of processing. Sometimes there is a simple vertical sequence of activities, and on other occasions various components or semi-processed materials are produced in parallel and assembled or somehow mixed together at a later stage to form the final product. At each stage economic decisions must be made about the appropriate level of quality. Each of these decisions has potential spill-overs so far as other stages of production are concerned. This is because the quality of each output is to some extent dependent on the quality of its inputs.

The question naturally arises as to whether the quality decisions at different stages can be decentralized. This question can be resolved into three distinct issues. First, whether in the absence of transaction costs, an efficient procedure could in principle be devised. Secondly, if it could, whether the transaction costs that would arise in practice are likely to make centralization cheaper instead. Thirdly, whether if decentralization is suitable, transactions costs are lower between the divisons of a single ownership unit, trading at shadow prices, or between independent ownership units which bargain with each other over arm's length prices.

Most of the existing literature on quality control and vertical integration (reviewed in section 1.5 and Casson, 1984) focuses upon this final issue. As such, it begs the important question of whether decentralization of any kind is compatible with efficient quality control. The analysis in this chapter affirms that quality decisions can, in principle, be decentralized, but suggests that under certain circumstances the incentive structure required may be prohibitively complex.

The issues raised by quality control are of much more than theoretical interest. Quality control skills are known to be a major element in the management skills of many leading multinationals. Quality control is a key factor in a number of other areas of economics too. The issues identified below reflect just some of the questions whose ultimate resolution may depend upon the development of a broad-based theory of quality control.

1 Why do some developing countries enjoy far greater success in export marketing of agricultural products than others, even though the quality of the crop, when harvested, appears to be the same in both cases (Jaffee, 1986a; 1986b)? Is deterioration of quality the result of organizational failures in the distribution channel (Brown, 1984)? If so, can vertical integration contribute to quality assurance, as it seems to do in other multi-stage processes?

2 Quality control is a major problem in many service industries (Inman, 1985; Moores, 1986). Customer complaints about 'quality of service' are much more difficult to resolve in some cases, though, than in others. In public transport systems, for example, it is fairly straightforward (though expensive) to resolve complaints about seating comfort by investing in new vehicles (or refurbishing existing stock). But it may be difficult to handle persistent complaints about the late arrival of scheduled services, and missed connections, without fundamental changes not only to scheduling but also to the routing of services, and perhaps even to the configuration of the system itself.

3 Most service industries are labour intensive, and many aspects of quality of service are directly determined by the quality of labour employed. Assessing the quality of workers' performance is often difficult, however, even with 'scientific' techniques of work measurement. This is particularly true where work is carried on in teams (Alchian and Demsetz, 1972). In a collaborative effort, overall performance is usually governed by the strength of the 'weakest link in the chain'. But identifying the weakest link – i.e. the poorest worker – can be extremely difficult. Better understanding of quality control may help identify situations where changes in employment policy are most likely to enhance the overall quality of the service provided.

4 Finally, how is it that the Japanese can manufacture high-quality standardized products at costs well below those of their US and European competitors (Baranson, 1981; Dunning, 1985b)? Do Japanese 'quality circles' have a genuine role in improving product quality, or are they simply a method of motivating a low-paid workforce to greater effort? If they are genuine, what precisely is their mechanism, and why have attempts to transfer the 'quality circle' concept to the West achieved such mixed results?

Obviously, it is impossible, within the scope of a single chapter, to deal thoroughly with all the issues raised above. Nevertheless, a model can be developed which is at once sufficiently general to show that the analogies drawn above do, in fact, reflect formal similarities between quite diverse phenomena, and yet sufficiently tractable to yield fairly simple formulae for its solution.

4.2   OUTLINE AND PLAN OF THE CHAPTER

The concept of quality is discussed in detail in the next section. It is argued that ultimately the demand for quality derives from the consumer, and in particular from the nuisance the consumer experiences when a product is treated as though it were good and it turns out unexpectedly to be bad. The intensity of the consumers' demand for quality influences the standards imposed by the final producer upon his own suppliers, and so on down the chain of supply. Detailed consideration of the chain of supply in section 4.4 identifies two main types of activity: transformation and sorting. Errors in transformation lead to defective output, while errors in sorting direct output into the wrong channel. It is shown that when sorting out defective items from satisfactory items, there exists a trade-off between accepting too many bad items and rejecting too many good ones. Optimization of sorting subject to this trade-off is the subject of section 4.5. A distinction is drawn between the power and toughness of a sorting strategy, and it is argued that power diminishes as capacity utilization of the sorting facilities increases. Optimization of transformation is the subject of section 4.6, and once again capacity utilization plays a crucial role. The analysis suggests that for the production system as a whole, the problem of co-ordinating quality decisions at different stages is closely allied to harmonizing investments in capacity throughout the system.

A scheme for decentralizing quality decisions is presented in section 4.7. The manager of each activity is paid a fixed price for each unit processed, and is charged a heavy penalty for any defect induced in processing. The scheme works well for transformation activities but, as shown in section 4.8, its implementation is problematic where sorting is concerned.

Section 4.9 compares centralized non-price decision making with decentralized decision making within the same ownership unit. The comparison is based upon the administrative costs of the two organizational forms. It is argued that centralization is appropriate to complex configurations of essentially simple activities, such as transformation, whilst decentralization is appropriate to simple configurations of relatively complex activities such as sorting.

Section 4.10 evaluates alternative ownership structures for quality control. It re-examines conventional arguments in favour of vertical integration and shows that it is no single factor, but rather a coincidence of factors, that discourages subcontracting and favours quality control. The four practical issues identified above are reconsidered in section 4.11, and a number of testable implications are deduced. The chapter concludes with suggestions for future research.

4.3   DEFINITION AND MEASUREMENT OF QUALITY

The concept of quality is not so simple as it first appears. It is useful to begin with the primitive concept of an 'attribute'. Most goods have a wide range of attributes – size, shape, weight, colour, and so on. Many of these attributes, though, are of little significance so far as the typical buyer is concerned. Attributes which are especially significant to the buyer may be termed 'characteristics' of the good (following Lancaster, 1966; 1979). Which attributes are significant to a buyer depends upon the function that the good is required to perform. Many goods serve more than one function, so that two or more distinct sets of characteristics may be significant. A motor car, for example, has as its principal function personal transport, so that characteristics such as speed, acceleration and luggage space are relevant; but it also has a function in conspicuous social display, so that characteristics such as styling and colour are important too.

Once the functions of the good are known, the concept of performance becomes relevant. Some levels of performance will be acceptable to the buyer, and others not. The division between acceptable and unacceptable is given by the standard to which the buyer expects the good to perform. It is assumed that for each characteristic there is a corresponding standard of performance. In the case of customized products, where the buyer himself has dictated the specification, he will, if sensible, have included certain minimum standards of performance into the specification. In other cases, the buyer's standard may be based upon claims advanced by the producer – for heavily promoted mass-produced goods, for example, the buyer may simply expect the good to do what the advertising says it will do. Failure to meet the buyers' standard – whether it is implicit or explicit, and whether formulated by the buyer or the seller – means that the product is unsatisfactory.

It should be noted that this approach to product standards is a psychological one rather than a legal one. It says, essentially, that the product is unsatisfactory if the buyer is disappointed with it. The approach does not require that there be default – in the legal sense – on the terms of a contract of sale.

The concept of standards works best when product performance is objective and measurable. It is less satisfactory for, say, works of artistic merit, where the most valued characteristics are difficult to define and impossible to measure. It also works best when all buyers set their standards at the same level. Differences between buyers' standards may emerge for cultural reasons. Japanese consumers, for example, are reputed to demand much higher standards of retail service than do European consumers. Buyers may also set different standards because of the way in which they utilize the product. A buyer who uses the product carelessly, or very intensively, may well find its performance worse than a buyer who uses it skilfully, or on only an occasional basis. Abuse of the product by buyers is of considerable concern to reputable producers, who fear that their good name may be tarnished by vociferous complaints from a few inept users of it.

Agreement on standards between buyer and seller is even more important than agreement between one buyer and another. If buyer and seller cannot agree upon common standards then endless disputes are liable to arise over product quality. Anticipation of these disputes will raise the transaction costs perceived by both parties, and so deter trade. Many governments have introduced national standards to avoid this difficulty, and international standards have even been agreed for some products – sometimes in the interests of consumers' health and safety, and in other cases to further the interests of producing nations in promoting international trade.

A buyer may well use several different standards of performance in respect of a given characteristic. The highest standard may correspond to 'excellence', the second to 'good', and the third to 'adequate'. This is an example of grading the product by recording the highest standard which it is able to achieve.

It is possible to think of standards as things which can, in the long run, be set with some sort of optimization in mind. In this chapter, however, standards are simply regarded as exogenous. They are culturally determined parameters which are common to all the producers and consumers involved. A more ambitious analysis of the role of quality considerations as a whole within economic life would have to allow for endogenous changes in standards. But that approach is well outside the confines of the present analysis.

Given the prevailing standards, the simplest way to represent the quality of a product is in terms of a matrix of zero–one values. The columns represent the characteristics and the rows represent the grades, ordered from the highest grade in the first row to the lowest grade in the last row. An element of unity in the ith row and jth column indicates that the product has achieved the ith grade in respect of the jth characteristic. Since by assumption, for any given characteristic the various grades are mutually exclusive and collectively exhaustive, the elements in each column sum to unity.

The most elementary case involves a single characteristic and a single standard of performance. This defines two grades – satisfactory and unsatisfactory – and the matrix, in this case, reduces to a two-element column vector. Where several characteristics are involved, the number of grades associated with each characteristic may vary. In this case the number of rows is set equal to the maximum number of grades which are used in respect of any of the characteristics, and dummy grades, below the minimum grades, are defined for characteristics using less than the maximum number of grades. Since the dummy grades are never actually observed, the corresponding elements are always set to zero.

When a product is produced on a one-off basis, the quality of a unit of the product is indistinguishable from the quality of the product as a whole. When several units of the same product are produced, however, it is quite likely that performance will vary across units. This variability of the units may be regarded as an additional attribute of the product. Variability may be accommodated by relaxing the zero–one constraint on the quality matrix. While each *unit* of product continues to be associated with a zero–one matrix, the *product as a whole* is associated with a real-valued quality matrix. This matrix describes a set of probability distributions, one for each characteristic. The element in the ith row and jth column of this matrix is equal to the probability that the jth characteristic will assume the ith grade.

It is a fundamental postulate of the theory developed in this chapter that the probabilistic quality matrix has a number of parameters which can be controlled by the management of the firm. Varying the parameters, it is assumed, affects the costs of the firm. Varying the probabilities, on the other hand, affects the firm's revenues. Thus increasing expenditure on supervisory services may raise the probability that a unit of output achieves the highest grade. Assuming that the price of the highest grade reflects a quality premium, this raises the expected revenue of the firm. The managers must therefore trade off the additional revenue from higher quality against the additional cost of more intensive supervision. In general, in a profit-maximizing firm, quality management involves setting the parameters of the quality matrix to equate marginal expected revenue to marginal cost. The consequences of this decision rule are explored below.

4.4   THE STRUCTURE OF A PRODUCTION PROCESS

Factors influencing the probabilistic quality matrix encompass both the design of the product and the actual process of production. Design and production are intimately related, but in the context of the model below, design factors are taken as given and the emphasis is placed upon control of the production process.

Quality control can be analysed using either a static or dynamic approach. The static approach is the simplest, and forms the basis of the analysis below. In this approach, it is assumed that the system can be effortlessly maintained in a steady state equilibrium, and that changes from one equilibrium to another – made in response to exogenous changes – incur no adjustment costs.

The typical production process comprises a complex of activities. All the activities are connected by flows of intermediate products. The crucial point is that each intermediate product stream is not homogeneous, but is a mixture of different elements. Thus a stream of car batteries supplied by an electrical component manufacturer to a motor vehicle assembly line comprises a mixture of car batteries that work and those that do not. Similarly, a stream of ethyl alcohol flowing from one part of a chemical plant to another is in fact a mixture of ethyl alcohol and various other chemicals that constitute impurities in the solution.

Each activity has, in principle, two quite distinct aspects. The first is *transformation* and the second is *sorting*. Transformation occurs when the composition of output – averaged over all the output streams – differs from the composition of the inputs – averaged over all the input streams. The interpretation of input and output is intended to be quite general. Thus transformation includes transportation (transforming location), storing (transforming in time) and the utilization of assets (transforming an asset into a depreciated asset by the generation of asset services).

Sorting occurs when the output streams have compositions that differ from one another in some systematic way. Thus a cracking and distillation process in an oil refinery that sends petroleum out down one pipeline and heavy oils down another is using physical and chemical processes to effect a sorting operation. A transportation system that sends parcels from London to Crewe on the train for Glasgow and parcels for Cardiff on the train to Swansea is effecting a sorting operation using a more conscious process.

Conventional economic theory is preoccupied with pure transformation processes. Sorting does not enter because each process generates only a single product. If this product is completely homogeneous then there is no need to subsequently sort through the output stream. But if the product is heterogeneous then the output stream contains a mixture of items, and it may then be advantageous to sort the items into separate streams later on. The fact that the process itself does not do this creates the problem of quality control, which the separate sorting process is required to resolve.

A pure sorting process does not involve transformation. Thus if the output stream from the transformation process contains a mixture of 'good' and 'bad' items, a pure sorting process does not affect the overall balance between them. The proportion of bad items – when averaged over all the output streams from the sorting process – is the same as the proportion of bad items in the stream received from the transformation process. What has happened is that the 'good' items have been concentrated in the 'good output' stream and the 'bad' items in the 'bad output' stream. The output streams from the sorting process are therefore much less of a mixture than is the original output stream from the transformation process. These streams can therefore be utilized with much greater confidence in the subsequent stages of production.

Sorting involves two logically distinct stages, but in practice both stages are often carried out by the same operative or the same piece of machinery. Consider a single stream which is input to a sorting process. The first stage is to label the individual items by assigning them to one of several categories or grades – as determined by the standards of performance applied to the product. The labelling involves an inspection process, which generates information on the item, and a decision rule which describes how the information is to be used to determine the label that is applied. The labelled items are passed on to a switching mechanism which recognizes the labels and directs the items into the appropriate output stream.

Sorting decisions will not, in general, be entirely accurate. Errors can occur at either inspection or switching. The model developed below focuses upon a simple decision between good and bad items. In this case, two types of error can be made: the type I error of rejecting a good item from the 'good output' stream, and the type II error of accepting a 'bad' item for the 'good output' stream.

It has been shown above that transformation activities that generate multiple products involve not only transformation, but sorting as well. Conversely, many sorting activities involve not only sorting, but transformation too. This transformation is effected by either the inspection process or the switching process. In some cases inspection does not affect the items themselves, but in many cases it does. The method of inspection may result in damage to some of the items, while in other cases it may provide the opportunity for a quick repair.

Sorting activities that involve transformation are quite complicated to specify because it is necessary to know whether the transformation that occurs can be detected by the inspection process. If the transformation occurs at the switching stage then it is unlikely to be detected. Thus a switching mechanism that damages items being directed along the 'good output' stream can undermine much of the work done by the preceding inspection process. If the transformation occurs at the inspection stage, then its consequence may depend upon whether the change is accidental or deliberate. Accidental damage, for example, may go undetected, but deliberate damage will almost certainly be detected. Thus sample items that are deliberately tested by trial use can be channelled to the 'bad output' stream, whilst the remains of items that have been tested to destruction can be channelled to a special 'waste products' stream.

To simplify the analysis, it is assumed in this chapter that production comprises only pure transformation and pure sorting activities. Each transformation activity takes a single input and transforms it into single output, whilst each sorting activity sorts a single stream into two streams, labelled 'good' and 'bad' respectively. The extension of the analysis to activities which combine transformation and sorting is considered briefly in section 4.10.

These assumptions are not quite so restrictive as they may seem. Many activities have either transformation or sorting as their primary rationale, and do not aim to achieve both simultaneously. Discussions of quality control often focus upon a simple vertical sequence in which a raw material is progressively transformed into a finished product; this is equivalent to a series of pure transformation activities. Other discussions focus upon the desirability of interpolating pure sorting activities somewhere in such a sequence. Both these issues can be discussed at an elementary level without recourse to models in which transformation and sorting occur within the same activity.

4.5 THE ECONOMICS OF PURE SORTING

Consider a profit-maximizing firm which purchases a product from subcontractors who produce under constant returns to scale and just break even. Customers buy only from the firm, and not from the subcontractors. Their demand is infinitely price-elastic, and affords the firm a parametric margin between purchase price and selling price equal to $p > 0$. Customers can identify two grades of product: 'good' and 'bad'. Bad product is identified by the adverse experience it generates. Customers demand, and receive, full compensation from the firm for all adverse experiences they endure. This compensation is equal to $\alpha_1 p$, where $\alpha_1 > 0$. In the special case where $\alpha_1 = 1$ the customer is effectively supplied the product at the wholesale price, wiping out the firm's margin exactly. Since customers are fully compensated, they perceive no risk in the use of the product.

The input purchased from the subcontractors comprises a mixture of good and bad products. The proportion of bad products, ϕ $(0 \leqslant \phi \leqslant 1)$ is exogenous, and is the same for all subcontractors. No compensation is available on bad items supplied, but so long as the proportion of bad items remains exogenous, this assumption is of little consequence. Individual items of the product are so highly divisible that the variance of the fluctuations in the firm's revenue stream due to variability of the quality supplied to customers is negligible.

The object of sorting is to channel good items – and only good items – into the 'good product' stream that is marketed under the brand name, and to channel bad items – and only bad items – into the 'bad product' stream that is marketed as unbranded output or 'seconds'. Customers are also potential users of the bad output, but they put this to an alternative use. This use does not allow them to discriminate between any good units of product which may inadvertently be mixed up with bad units in the supplies of unbranded output. Customers' demand for unbranded output is perfectly elastic at a parametric margin $(1 - \alpha_2)p$, where $100\alpha_2$ $(0 \leqslant \alpha_2 < 1)$ is the percentage discount relative to the good product. It is assumed that $\alpha_1 > \alpha_2$, because otherwise the sorting of output prior to use would be pointless. It is the fact that the value of bad output, when used on the assumption that it is good, is less than the value of bad output when used on the assumption that it is bad, that makes it efficient to distinguish the good output from the bad prior to utilization taking place.

As noted earlier, two types of error can be made in sorting: the type I error of rejecting good output and the type II error of accepting bad output. The conditional probability of a type I error, $a_1 (0 \leqslant a_1 \leqslant 1)$ is the probability that, given a good item, it will be rejected, while the conditional

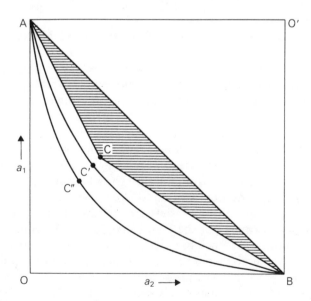

FIGURE 4.1   Trade-off between type I and type II error probabilities

probability of a type II error, $a_2 (0 \leqslant a_2 \leqslant 1)$ is the probability that, given a bad item, it will be accepted.

It is assumed that all items are sorted. The most arbitrary form of sorting is to make no observations on the items whatsoever and simply reject at random a proportion $\varrho (0 \leqslant \varrho \leqslant 1)$ of all the output. This associates a type I probability $a_1 = \varrho$ with a type II probability $a_2 = 1 - \varrho$. The trade-off between type I and type II errors generated by varying ϱ is illustrated by the diagonal line AB in figure 4.1.

It is assumed that both types of error cannot be simultaneously eliminated – i.e. completely error-free measurement of quality is impossible. On the other hand, it is possible to do better using observation than without observation. Specifically it is assumed that there is at least one point lying below AB, and excluding the no-error origin O, that can be attained using a suitable test. Let this point be denoted C.

Randomized test procedures can be used in which different types of test are applied with given probabilities. Non-randomized tests are referred to as pure tests, to avoid confusion. To illustrate, randomized procedures which combine the pure test C with the rule of rejecting everything, represented by A, generate the line AC. Each point on the line AC represents a combination of the two pure tests which attaches different probability weights to them. Combining C with all the arbitrary pure tests represented by the line AB generates the convex set represented by the shaded area ABC.

The pure test represented by C is a sensible test in the sense that it improves upon the arbitrary procedures along AB. For every sensible test, however, there is a corresponding silly test that does worse than the procedures along AB. A silly test is obtained from a sensible test by reversing the test criterion so that everything that was previously accepted is now rejected, and vice versa. Thus a sensible test with probability errors $a_1' + a_2' < 1$, generates a silly test with probability errors $a_1^* = 1 - a_1', a_2^* = 1 - a_2'$, such that $a_1^* + a_2^* > 1$. Silly tests have received explicit attention in statistical decision theory, but since they are demonstrably inefficient relative to arbitrary tests they will be ignored here.

In general there may be many sensible pure test procedures such as that represented by C. The convex hull formed by these points together with the points A and B has a lower boundary which is convex to the origin O. This lower boundary is the efficiency frontier for the test procedures. When there are infinitely many pure test procedures a smoothly curved frontier such as AC'B may result. It is assumed that as expenditure on resources devoted to sorting is increased, so this boundary, whilst remaining fixed at A and B, shifts outwards continuously in the direction of O. This is because additional resources permit more accurate observations, and more accurate observations allow more powerful tests of quality to be performed. The shift is illustrated in the figure by the transition from the curve AC'B to AC''B.

The precise details of the mechanism are not strictly relevant, but an example may clarify the situation. Suppose that when an item is inspected, a measurement is recorded on an attribute which is believed to be correlated with its quality. When the item is good, the attribute ζ is distributed with density function $f(\zeta, \mu_1, \sigma_1)$ where μ_1 is a location parameter and σ_1 a dispersion parameter. When the item is bad, on the other hand, the density function is $f(\zeta, \mu_2, \sigma_1)$ where $\mu_2 < \mu_1$. The pure test criterion:

accept the item if $\zeta \geqslant \zeta^*$
reject the item if $\zeta < \zeta^*$

generates the type I and type II error probabilities

$$a_1 = \int_{-\infty}^{\zeta^*} f(\zeta, \mu_1, \sigma_1) = F(\zeta^*, \mu_1, \sigma_1)$$

$$a_2 = \int_{\zeta^*}^{\infty} f(\zeta, \mu_2, \sigma_1) = F(\zeta^*, \mu_2, \sigma_1)$$

Under suitable conditions on f, varying ζ^* over the real line determines a spectrum of pure test procedures which is represented by a continuous negatively-sloped locus of points joining A to B and lying on or below the diagonal AB. The corresponding efficiency frontier may be identified with the lower boundary of the convex hull formed by the points on the locus and the points on the diagonal AB. As resource inputs are increased, the dispersion parameter is reduced to $\sigma_2 < \sigma_1$, increasing the power of test procedures for at least some values of ζ^*. The mechanism is illustrated by the comparison of the upper and lower graphs in figure 4.2. In terms of figure 4.1, the effect is to push out the efficiency frontier in the direction of O.

To generate a computable model it is useful to specify a simple functional form for the efficiency frontier. This is not so easy as it may seem, however, because one of the parameters needs to be an index of the convexity of the frontier. It is difficult to find a functional form which satisfies the twin conditions that its graph passes through points A and B and that it is easy to differentiate it with respect to its index of convexity. In the model presented below, the first of these conditions has been relaxed, in order that the second can be very easily satisfied.

It is assumed that the respective type I and type II error probabilities are given by

$$a_1 = x_1/2x_2 \tag{4.1a}$$
$$a_2 = 1/2x_1 x_2 \tag{4.1b}$$

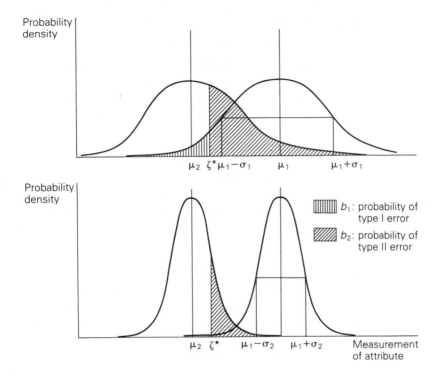

FIGURE 4.2 Geometric interpretation of type I and type II errors

where x_1 is an index of the toughness of the test criterion, and x_2 is an index of the power of the test. A tough test is one that gives a low probability of a type II error. A powerful test gives a low probability of a type I error for a given probability of a type II error. To support the interpretation of a_1, a_2 as probabilities, it is necessary that $x_2 \geqslant x_1 \geqslant 0$. It is also required that, for a given value of x_1, there must be at least one test procedure that is sensible (i.e. $a_1 + a_2 < 1$); this implies that $x_2 > 1$.

Let θ_0 be the probability that a unit of output emerges from the sorting process as good output labelled as good, θ_1 the probability that it emerges as bad output labelled as bad, and θ_2 the probability that it emerges as good or bad output labelled as bad. The laws of probability imply that

$$\theta_0 = (1 - a_1)(1 - \phi) \tag{4.2a}$$
$$\theta_1 = a_2 \phi \tag{4.2b}$$
$$\theta_2 = a_1 (1 - \phi) + (1 - a_2)\phi \tag{4.2c}$$

The expected revenue generated by a unit output channelled through the sorting process is

$$v = (\theta_0 + (1 - \alpha_1)\theta_1 + (1 - \alpha_2)\theta_2)p$$

which, using equations (4.2), can be expressed as

$$v = [1 - \alpha_2\phi - \alpha_2(1 - \phi)a_1 - (\alpha_1 - \alpha_2)\phi a_2]p \qquad (4.3)$$

The terms in the square brackets in equation (4.3) may be interpreted as follows. The first term shows the revenue generated if all the output is good, and just one unit of good output is supplied for a unit margin. The second term shows the revenue lost when a proportion of the output is bad and is sold off as such. The third term shows the revenue lost when some of the good output is sold off as bad by mistake. The final term shows the revenue lost when bad output that should have been sold off is supplied as good output by mistake.

With respect to the cost structure of the sorting process, two crucial assumptions are made. The first is that variations in the toughness of the test are costless. In other words setting high standards is not itself difficult: it is discriminating between the items that meet these standards and those that do not that is problematical. The second is that the power of the test, x_2, increases with the capacity of the sorting activity. Capacity is measured by the stock of physical and human capital that is devoted to sorting. This stock is fixed in the short run, but variable in the long run, when additional units of capacity services can be procured at a parametric price $w > 0$. Let the rate of throughput of items be $y > 0$ and the amount of capacity be $z > 0$; then capacity utilization is measured by

$$u = y/z \qquad (4.4)$$

It is assumed that

$$x_2 = 1/u^\beta \qquad (4.5)$$

where $\beta \geqslant 1$ is a technological parameter. Equation (4.5) implies that when capacity is infinite, so that utilization is zero, the power of the test is also infinite, so that both type I and type II errors are zero. On the other hand, when capacity is fully utilized, the power of the test is unity, which means that the test is no better than a procedure which arbitrarily rejects a certain proportion of the output irrespective of its observable characteristics. The precise relation between capacity utilization and power is illustrated in figure 4.3.

the total cost of the sorting process is

$$c = wz \qquad (4.6)$$

while total revenue is

$$r = vy \qquad (4.7)$$

Profit

$$\pi = r - c \qquad (4.8)$$

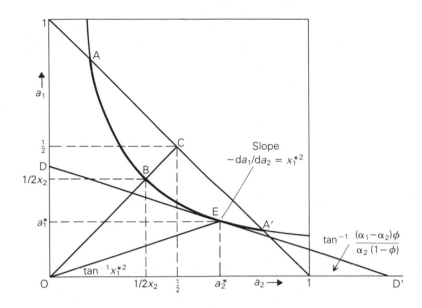

FIGURE 4.3   Determination of the optimal toughness of a test for a given level of power

is maximized in the short run by choosing x_1 and y, with z fixed. In the long run, since there are constant returns to the scale of throughput, profit is maximized by choosing x_1 and z for a given y. In each case, the solution for x_1, y and z determines the power of the test x_2, the capacity utilization, u, and the probabilities of the two types of error, a_1, a_2. These probabilities can in turn be used to calculate the mixtures of good and bad items in each of the output streams, as determined by the probabilities θ_0, θ_1 and θ_2.

Solving the first order conditions for short-run maximum of profit gives the equilibrium values

$$x_1^* = [(\alpha_1 - \alpha_2)\phi/\alpha_2(1 - \phi)]^{\frac{1}{2}} \tag{4.9}$$

$$x_2^* = [(\alpha_1 - \alpha_2)\alpha_2\phi(1 - \phi)]^{\frac{1}{2}}/(1 - \alpha_2\phi) \tag{4.10}$$

$$u^* = 1/x_2^{*1/\beta} \tag{4.11}$$

$$y^* = u^*z \tag{4.12}$$

whence

$$a_1^* = 1/2\,\alpha_2(1 - \phi)(1 - \alpha_2\phi) \tag{4.13}$$

$$a_2^* = 1/2\,(\alpha_1 - \alpha_2)\phi(1 - \alpha_2\phi) \tag{4.14}$$

The corresponding long-run equilibrium is

$$x_1^{**} = [(\alpha_1 - \alpha_2)\phi/\alpha_2(1-\phi)]^{1/2} \tag{4.15}$$

$$x_2^{**} = \{[(\alpha_1 - \alpha_2)\alpha_2\phi(1-\phi)]^{1/2}(\beta p/w)\}^{\beta/(\beta+1)} \tag{4.16}$$

$$u^{**} = 1/x_2^{**1/\beta} \tag{4.17}$$

$$z^{**} = u^{**}y \tag{4.18}$$

whence

$$a_1^{**} = (1/2)[(\alpha_1 - \alpha_2)\phi/((\alpha_2(1-\phi))^{2\beta+1}]^{1/2(\beta+1)}(w/p\beta)^{\beta/(\beta+1)} \tag{4.19}$$

$$a_2^{**} = (1/2)[\alpha_2(1-\phi)/((\alpha_1 - \alpha_2)\phi)^{2\beta+1}]^{1/2(\beta+1)}(w/p\beta)^{\beta/(\beta+1)} \tag{4.20}$$

It is readily established that under the assumed restrictions on the values of the parameters α_1, α_2, β, the second-order conditions for a maximum of profit are satisfied.

Comparing equations (4.9) and (4.15) shows that the toughness of the test is the same in both the short run and the long run. It is only the power of the test that is different in the two cases. The power of the test differs because the opportunity cost of raising the power is different. In the short run the opportunity cost is given by the value of the output that must be sacrificed to reduce the utilization of a given amount of capacity, while in the long run the opportunity cost is governed by the price of additional capacity.

The determination of the optimal toughness of the test is illustrated in figure 4.3. The axes measure the error probabilities a_1, a_2, as in figure 4.1. The efficiency frontier is represented by the curve ABEA′, which is convex to the origin O. The power associated with this frontier is measured by the ratio of the lengths OC/OB. The functional form for the efficiency frontier implied by equations (4.1) equates the slope of the frontier to the square of the toughness of the test. The iso-revenue line DD′ is a straight line whose slope is equal to the ratio of the additional revenue gained by reducing the conditional probability of a type II error to the additional revenue gained by an equal reduction in the conditional probability of a type I error. The marginal revenue associated with the type II error is the gain from selling a bad item as bad instead of good, $(\alpha_1 - \alpha_2)p$, multiplied by the probability that the item is bad, ϕ; the marginal revenue associated with the type I error is the gain from selling a good item as good instead of bad, $\alpha_2 p$, multiplied by the probability that the item is good, $1 - \phi$.

The higher is the level of revenue, the lower is the iso-revenue line. The lowest attainable iso-revenue line, DD′, is tangent to the efficiency frontier at E. The slope of the ray OE measures the square of the optimal toughness of the test. The coordinates of E measure the optimal error probabilities a_1^*, a_2^*.

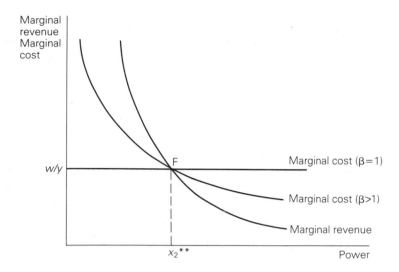

FIGURE 4.4   Determination of the optimal power of a test in the long run

Using this diagram it is easy to see that an increase in the probability of bad items will increase the steepness of the iso-revenue line and hence lead to a tougher test criterion. The same effect would be produced if the penalty associated with misrepresenting a bad item as good were increased, or if the price penalty associated with supplying a good item as bad were reduced. Notice that these effects apply both in the short run and in the long run, and are independent of the level of capacity, the cost of capacity services and the scale of throughput.

These independence properties are a reflection of the fact that the toughness can be solved for using a single first-order condition. The optimal toughness can then be substituted into the other first-order condition to give a single equation in a single unknown, from which the optimal power of the test can be determined. The determination of the optimal power is illustrated in figure 4.4. It is a long-run equilibrium that is shown. In the special case where $\beta = 1$, the marginal cost of power, for a given level of throughput, is equal to the marginal cost of capacity services, normalized by the rate of throughput, and is therefore constant at a level w/y. When $\beta > 1$, the marginal cost diminishes with respect to power, and as β tends to infinity the marginal cost schedule tends towards a hyperbolic form. The marginal revenue schedule, however, diminishes always as the reciprocal of the square of the power, and hence cuts the marginal cost schedule from above at a point such as F. The ordinate of F determines the optimal power of the test.

These results are prefaced on the existence of interior maxima ($0 <$ $a_1^*, a_2^*, u^*, a_1^{**}, a_2^{**}, u^{**} < 1$). Plausible values for parameters such as the input prices will generate interior maxima, but it cannot be guaranteed that sensible solutions exist for all values of these parameters.

4.6   THE ECONOMICS OF PURE TRANSFORMATION

The economics of transformation is much simpler than that of sorting. The case discussed here is particularly simple, because all that happens is that a single stream of input mixture is transformed into a single stream of output mixture. Bad items in the input mixture are transformed into bad items in the output mixture. Good items in the input mixture are transformed into either good or bad items in the output mixture. The probability that a good item is rendered defective during the transformation process increases with the level of capacity utilization. When capacity utilization is zero, the probability of introducing a defect is zero, whilst when capacity utilization is unity the probability of introducing a defect is unity – i.e. full capacity operation renders all the output defective.

Following the previous notation, let the probability of finding defective input be ϕ and the probability of finding defective output be θ ($0 \leqslant \phi, \theta \leqslant 1$). Let a be the probability of introducing a defect ($0 \leqslant a \leqslant 1$); then

$$\theta = a(1 - \phi) + \phi \tag{4.21}$$

Let u be capacity utilization, y throughput, and z capacity. It is assumed that

$$a = u\gamma \tag{4.22}$$

where

$$u = y/z \tag{4.23}$$

and $\gamma \geqslant 1$ is a technological parameter.

It is assumed that there are two components of cost. Direct processing cost, c_1 incurred in respect of energy, etc., is directly proportional to throughput

$$c_1 = w_1 y \tag{4.24}$$

where $w_1 \geqslant 0$ is the parametric price of processing services. The cost of capacity services, c_2, is directly proportional to capacity, as before,

$$c_2 = w_2 z \tag{4.25}$$

where $w_2 > 0$ is the parametric price of capacity services.

The margin between the price of the input and the price of the output is $p > 0$, but defective output incurs a penalty of αp, so that if $\alpha = 1$ the output is supplied at the same price at which the input is purchased. No compensation is available for defective input, however. The firms' average margin is therefore

$$v = (1 - \alpha\theta)p \qquad (4.26)$$

Revenue imputed to transformation is

$$r = vy \qquad (4.27)$$

total cost

$$c = c_1 + c_2 \qquad (4.28)$$

and profit

$$\pi = r - c \qquad (4.29)$$

In the short run, capacity, z, is fixed and profit is maximized by choosing the level of throughput y. This in turn affects capacity utilization, u, and hence the induced defect rate, a. In the long run, capacity is variable and the firm operates under constant returns to the rate of throughput. The level of output, y, is therefore taken as given, and profit is maximized by choosing the capacity, z. This in turn influences the capacity utilization, u, and hence the defect rate, a.

Solving the first-order condition for a short-run maximum of profit with respect to y gives

$$a^* = (1 - \alpha\phi - (w_1/p))/\alpha(1 - \phi)(\gamma + 1) \qquad (4.30)$$
$$u^* = a^{*1/\gamma} \qquad (4.31)$$
$$y^* = u^*z \qquad (4.32)$$

By comparison, the first-order condition for a long-run maximum of profit with respect to z, with y given, implies that

$$a^{**} = (w_2/p\alpha(1 - \phi)\gamma)^{\gamma/(\gamma + 1)} \qquad (4.33)$$
$$u^{**} = a^{**1/\gamma} \qquad (4.34)$$
$$z^{**} = y/u^{**} \qquad (4.35)$$

Given the restrictions on the parameters, the second-order conditions are always satisfied.

Equation (4.30) shows that the induced defect rate is smaller, the greater is the penalty for defective output, α. A high price of processing services, w_1, also reduces the defect rate because it diminishes the net revenue from the additional output generated by higher capacity utilization. The defect rate is also smaller the faster the defect rate accelerates with respect to capacity utilization, as measured by the value of γ.

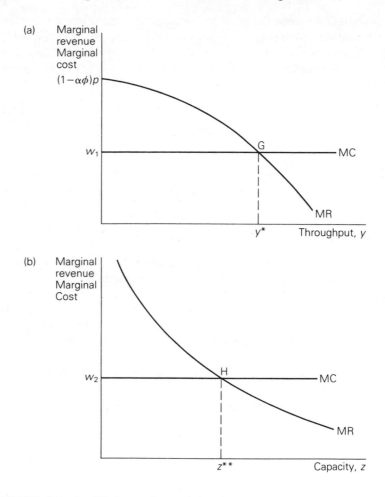

FIGURE 4.5   Equilibrium of transformation: (a) determination of optimal throughput in the short run; (b) determination of optimal capacity in the long run

In the short-run situation the defect rate is determined by the level of throughput. The determination of the optimal throughput is illustrated graphically in figure 4.5(a). The marginal cost of throughput is equal to the price of processing services, which is constant. When throughput is zero, and hence capacity utilization is zero, the induced defect rate is zero, and hence marginal revenue at zero output is equal to the margin on good output reduced by the expected penalty due to defective items bought in from suppliers. As output increases, capacity utilization increases and the loss of marginal revenue induced by a higher proportion of defective items accelerates. Thus the marginal revenue schedule accelerates downwards and intersects the marginal cost schedule at G, whose ordinate determines the optimal throughput, y^*.

Equation (4.33) shows that in the long run too the induced defect rate is smaller the greater is the penalty incurred by defective output, α. It is also lower, the lower is the price of capacity services, w_2, and the lower the defect rate in the supplies, ϕ. In the long run, the optimal defect rate is determined by the amount of capacity installed for the given level of throughput. The marginal cost of capacity is constant at the price of capacity services (see figure 4.5(b)). The marginal revenue of capacity diminishes at a decreasing rate, due to the fact that higher capacity means lower capacity utilization, and lower capacity utilization diminishes the induced defect rate at a diminishing rate. The marginal revenue schedule is asymptotic to the horizontal axis. It intersects the marginal cost curve at H, whose ordinate determines the optimal capacity z^{**}.

Finally, it should be noted that, as before, the results are prefaced on the existence of an interior maximum $(0 < a^*, a^{**} < 1)$. Given reasonable values for the parameters – and for input prices in particular – interior maxima exist, though they cannot be guaranteed under all conditions.

4.7   DECENTRALIZATION OF QUALITY CONTROL IN MULTI-STAGE TRANSFORMATION

This section considers whether it is possible to devise a system of incentives that allows decisions with quality implications to be decentralized to the managers of individual activities within a production process. Attention is focused on a simple case in which n strictly complementary pure transformation activities are involved. The precise configuration of these activities is not specified. One simple possibility is a vertical sequence comprising n successive stages which convert a raw material into a finished product. Another possibility is a set of n parallel activities producing components which are simply collected together to form the finished product. The terminology employed below is consonant with a configuration of this second kind.

It is assumed that a defect introduced at any stage is sufficient to render the finished product defective. For the sake of simplicity it is assumed that only a small proportion of items are rendered defective at any stage, so that the defect rate in the finished product can be approximated by the sum of the defect rates relating to the individual activities:

$$\theta = \sum_{i=1}^{n} a_i \qquad (4.36)$$

where a_i is the proportion of items rendered defective by the ith activity

$(i = 1, \ldots, n)$. Using the subscript i to specify the ith activity throughout, the natural generalization of the single-activity transformation model is as follows:

$$a_i = u_i \gamma \qquad\qquad (i = 1, \ldots, n) \qquad\qquad (4.37)$$

$$u_i = y/z_i \qquad\qquad (i = 1, \ldots, n) \qquad\qquad (4.38)$$

$$c_{1i} = w_{1i} y \qquad\qquad (i = 1, \ldots, n) \qquad\qquad (4.39)$$

$$c_{2i} = w_{2i} z \qquad\qquad (i = 1, \ldots, n) \qquad\qquad (4.40)$$

$$v = (1 - \alpha\theta)p \qquad\qquad\qquad (4.41)$$

$$r = vy \qquad\qquad\qquad (4.42)$$

$$c = \sum_{i=1}^{n} (c_{1i} + c_{2i}) \qquad\qquad\qquad (4.43)$$

$$\pi = r - c \qquad\qquad\qquad (4.44)$$

The short-run maximization of profit involves choosing the appropriate value of output, y, conditional upon the fixed capacities $z_1, \ldots, z_n$. From equations (4.36)–(4.44), the solution is

$$y = [(1 - (\sum_{i=1}^{n} w_{1i}/p)/\alpha(\gamma + 1) \sum_{i=1}^{n} z_i^{-\gamma}]^{1/\gamma} \qquad\qquad (4.45)$$

The question arises as to whether it is possible to specify a price system such that the manager of each activity, by maximizing the profit imputed to his activity, spontaneously chooses to operate at exactly this scale of production. Such a system does in fact exist. It comprises two elements: (a) a penalty equal to αp, levied on each item rendered defective by the activity concerned; and (b) a fee for processing each unit of output, irrespective of quality, determined by the condition that the marginal revenue of the ith activity shall just equal its marginal cost at the scale given by (4.45).

The appropriate fee is

$$f_i = [(\gamma/(\gamma + 1))(p - \sum_{i=1}^{n} w_{1i}) z_i^{-\gamma}/ \sum_{i=1}^{n} z_i^{-\gamma}] + w_{1i} \qquad\qquad (4.46)$$

In principle, a third element could be introduced, namely a lump sum subsidy sufficient to allow the activity to break even after paying the penalties levied for bad quality. Such an element is not strictly necessary, however, because the fixed fee provides the manager of the activity with sufficient quasi-rent to cover his penalty costs and leave him with a profit of

$$h_i = ((\gamma - 1)/(\gamma + 1))(p - \sum_{i=1}^{n} w_{1i}) z_i^{-\gamma}/ \sum_{i=1}^{n} z_i^{-\gamma} \qquad\qquad (4.47)$$

on each unit of output. If, however, the headquarters division seeks to maximize its own imputed profit by allowing individual transformation activities to do no better than break even, then headquarters may impose a lump sum tax on the ith activity equivalent to h_i on each unit. Under this arrangement, the activities as a whole receive a fee income, on each unit, of

$$f = \sum_{i=1}^{n} f_i = (\gamma/(\gamma+1))(p - \sum_{i=1}^{n} w_{1i}) \sum_{i=1}^{n} w_{1i} \qquad (4.48)$$

out of which they pay penalty payments of

$$g = \alpha p \theta = (1/(\gamma+1))(p - \sum_{i=1}^{n} w_{1i}) \qquad (4.49)$$

lump sum taxes of

$$h = \sum_{i=1}^{n} h_i = ((\gamma-1)/(\gamma+1))(p - \sum_{i=1}^{n} w_{1i}) \qquad (4.50)$$

and incur direct costs of

$$k_1 = \sum_{i=1}^{n} (c_{1i}/y) = \sum_{i=1}^{n} w_{1i} \qquad (4.51)$$

Headquarters receives an average revenue from customers of

$$v = (\gamma p + \sum_{i=1}^{n} w_{1i})/(\gamma+1) \qquad (4.52)$$

and makes net payments to activity managers, per unit, of

$$f - g - h = \sum_{i=1}^{n} w_{1i} \qquad (4.53)$$

leaving a surplus on the whole operation of

$$s = (\pi/y) = (\gamma/(\gamma+1))(p - \sum_{i=1}^{n} w_{1i}) \qquad (4.54)$$

The long-run maximization of profit involves choosing the appropriate capacities $z_1, \ldots, z_n$ conditional upon the output, y, and the first-order condition gives the solution

$$z_i = (\alpha\gamma p/w_{2i})^{1/(\gamma+1)} y \qquad (4.55)$$

Decentralization in the long run can be effected by imposing the same penalty as before for bad quality, αp, and setting the processing fee for the ith activity at

$$f_i' = w_{1i} + (\gamma+1)(\alpha p(w_{2i}/\gamma)^\gamma)^{1/(\gamma+1)} \qquad (4.56)$$

Each activity just breaks even and headquarters earns a surplus on each unit of

$$s_i' = p - \sum_{i=1}^{n} w_{1i} - (\gamma + 2)(\alpha p / \gamma^\gamma)^{1/(\gamma+1)} \sum_{i=1}^{n} w_{2i}^{\gamma/(\gamma+1)} \qquad (4.57)$$

Although the processing fees are different, therefore, it can be seen that in both the short run and the long run, a pricing system exists that will efficiently decentralize quality control.

4.8   DECENTRALIZATION OF SORTING DECISIONS

The extension of the previous model to encompass sorting activities encounters analytical difficulties. These are caused by the complexity of the relationship between the penalty structure which applies to the output channels and the marginal value to the firm of high quality in the input channel. Given that a simple relationship of this kind could be established, the decentralization of sorting would be fairly straightforward. The incentive framework would require each sorting activity to impose quality penalties on the supplying activity. At each stage the penalty structure would reflect the marginal contribution to the profit of the overall process of an improvement in the quality of output passed on to the next activity. This incentive structure would apply not only to processes composed entirely of sorting activities, but also to processes which include a mixture of transformation and sorting. In practice, the derivation of the appropriate incentive structure is prohibitively complicated in even quite simple cases.

Similar analytical difficulties are encountered when sorting and transformation occur within the same activity. There are two important examples of this. First, as was noted earlier, any multi-product transformation activity must contain an element of sorting in so far as the contents of the output channels are genuinely different. Secondly, the common practice of quality control by sampling inspection involves transforming the sampled items to some degree, so that the higher the sampling proportion the greater, other things being equal, is the proportion of the input that is 'damaged' during sorting.

Inspection by sampling is typically applied to batch processes. Every batch is sampled. A statistic computed from the sample is assumed to be correlated with the average quality of items within the batch. The entire batch is accepted or rejected on the basis of this statistic. Thus, in terms of the sorting model presented earlier, the batch is analogous to the item and the sample statistic fulfils the role of the observable characteristic. Using this procedure, the power of the test is greater the higher is the sampling proportion, although the power will normally increase with respect to the sampling proportion at a diminishing rate. Since an increase in the sampling proportion increases the rate of damage, there exists a trade-off between the power of the test and the level of damage. The power of the test itself, however, is just one aspect of the trade-off between two types of error probability. The trade-off is, in fact, a three-way affair, involving the type I error probability, the type II error probability and the proportion of output which, for given error probabilities, will be directed into the 'good output' channel.

Despite these complexities, it is once again possible to visualize, heuristically, how for a given activity the marginal valuation of input quality will be related to the penalty structure associated with the output channels. Extending this idea to a complex of activities, some or all of which combine sorting and transformation, it is possible, in principle, to devise a system of incentives in which the quality penalty structure associated with each channel reflects the marginal contribution of quality in that channel to the profitability of the overall process. The conclusion must be, therefore, that there are no fundamental obstacles to the decentralization of quality decisions within even quite complex production processes.

4.9   SYSTEM COMPLEXITY AND ADMINISTRATIVE COSTS

The preceding analysis presumes the absence of all transaction costs. The impact of transaction costs on the decentralization of quality control is the subject of this section and the next. This section is concerned purely with the question of decentralization within a single ownership unit. The object is to evaluate centralized non-price decision making against a system in which the central authority sets only shadow prices and each activity becomes a quasi-autonomous profit centre. It is assumed that the production system is self-contained in intermediate products. It is also assumed that shadow prices are set by balancing the aggregate supplies and demands revealed at various trial prices. Finally, it is assumed that managers supply the same amount of effort and integrity under both regimes.

Under these conditions, two factors assume critical importance. The first is the cost structure of price making in intermediate product markets, and in particular the role of indivisibilities in associating a substantial fixed cost with the determination of each price or quality premium. The predominance of fixed costs within total costs means that the total costs of price making are roughly proportional to the number of prices required, which in turn is equal to the number of different intermediate products – including different grades of the same product – that are traded.

The second factor is the cost savings that emerge from breaking down the single highly complex decision problem facing a central planner into a number of much simpler problems concerned with how to adjust quality in response to shadow prices within a single activity. These savings are likely to be greatest when a single activity is just sufficient to absorb the full attention of a single manager, and when many such activities are involved in the process as a whole, so that central planning is much more than any one manager can cope with.

Comparing the costs and benefits of decentralization indicates that decentralization is more advantageous when the process comprises a large group of complex activities whose interrelationships are fairly simple, so that the number of intermediate products is relatively small compared to the number of activities involved. The situation most favourable to centralization, on the other hand, involves a relatively small number of fairly simple activities with a large number of intermediate product flows between them. In other words, a complex configuration of a small number of simple activities favours centralization.

In the hierarchy of complexity amongst activities, pure transformation appears at the bottom, with pure sorting above it and combined sorting and transformation at the top. This suggests that the processes most likely to be centralized involve a complex configuration of pure transformation activities, whilst those most likely to be decentralized involve a simple configuration of combined sorting and transformation activities.

These conclusions are fairly robust to the relaxation of the earlier assumptions about the way that shadow prices are formed. Altering these assumptions alters the general balance of advantages between centralization and decentralization, but has little effect on the way that system complexity impacts on decentralization.

The opening up of a production system to allow imports and exports of intermediate products favours decentralization, because external market prices provide an appropriate benchmark for setting internal prices, and so reduce the costs of the price-making mechanism. In certain cases direct inter-divisional bargaining may be the favoured method of setting shadow prices. The availability of this option strengthens the case for decentralization, particularly where a large number of separate activities participate as buyers and sellers of an intermediate product, because bargaining then takes place in an essentially competitive environment. Managerial motivation may also be improved by decentralization because profit centres provide the basis for relating the rewards of the individual manager more closely to his performance.

4.10   THE ROLE OF OWNERSHIP STRUCTURE

This section evaluates a system of decentralized decision making within a single ownership unit against a system in which every activity is undertaken by an independent ownership unit. In the case of independent ownership, each activity obtains its supplies from one or more subcontractors. The analysis builds upon earlier work by Klein, Crawford and Alchian (1978), Monteverdi and Teece (1982), and Williamson (1975; 1985), as summarized in section 1.5. The factors most likely to discourage subcontracting and favour integration are

(a) missing property rights and, in general, the costs of enforcing property rights through the courts;
(b) uncertainty of the user about the proportion of defective items which will, on average, be supplied to him;
(c) the ease with which the supplier can switch to other customers in the event of a disagreement with an existing user; and
(d) random variations over time in the quality of supplies.

When considered singly, these factors are not particularly important. It is only when they occur jointly that their effect becomes significant.

(a)   Costs of Enforcing Property Rights

Consider, for example, the costs of enforcing guarantees of product quality. Superficially, it seems that efficient subcontracting calls for a legally enforceable commitment by the supplier to refund damages arising from defective items. But even if no such commitment can be enforced, there are circumstances under which it pays the supplier to honour the commitment voluntarily so that the efficiency of subcontracting is not impaired at all. For suppose the contrary to be the case, that the supplier refuses to make any commitment, the immediate effect is to transfer the cost of defects from the supplier to the user. But if the user has accurate knowledge of the quality of the supplier's output stream, the user can recalculate the value of the supplier's output stream in the absence of the commitment and, as a result, he will reduce the amount he is willing to pay by the expected cost of the damages. This means that the cost of the defects is ultimately borne by the supplier, whether he agrees to pay damages or not.

If the supplier does not perceive that the proportion of damages he offers to bear affects the price he can obtain for his output stream, then he may feel encouraged, once he has reduced his commitment to pay damages, to increase the proportion of defective items in his output. Since the user is willing to pay a premium simply to keep bad items out of the supplier's 'good output' stream – where their value is much lower than in the 'bad output' stream – the user will respond to such a move by reducing the price he offers for 'good output' by an amount that cuts the supplier's revenue by more than his saving in damages. The supplier is, in effect, sub-optimizing profit because he deceives himself about the user's response to bad output. The high proportion of defective items in his 'good output' stream is socially wasteful, and the cost of this waste is borne by the supplier himself.

A similar result applies if the supplier has a policy of paying damages only if the user takes him to court. The expected legal costs faced by the user reduce the value of the output stream, whilst the fact that the damages are ultimately paid means that the supplier does not reduce his own compensation costs. The user's expected legal costs are passed back to the supplier in a lower price, and the social waste involved in contesting the claims is borne by the supplier himself.

Under such conditions the supplier has a strong incentive to compensate the user fully for defective items, even though any guarantee he gives cannot be legally enforced. The problem of unenforceable guarantees, therefore, is not that the supplier will not honour them. The problem, if anything, is that the supplier may find it difficult to convince the buyer that he still intends to honour them, even though he cannot be compelled to do so.

(b)   Uncertainty about the Quality of Goods

Uncertainty about the quality of supplies is of little consequence to the user so long as he is fully insured through legally enforceable guarantees. Even with user uncertainty and unenforceable guarantees, the supplier may still voluntarily compensate the user, in order to retain his goodwill and not prejudice future contracts. This is particularly important when the supplier cannot easily switch to another customer in the case of a dispute with an existing user. The vulnerability of the supplier may indirectly be an advantage to him, in fact, as it may increase the credibility of his commitment to compensate the user, as referred to above.

(c)   The Ease of Switching to other Customers

There may be a problem for the user, however, if his supplier finds it easy to switch users, while he finds it difficult to switch suppliers. Under these circumstances – where factors (a)–(c) appear in conjunction – subcontracting may become inefficient relative to integration.

(d)   Random Variations in the Quality of Supplies

Random variations in the quality of supplies can arise for one of two main reasons. The first is indivisibility in the product. When each transaction involves just a few units of the product, average quality can vary significantly between successive transactions. Such variations are disliked by risk-averse consumers. They are also a potential threat to production processes whose efficient operation depends crucially upon maintaining continuity of flow. Under these conditions, guarantees of quality assume especial importance to the user. As a result, the inefficiencies of subcontracting associated with factors (a)–(c) above become particularly acute in this case.

When circumstances (a)–(c) are present, the user is liable to distrust the supplier, since he perceives that the supplier may have an incentive to mislead him about quality. When quality varies over time, continual vigilance is required of the user, and this encourages him to continually replicate the sorting activities performed by the supplier. This wasteful duplication of sorting activity means that subcontracting is particularly disadvantageous when the supplier's production process does not settle down into a steady state.

It should be noted that the statistical literature on quality control takes as its starting point random variations of the kind implied by factor (d). Output is regarded as indivisible. Production is regarded as a potentially unstable process, in the sense that it can easily become 'out of control', and remain 'out of control' indefinitely. Quality control is an on-going process which monitors output, identifies and diagnoses problems, and adjusts the parameters of the production process accordingly. This dynamical view of quality control accords much more with the literature on management, time series analysis and engineering feed-back control than it does with the literature of economics. It has its own important implications for organizational structure and behaviour within the firm, but there is insufficient space to pursue the matter further within the confines of this chapter.

4.11   PRACTICAL APPLICATIONS

It is appropriate to conclude this chapter by returning to the practical issues raised at the outset.

(a)   The Failure of Agricultural Export Marketing
in Developing Countries

A major reason for the failure of many agricultural export marketing strategies seems to be that the activities that make up the distribution channel are structured in the wrong way. It may appear at first sight that export marketers have little choice about the structure of their activities. Whilst this may be the case regarding transformation activities such as transport, storage and ripening, it is not the case so far as sorting is concerned. Sorting can be carried out at many different stages throughout the channel, or it may not be carried out at all. Sorting efforts may be concentrated at the upstream stages of the channel nearest to the grower, or at the downstream stages nearest to the consumer. An important aspect of channel management is to decide at which stages sorting activities should be carried out.

Another important aspect is to discover consumer attitudes in order to set the appropriate standards and decide the number of different grades that will be marketed. Economic judgements also have to be made about the appropriate degree of toughness in the sorting procedures, and about investments in sorting capacity which will provide tests of the appropriate power.

Decisions of this kind may require entrepreneurial skills which are specific to certain individuals or organizations. Governments which intervene in export marketing may give control over distribution to organizations which lack these skills. This may at once explain the apparent failure of many government export boards and the success – in terms of private profitability, at any rate – of a small number of large oligopolistic companies which specialize in food processing and distribution. The success of these companies is sometimes explained in terms of the advantages of vertical integration (Read, 1986). In the case of highly perishable products such as bananas this may well be the case. But there are other instances where companies are successful even though they control only a small part of the distribution channel.

The analysis above suggests that the subcontracting of sorting activities may well be efficient, unless there are simultaneously problems of imperfect property rights, buyer uncertainty, and easy customer-switching by suppliers. These problems are not particularly acute in the case of most agricultural products – indeed one of their features is that quality is fairly easy to assess by inspection, so that buyer uncertainty is not so great a problem as in some industries. (There are exceptions though – it is often difficult, for example, to detect whether flowers have been 'forced' to be ready for a festival season.) Suppose that the advantage of the successful firm lies not in vertical integration but simply in the possession of proprietary know-how relating to quality control. If the firm finds it difficult to license this know-how, it will attempt to own and control all those sorting activities where its know-how is applicable. If it is generally applicable throughout the channel then, in the absence of other constraints, the firm will own and control the entire channel. The strategy will be pursued even in the absence of operating economies of vertical integration. If there are constraints which prevent ownership at certain stages, then the firm may simply own all the other stages instead. In the case where upstream ownership is in the hands of the exporting country's government, the firm may even develop special skills to correct for the errors in sorting perpetrated at the upstream stages. From the firm's point of view, the only problem with this strategy is that it may be difficult to bargain with the government – or any other owners involved in the channel – to secure an adequate reward for its own investment in quality control.

(b) Quality Control in Service Industries

Consider now the problem of quality of service in transportation systems. Most transportation systems are configured as a network connecting various nodes. The nodes figure as the origins, destinations and junctions for different routes which traverse the network (Daughety, 1985). To fix ideas, assume that scheduled services for the conveyance of passengers and freight operate along each route. Each line element in the network, connecting two adjacent nodes, has a certain traffic capacity. The amount of traffic over the line is determined by the number of different routes that share its use, by the frequency of services on each route, and the average loading on each service. As the amount of traffic over the line increases relative to its capacity, so the incidence of delays rises, because of congestion. When the capacity limit is reached, all the traffic is delayed. In terms of the formal model, the network may be regarded as a complex of transformation activities, and the proportion of traffic delayed over each line may be identified with the activity's defect rate.

The overall performance of the system is measured by the total amount of traffic that is delayed. Good performance depends crucially upon appropriate capacity investments being made on each line element. This ensures that major bottlenecks are eliminated and also that wasteful expenditure on underutilized capacity is avoided as well. Because it is mainly transformation activities that are involved, decentralization of quality control is, in principle, fairly easy. Detailed records of time-keeping can be used to determine the frequency with which traffic delays occur on each line element, so that a system of charges for line use and penalties for delays can be easily implemented. The main objection to decentralized ownership of the network is that bargaining problems may emerge in the negotiation of prices. If, however, the network structure allows plenty of opportunity for switching traffic to other routes – or if it is easy to add new elements to the network – then prices may be determined within a reasonably competitive environment.

So far the discussion has focused upon infrastructure investment co-ordination as the key to system performance. In this context it is transformation activity rather than sorting activity which is crucial. Although sorting of traffic does occur at junctions, sorting errors are most unusual in this context. Sorting is, however, important in loading individual consignments onto the right service to begin with, and trans-shipping them where connections have to be made with other services. Here there is an obvious – though crucial – distinction between passenger and freight traffic, because while passengers can sort out connections for themselves, freight traffic requires specialized personnel. Sorting problems are particularly acute for small consignments such as letters and parcels, and much less significant for bulk consignments such as oil and coal.

So far as passengers are concerned, there is no incentive problem in delegating sorting because passengers bear the full consequences of their own mistakes. But where freight is concerned, it is necessary to have a system of identifying where sorting errors are made and to devise rewards and punishments for those involved. Identifying the source of errors is potentially difficult where a large volume of miscellaneous consignments is concerned, as it may involve pooling information from various sources. In particular, people to whom traffic has been misdirected may have to be offered financial incentives not to steal or destroy the items, but to return them to a special bureau that will investigate the error. Disciplining bad sorting has the added complication that the sorting may have been carried out under undue pressure of time caused by delays to scheduled services. Since the scope for disagreements over responsibility for errors is so great, decentralization of freight sorting activities calls for a very high degree of trust, and so in many cases centralized control within a single ownership unit will be the preferred solution. It may be concluded that the tendency towards centralization within transportation networks will be greater when small-consignment miscellaneous freight traffic predominates than when bulk freight or passenger movements predominate instead.

(c)   Quality of Labour in Service Industries

A prominent feature of service industries is that many employees are in direct contact with the customer. In manufacturing, where the shop-floor worker has no direct contact with the customer, it is possible to interpose a sorting process between the employee and the customer in which the products of careless or unskilled workmanship can be weeded out. In service industries, sorting cannot be carried out like this, and so it is essential to ensure that the quality of work delivered by the employee who is in contact with the customer is maintained at the highest possible level.

One way of achieving this quality of service is through close supervision. A supervisor, however, is an indivisible resource, and cannot be in more than one place at once. When the service outlet involves a large group of employees it may be economic to employ a full-time supervisor. But if the employee typically works alone in a one-to-one situation with the customer, the costs of supervising each employee become prohibitive. It is arguable that with the increasing automation of many service industries, and in particular with the growth of off-site servicing work – e.g. in maintaining domestic consumer durables – many service employees now fall into this category.

If quality control cannot be effected by sorting the output, and supervision is uneconomic, the natural response is to concentrate on sorting out the most suitable employees through the recruitment process. This, however, imposes exceptional demands on recruitment skill. Employment protection legislation means that in many countries it is difficult to dismiss workers unless definite proof can be given of persistently unsatisfactory work, and the very nature of unsupervised service employment makes such evidence difficult to acquire. Under these circumstances, a type II error of recruiting an unsuitable employee becomes extremely costly. One obvious response is to increase the toughness of the recruitment test, by inflating the educational and other qualifications required. Another response is to use part-time workers who enjoy less employment protection. To increase the power of the recruitment test it may be appropriate to have specialist agencies to provide a preliminary screening of job applicants. It can be argued that some MNEs in the service industries derive their profits mainly from their ability in recruiting suitable employees and thereby guaranteeing a uniformly high standard of service to their customers.

One of the consequences of these policies is to improve the quality of service to the customer at the expense of denying jobs to people whose limited qualifications make them appear to be too much of a risk. This is perhaps one reason why in some countries, such as Britain, expansion of the service industries has created a modest number of new jobs for well-qualified people but has not provided sufficient employment to absorb all those made redundant from manufacturing industry.

(d) The Japanese versus Western Philosophy

Although Japanese production philosophy has proved difficult for Western observers to understand (see, for example, Abegglen, 1973; Clark, 1979; Johnson, 1982) it seems reasonable to postulate that many Japanese practices reflect the systems approach to quality control analysed in this chapter. The Japanese have directed indigenous resources towards industries which assemble manufactured products from components which afford substantial economies of scale. These scale economies are typically associated with the use of indivisible high-speed automated machinery whose capacity is large relative to the world market for the product. The Japanese have been quick to appreciate that mechanization affords greater precision and a more uniform quality of output than is available from labour-intensive methods. They have followed through the logic of the simple proposition that the quality of an assembled product is no better than the quality of the components from which it is made. By concentrating upon quality control at the upstream stages of production, rather than the downstream stages favoured by their Western competitors, they have made inspection much easier, diagnostics more straightforward, and have avoided the costs of replacing defective components by taking apart and reassembling the finished product.

Components requiring expensive dedicated machinery are usually produced by the assembling firm – probably because the high level of sunk costs required would place a subcontractor in a vulnerable bargaining position. Components produced using more labour-intensive methods, on the other hand, are often subcontracted. Subcontracting components whose quality affects the overall performance of the finished product is potentially hazardous, however. A high degree of trust is necessary to avoid wasteful duplication of the subcontractor's own quality procedures. In Japan, this trust is founded partly on the economic power of the client firm, which offers the prospect of regular future transactions if current supplies are satisfactory. The subcontractor may also be required to supply the client exclusively, so that if contracts are terminated, the subcontractor's costs of switching to another client will be high. The client will normally use several subcontractors, so that he cannot easily be held hostage by a withdrawal of supplies by any one of them. Since labour-intensive processes rarely afford significant economies of scale, the cost penalties incurred by this strategy are only slight. Additional sanctions include extending short-term credit to the subcontractor, and acting as a procurement agency for some of the subcontractor's supplies. Underpinning the entire arrangement, however, is an implicit assurance to the subcontractor that if he expands his capacity to meet all the client's needs then the client will continue to patronize him, and will not exploit any temporary excess capacity in the subcontracting operation to bid down the price. This is consistent with profit maximization by the client firm over a long-term horizon, since it maintains his reputation and assures the availability of future supplies.

Because labour-intensive manufacturing typically calls for many production workers to work together in the same factory, quality of workmanship can be achieved economically through close supervision. But capital-intensive production requires mainly skilled personnel to service the machinery, often working alone under conditions which make supervision difficult. This creates the problem of recruiting responsible service personnel alluded to above. The 'quality circle' concept seems to be one aspect of the Japanese solution to this problem. It involves motivating workers in such a way that they effectively supervise themselves. The quality circle therefore achieves for skilled workers what close supervision and conventional economic incentives achieve for unskilled workers. It is a complement to, rather than a substitute for, other methods of motivating employees.

4.12 CONCLUSIONS AND IMPLICATIONS FOR FUTURE RESEARCH

This chapter has examined quality control in the context of an economic model in which all factor services, intermediate products and final products are essentially mixtures of good and bad items. A mixture can be altered by either transformation or sorting. The basic model presented above has diverse practical applications. The range of applications can be readily extended simply by recognizing that labelling the content of the mixtures as 'good' and 'bad' is inessential. By dropping the labelling, and allowing any number of pure constituents to be mixed, transformation can be identified as any activity that produces a new mixture from existing mixtures, and sorting as simply multi-product transformation of which each product is a different mixture. This affords a comprehensive generalization of the theory of production, which is applicable to practically any industry.

The theory can not only be generalized, but also specialized to handle particular problems more satisfactorily. So far, for example, it has been assumed that capacity utilization is the only factor affecting the rate at which defects are induced during transformation. There is considerable evidence, however, that another factor is the defect rate in the input stream. More specifically, it is suggested that defect items entering an activity cause breakdowns which render other items defective too. This effect has important implications for the management of quality. It implies that rigorous quality control at the earliest stages of production is crucial if a catastrophic accumulation of defective items at later stages is to be avoided.

Knock-on effects of this kind suggest the need for a fully dynamic analysis of how quality is determined. The approach in this chapter has been essentially static. Statistical literature on quality control adopts a more dynamic approach, and building a bridge between the economic and statistical literature must be a high priority in future research.

5

Contractual Arrangements for Technology Transfer: New Evidence from Business History

5.1 INTRODUCTION

The economic theory of the MNE, it was suggested in chapter 1, is the basis for a general theory of the choice of contractual arrangements. It was pointed out in chapter 2, however, that most writers have so far analysed contractual arrangements as if managers were always faced with a polarized choice between equity and non-equity arrangements or, more generally, between the 'hierarchy' and the 'market'. In practice, the choice is over a spectrum of contractual arrangements, some of which are more 'firm-like' than others.

This is very apparent in the study of business history. The historian deals with archival evidence on the specific details of contractual arrangements, and the concepts of markets and hierarchy are far too abstract for his purposes. Even if these abstractions are rendered more concrete by using categories such as licensing and majority-owned direct investment, these categories are still too broad.

It was pointed out in chapter 1 that one of the strengths of the economic theory of the MNE is its practical relevance, but to be relevant to business history a more refined typology of contractual arrangements is required. Now in principle, the number of contractual arrangements that can be devised is limited only by the imagination and ingenuity of entrepreneurs. Fortunately for the analyst, however, in practice most contractual arrangements conform (approximately) to one of a relatively small number of types. This is because firms that rely upon standard forms of contract can economize on specification and negotiation costs; in particular, they avoid the suspicion that they are offering their partner a non-standard contract because they have built a loophole into the contract that they can later exploit to their own advantage.

A complete account of the choice of contractual arrangements requires a fully-fledged theory of transaction costs, in which each possible arrangement can be explicitly costed. Pending the development of a theory as sophisticated as this, however, a preliminary exercise can be conducted that highlights many of the issues involved.

The simplest way to appraise a spectrum of contractual arrangements is to identify a small number of key strategic issues, and to see how successfully each arrangement can handle each of these issues. If all the issues were equally important in all situations, then each arrangement could be given a 'score' for its overall performance, equal to the number of issues it can resolve, and the theory would predict that the highest-scoring arrangement available in any situation would be chosen.

In practice, however, the relative importance of the strategic issues will vary from one situation to the next. The kind of issue that is paramount in any given situation depends upon the motive that leads the firm to seek international involvement in the first place. It is assumed in this chapter that the motive is the international transfer of a proprietary advantage. The term 'proprietary advantage' is construed quite broadly. It includes technology – both patented and unpatented – reputation – including brand names and customer loyalty – managerial skills, and indeed any kind of expertise in which the firm enjoys some degree of monopoly power.

The exercise presented in this chapter demonstrates how a simple scoring system can be devised which predicts the form of contractual arrangements chosen by particular firms in specific historical contexts. Section 5.2 reviews some of the basic concepts and section 5.3 develops the scoring system itself. The remaining sections of the chapter are devoted chiefly to the interpretation of recently researched case study evidence. It is shown that the scoring system works well in most of the cases concerned, though further applications may well reveal some shortcomings in the system.

5.2   BASIC CONCEPTS

The exploitation of a proprietary advantage normally involves a firm in two quite distinct activities in the host country: namely production and marketing. If necessary, quite separate contractual arrangements can be made for each of these activities. The character of the marketing function depends very much on whether the product is a final product or an intermediate product, and on whether it is purchased privately or by a public agency. Final products for private purchase are typically distributed through wholesalers and retailers, whilst intermediate products for private use are often supplied in bulk direct to downstream firms. Products purchased by a public agency are usually supplied in bulk, whether they are for final or for intermediate use, although there are some exceptions. The analysis below focuses upon a final product sold for private purchase. It identifies marketing with advertising to private consumers and with the management of a wholesale and retail distribution channel. The examples given in section 5.5, however, show how the general principles can be applied to other cases too.

There are two main approaches to analysing contractual arrangements. The first concentrates on the allocation of *risk* between the parties, as reflected in the *ownership* structure. The second concentrates upon the allocation of *managerial responsibility*, as reflected in the structure of *control*. There is, of course, a connection between the two, since effective incentives require each party to bear a share of those risks that are affected by the quality of its decisions. This connection does not, however, imply a complete coincidence between the structure of ownership and the structure of control.

The dominant approach in the literature – and the one followed here – focuses upon managerial responsibilities and the structure of control. Outright control of a foreign subsidiary can be obtained with less than 100 per cent of the equity. Indeed, most empirical work on MNEs focuses upon majority-owned foreign affiliates rather than just upon wholly-owned affiliates, and this is the concept of the MNE adopted here. Likewise, the concept of a joint venture must be interpreted as implying a measure of shared control. In this chapter the concept of joint venture is defined in such a way that both parties have some influence upon the price and quality of the joint venture's products.

Rugman (1981) places extreme emphasis on the importance of outright control of production. In practice, however, joint ventures are a very significant form of international involvement too (Friedmann and Kalmanoff, 1961; Franko, 1971, 1973 1982; Tomlinson, 1970). Some writers tend to regard joint ventures as a 'second best' solution imposed by host government requirements, but there is growing recognition of the fact – fully supported by historical studies – that joint ventures are often a 'first best' strategy for an investing firm (Beamish, 1984; Dunning and Cantwell, 1982; Harrigan, 1985; Hladik, 1985; Killing, 1983). Other arrangements considered in the literature include industrial co-operation (Buckley, 1985a; Paliwoda, 1981), management contracts (Brooke, 1985; Gabriel, 1967) licensing (Contractor, 1981, 1983; Telesio, 1979), subcontracting (Sharpston, 1975) and sales franchising.

All of these arrangements are typically regarded as 'alternatives' to the MNE.

For analytical purposes it is convenient to distinguish six main types of contractual arrangement, based upon different ways of partitioning responsibility for production and marketing. The various permutations are derived from the scheme shown in figure 5.1, and their structure is indicated in table 5.1. Where a partner is involved, it is assumed – unless otherwise stated – that the partner is indigenous to the host economy.

An industrial co-operation agreement is defined as a joint venture where the parent firm's equity involvement is only short term (e.g. 'turn-key' projects, equity 'fade out' arrangements). An additional feature in such an agreement may be a clause which specifies, for example, that payments to the parent are not to exceed certain amounts, or are to be made through counter-trade.

Under a licensing arrangement, a company sells the right to exploit its advantage within specified limits in return for a fixed fee. The fee is normally related to the licensee's rate of output, though this is not implied by the definition. The definition of licensing employed here, though, does imply that if the licensor also takes an equity stake in the licensee, then this is not with the object of acquiring control, but to avoid the risk that the licensee profits at the licensor's expense because the fee structure is wrong. The licensor cannot, therefore, control the price and quality of the licensee's product on a day-to-day basis, although he may build into

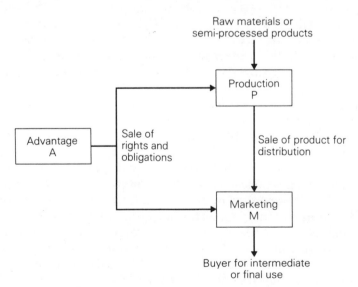

FIGURE 5.1　The structure of contractual arrangements

TABLE 5.1 Definitions of contractual arrangements

| | Control allocated to | | | |
Arrangement	Parent	Partner	Other partner	Comment
Main types				
Outright control	APM	—	—	Parent's equity stake need not be 100 per cent but is sufficient to give outright control
Joint venture	APM	PM	—	Parent's equity stake need not be 50 per cent, but is sufficient to give some control over quality and price of product
Industrial co-operation agreement	APM	PM	—	Similar to joint venture, but with time limit on equity holding and possible restriction on nature and timing of payments to parent
Subcontracting	AM	P	—	Partner receives mainly a fixed fee for each finished unit supplied to parent
Sales franchising	AP	M	—	Partner purchases product from parent mainly for a fixed fee
Licensing and production franchising	A	PM		Parent receives mainly a fixed fee for each unit produced (or sold)
Some other possibilities				
Chain management	A	P	M	
Interlocking joint ventures	APM	P	M	

A: advantage, P: production, M: marketing (see also figure 5.1).

the licensing agreement restrictive clauses which would limit the licensee's discretion if they could be enforced.

Under subcontracting, only production is delegated to another firm, and the product is returned to the parent firm for marketing. The subcontractor does not have the right to use the proprietary advantage to produce goods on his own account. The subcontractor is paid a fixed fee, and any equity stake held by the parent firm in the subcontractor is insufficient to allow quality control through direct supervision of production.

Under sales franchising, it is the marketing and not the production that is delegated to another firm. The franchisee is supplied with units of the product on a fixed scale of charges (usually related to quantity) and promotes and sells the product subject to whatever restrictive covenants are imposed by the franchising agreement. Note that 'franchising' in service industries such as 'fast-food' retailing in fact corresponds to licensing, as defined above, since the 'franchisee' both produces and sells the product.

A management contract is defined as a licensing or subcontracting arrangement that allows the other party to produce as much as he likes of the product. In other words, the other party pays for training in production and is then free to use this training how he likes. No rational profit-maximizing firm would be willing to pass on its advantage to a potential rival on these terms, unless its management believes either that the partner will never learn sufficient to become a serious rival, or that the advantage is about to become obsolete in any case. It is assumed below, therefore, that if the advantage is a significant one, the management contract will be subject to such restrictions that it conforms to one of the other types of arrangement instead. Typically the management contract will be a component of an industrial co-operation agreement.

If, on the other hand, the advantage is not a significant one, then the firm's degree of monopoly is relatively small. The firm is essentially competing against rival firms to sell training services to the host economy. Whilst problems such as buyer uncertainty may still remain, the strategic problems are sufficiently different for this case to be outside the scope of this paper.

In principle, sales franchising can be combined with subcontracting by delegating one firm to do production and another to do the marketing. The parent's role is simply to authorize each firm to handle the product, and possibly to assist in co-ordination by, for example, arbitrating in disputes over the quality of the product supplied by the subcontractor to the franchisee. Such an arrangement may be called 'chain management'; the structure of control is indicated in the entry under 'some other possibilities' at the bottom of table 5.1. A variant of this arrangement is for the parent firm to enter into separate joint venture arrangements with the subcontractor and the franchisee; the structure of control associated with this arrangement is shown in the bottom line of the table.

The discussion above has drawn attention to some distinctions which are normally glossed over in the theoretical literature. There is one further distinction which needs to be made, namely the distinction between a subsidiary created as a 'green field' investment and a subsidiary acquired through takeover or merger. This is an issue which has recently been the focus of interesting empirical work (Caves and Mehra, 1985; Davidson, 1980; Khoury, 1980; Kogut and Singh, 1985; Wilson, 1980).

The distinction is important because a subsidiary recently acquired by takeover or merger is unlikely to share the same capital infrastructure, managerial procedures and cultural attitudes as the parent firm. The distinction becomes less important over time as the new acquisition becomes assimilated into the parent's group. An analogous distinction arises in many other contexts. A joint venture formed by buying into a foreign company may perform very differently from a joint venture formed as a 'green field' partnership with the same firm. A licensing arrangement with a company formed by management buy-out from the parent firm may perform very differently from the same arrangement with a totally independent company, and so on. It is in the case of outright control of a foreign subsidiary, however, that these differences are most likely to be acute. The analysis below, therefore, distinguishes between 'green field' investments and acquisitions of foreign subsidiaries, but does not make the same distinction in respect of other types of contractual arrangement.

Much of the theoretical literature has been preoccupied with explaining why outright control of a foreign subsidiary – however obtained – may be preferred to all other arrangements. This approach reflects the preoccupation of modern writers with explaining the rapid post-1945 growth of MNEs. This is most unfortunate for the business historian since before 1939 many firms avoided owning overseas subsidiaries because of the difficulties of international communication and the political instability of the inter-war period.

Since there are several contractual alternatives to outright ownership, it is insufficient to explain the choice of one of these alternatives by showing that it is superior to outright ownership; it is necessary to show that the chosen alternative is superior to each one of the other arrangements as well. There is now increasing recognition of the choices to be made between different alternatives to outright ownership (see Oman, 1984; UNCTC, 1983). Few writers, however, have presented an integrated analysis in which each arrangement is evaluated against all other possible arrangements (for early attempts, see Casson (1979) and Dunning (1981)). This chapter takes a further step in this direction.

5.3   STRATEGIC ISSUES

The strategic issues connected with the exploitation of a proprietary advantage are of two main kinds. Some arise because, *within each country*, production and marketing activities are complementary, and others because, *across countries*, the different marketing activities are potentially rivalrous. These strategic issues are discussed below. The economic theory which underpins the discussion is that presented in chapter 1.

Before proceeding with the discussion, the reader may like to take a preliminary glance at table 5.2. This table summarizes the results that follow. As noted earlier, the importance of particular strategic issues depends upon the characteristics of the situation. It is these characteristics, therefore, that ultimately govern the rational choice of contractual arrangements. The characteristics identified by the theory are listed in the left-hand column of the table. Eighteen characteristics are identified altogether, and they fall naturally into four groups. A more detailed analysis might possibly generate one or two more relevant characteristics, whilst a more superficial analysis would certainly provide considerably fewer. The listing of the characteristics accurately reflects the present state of development of the theory, however, and contains sufficient detail to meet the practical needs of most historians. The main types of contractual arrangement available are listed in the column headings on the right of the table. Generally speaking, the measure of control exercised by the parent firm diminishes when reading the contractual arrangements from left to right.

When interpreting the table it is important to recognize that terms such as 'joint venture', 'industrial collaboration agreement', etc., carry the meanings given in the earlier definitions and not necessarily the meanings they have in common parlance. A subcontracting arrangement as defined in this chapter, for example, might not be described by its signatories as a subcontracting arrangement, but as, say, an industrial co-operation agreement. Conversely, an agreement hailed as 'industrial co-operation' might not correspond to industrial co-operation as defined in this paper, but to subcontracting. The propositions advanced below, therefore, must be interpreted as deductions obtained by applying the behavioural postulates of economic theory to particular definitions. They are not to be interpreted as an attempt to make inductive generalizations from the empirical evidence.

TABLE 5.2 Characteristics affecting the choice of contractual arrangements

	Contractual arrangement						
	Outright control		Joint venture	Industrial collaboration	Subcontracting	Sales franchising	Licensing
Characteristic	Green field	Merger					
Nature of advantage							
Involves work organization and management	+	0	0	0	-	0	-
Protection and codification difficult	+	+	0	0	-	-	-
Further improvements likely from experience	+	+	0	-	-	-	-
Nature of firm							
Capital is difficult to obtain	-	-	0	0	0	0	+
Management skills are narrow	-	-	0	0	+	+	0
Nature of industry							
Output mobile and demand very inelastic	+	+	0	0	+	-	-
Inputs mobile and supply very inelastic	+	+	0	0	-	+	-
Quality very variable	+	0	0	0	-	+	-
Quality difficult to judge by inspection	+	+	+	+	-	-	-
Perishable or delicate output	+	+	+	+	-	-	+
Monopolized distribution channel	+	+	0	0	-	-	+
Economies of scope in marketing	-	-	0	0	-	+	0
Nature of countries (and industry)							
Large difference in production environment	-	+	+	+	+	-	+
Large difference in marketing environment	-	+	+	+	-	+	+
Large scope for transfer pricing gains	+	+	0	0	-	-	-
Host government dislikes foreign control	-	-	0	+	0	0	0
Political relations make expropriation risk high	-	-	0	+	0	0	+
Difficult communications	-	-	-	-	0	0	+

A contractual arrangement that successfully resolves the strategic issues associated with a particular characteristic earns a positive sign; the sign appears in the row corresponding to the characteristic and the column referring to the arrangement. An arrangement that makes only a modest contribution to resolving the relevant problems earns a zero sign. If the arrangement makes no contribution to resolving the problems, or even exacerbates them, then it has a negative sign.

The most important strategic issues considered by the economic theory of the MNE arise because many proprietary advantages are knowledge-based, and their profitable exploitation depends upon the firm maintaining monopoly power. Any attempt to exploit a knowledge-based advantage by a non-equity arrangement encounters the 'buyer uncertainty' problem. Attempts to overcome this problem may well lead to premature dissipation of the advantage and consequent loss of monopoly rents. The problem of preserving the advantage is most acute when the advantage is difficult to patent – either because the scope of patent protection is limited or because the advantage, though patentable, is difficult to formalize and codify. In some cases the advantage can be protected by other barriers to entry, such as exclusive access to essential inputs, or strategic investment in overcapacity when production affords economies of scale. If these other barriers to entry are not available, however, then the advantage must be protected by secrecy. This strongly favours outright control of a subsidiary, or at very least a joint venture arrangement which provides the firm with effective sanctions against its partner if the advantage is stolen.

Knowledge often generates other knowledge. At a mundane level, the exploitation of a new technology in production can provide valuable experience which leads to further improvements and so renders the original 'new' technology obsolete. Before a new technology has become routinely standardized, therefore, there is an additional risk in using non-equity contractual arrangements, namely that subsequent improvements in technology generated by production experience may not accrue to the parent firm.

Given that the advantage is protected by a barrier to entry, it remains to ensure that the monopoly power is exploited to the full. If the parent firm's product is easy to transport, and tariff barriers are low, then the home plant and the overseas plant (or two overseas plants) may compete to supply the same market. Competition will tend to be particularly intense in markets which are roughly equi-distant from the plants. To preserve monopoly profits, the managers of the different plants must collude. They may reserve particular markets for particular plants, or maintain agreed minimum prices in each of the markets. Such collusion could in principle be achieved by imposing cartel membership or an analogous marketing restriction upon licensees. In practice, however, the effective implementation of collusion calls for either outright control, or a network of joint ventures and/or subcontracting arrangements. All of these arrangements provide the parent firm with some measure of direct control over the international marketing of the product.

A firm with monopoly power derived from a proprietary advantage frequently enjoys monopsony power in purchasing the inputs which are used most intensively in the monopolized activity. If the inputs are mobile, however, and their total supply inelastic, potential monopsony rents can be dissipated by competition for the inputs between the firms who are authorized by the monopolist to exploit the advantage. Under such conditions, purchasing policies of authorized users need to be co-ordinated, and this favours the use of an equity stake. Such controls can also be imposed through restrictive clauses in non-equity arrangements, but they are difficult to police because the information needed to detect infringements is hard to obtain.

If the parent firm is newly founded, small, or for other reasons lacks reputation in the capital market, it will find it difficult to raise funds. This difficulty will be compounded if potential investors in the source country have a poor opinion of the economic prospects of the host country. Under such conditions, most of the capital will have to be supplied by the host country. Potential investors in the host country may well take a more optimistic view of their economic prospects than do investors in the source country, and so may be prepared to invest where foreigners are not. When the parent firm has little reputation, however, local capital will be forthcoming only if the parent firm takes a partner who has the confidence of local financiers. This encourages a joint venture or non-equity arrangement. The advantage to the parent firm of non-equity involvement is that the parent's capital contribution is limited mainly to working capital. Joint ventures require a more substantial capital contribution, but this is still less than the contribution required for outright purchase of a subsidiary. Non-equity involvement, and to a lesser extent joint ventures, will be favoured, therefore, by companies which are new, small or for other reasons are unable to raise substantial capital in their own name.

The successful exploitation of the firms' advantage may require production technology, work organization, management practices, etc., to be adapted to the local environment (Teece, 1977). The costs of adaptation through 'learning by doing' may be prohibitively high, in which case the firm must either acquire a going concern with suitable experience, or find a local partner. To encourage the partner to co-operate fully, he must be given some financial stake in the local operations. The problem of adaptation is most acute when the host environment is very different – e.g. there are differences in climate, in labour law and custom, and in the relative scarcity of different inputs (especially skilled labour).

Such conditions discourage foreign involvement through 'green field' investment.

Acquiring knowledge of the local market environment is very important when there are cultural differences between the source and host countries, when channels of wholesale and retail distribution are differently organized, and when the nature of indigenous substitutes for the product is different too. Such differences may call for an adaptation of product design, the adoption of new distribution logistics, and the modification of advertising strategy. The same principles which apply to the acquisition of local production know-how also apply in this case, but their implications are slightly different. One difference arises because the subcontracting option provides local production know-how, but not local marketing know-how, since under subcontracting, ownership of the product reverts to the parent firm before marketing is undertaken. Subcontracting does not, therefore, resolve the marketing problem. The sales franchising option, on the other hand, provides the requisite local marketing know-how.

It may be possible for the firm's management team to acquire skill *either* in adaptation of production *or* in adaptation of marketing, but difficult for it to have skill in *both*. The range of talents required may be too diverse. This encourages the firm to contract out one or other of these activities, i.e. to rely upon subcontracting or sales franchising. In some cases, there may be local firms which have skill in adapting both production and marketing activities, but only in respect of their own countries. If there are strong reasons for keeping production and marketing integrated, then this may encourage the firm to license a different local firm in each host country.

An important reason for integrating production and marketing is that it helps to resolve bilateral monopoly power. Distribution channels often exhibit economies of scale, so that one local firm comes to dominate the channel in each host country. Since the parent firm may well have a monopoly of the product, this creates a bilateral monopoly problem in the wholesale market. When two parties are locked into a situation of this kind, it is more efficient to negotiate a single long-term contract rather than a sequence of short-term contracts. Given the difficulties of enforcing long-term contracts, however, the simplest strategy may be to financially consolidate the two activities.

Against this, however, must be set the difficulty of controlling a marketing channel which deals not with a single product, but with a wide range of different products (e.g. groceries, or hardware). When there are economies of scope in a distribution channel – i.e. economies achieved by increasing the variety of products handled – there are significant advantages in allowing distribution to be handled by an independent specialist firm. This encourages sales franchising in particular.

Problems of quality control arise when the customer requires products to be supplied to very precise specifications and when the technology harnessed in production generates natural variability. As noted earlier, problems also arise in the early stages of a new production process when 'trial by error' learning is still going on. New products can also create problems for consumers who have not learnt how to use them properly. Disagreements between producers and their customers over responsibility for product failure are quite common where new products are concerned.

Quality control is most effective when administered through close supervision of the production process, since this avoids inferior quality items being produced in the first place. The key tactic here is to ensure that the parent firm's proprietary advantage in production is effectively transferred to the local production unit, and that staff trained by the parent firm supervise the production. Similar principles apply in respect of marketing. If consumer perceptions of the product can be damaged by accidents, delays or incompetence in the distribution channel, then it is important that trained staff supervise the marketing process too. Outright control, joint ventures, industrial co-operation agreements and management contracts normally provide this assurance, whereas the other contractual arrangements do not. In the case of outright control obtained through acquisition, however, the assurance is qualified by the risk that managers of the local subsidiary may be difficult to retrain in new attitudes to quality control, and may provide lax supervision as a result.

Quality control after production is completed is less effective, since it involves disposing of, or reprocessing, faulty items whose defects might have been avoided by better supervision. The quality of a finished product is often difficult to assess by superficial inspection, and so costly procedures may be involved which test to destruction a sample of the products. Subcontracting is preferable to licensing and franchising in this respect, because the product is returned to the parent firm before sale, so that quality testing can be brought under direct control.

Operational integration between production and marketing involves forward planning to eliminate bottlenecks in production which impede distribution (and vice versa). Forward planning allows these sequential operations to run smoothly without large precautionary holdings of inventory. Forward planning is most important when there are economies of continuous flow in production, when stock-outs create substantial inconvenience to customers, and when the product is delicate or perishable, and therefore difficult to hold as inventory.

Given the problems of enforcing forward contracts, operational integration is facilitated by bringing production and marketing under common control. Outright ownership brings production and marketing under the common control of the parent firm, whilst licensing brings them under the common control of the licensee. Other contractual arrangements involve some degree of separation of control between production and marketing, and so cannot fully resolve this problem.

Bringing production and marketing under the common control of the parent firm also facilitates the repatriation of the profits through transfer pricing, whereas bringing them under the common control of the licensor does not. All contractual arrangements other than outright ownership involve some element of arm's length pricing of knowledge, and this prevents profits being repatriated in the guise of payments for over-priced knowledge. This is important when the fiscal policies of the host country treat profits and licence fees differently.

Not only do some contractual arrangements involve separation of control, but they also permit a separation of control that is likely to lead to conflict. Even with outright control, conflicts between parent and subsidiary managements are likely to occur, especially when the subsidiary has been acquired by a takeover which was resisted by its management. Conflicts seem, at first sight, to be an almost inevitable outcome of joint ventures, although it is probably easy to overstate this risk. Joint ventures may benefit from a co-operative 'mystique' which attaches to them and is common to many different cultures (Franko, 1973). This mystique may beneficially influence managerial behaviour, at least in the early 'honeymoon' period of operation. It should also be recognized that sensible owners of a joint venture will refrain from day-to-day interference in its operations, and will delegate as much as possible to line managers. They will encourage managers to develop loyalty to the venture itself rather than to any of the owning companies. The avoidance of managerial conflict, therefore, while it encourages a green field investment strategy, and discourages joint ventures, may only marginally influence the choice between these two arrangements.

Joint ventures undertaken in conjunction with local enterprises are more likely to be viewed favourably by the host government than is outright control – particularly if the joint venture partner is a state-owned enterprise. This seems to be particularly true of countries which are sensitive to economic 'dependency' – these include countries with military governments who think in terms of strategic self-sufficiency, countries with radical left-wing governments, and countries with a recent experience of colonization.

A state-owned partner may not only be ideologically preferable, but may also be favoured because it provides the government with a source of 'inside information' on the behaviour of the parent firm. Most governments will also prefer non-equity contractual arrangements to outright foreign control. Industrial co-operation agreements are especially favoured because they typically involve the government in some capacity such as underwriter, they often commit the parent firm to counter-trade which assists export marketing by the host country, and they insure against adverse balance of payments effects from large unpredictable profit repatriations which could threaten a managed exchange rate regime. Industrial co-operation agreements are therefore particularly attractive to the governments of centrally planned economies.

From the point of view of the parent firm, conforming with government priorities does not eliminate political risk. If there is a disagreement with the government, for example, the firm's equity stake may be held hostage by the government. Also, if there is a change of government, the new government may not be sympathetic to a project for which the previous government has taken credit. The political risks are greatest for outright ownership, but they may still be significant for joint ventures too. Political risks are lowest for non-equity contractual arrangements, especially for the least controversial forms such as subcontracting.

When countries have different languages and cultures, frequent face-to-face contact between managers may be necessary in order to avoid misunderstandings. But if they are geographically distant, or for other reasons personal travel between them is difficult, then frequent face-to-face contact may be very costly. Some arrangements, such as outright control, call for frequent contact over matters of detail, whereas other arrangements, such as licensing, do not. Outright control, therefore, may be easier to effect between neighbouring countries with a common culture, but so difficult to effect between distant countries with different cultures that alternative arrangements such as licensing are preferred.

5.4 APPLICATION OF THE THEORY

The results summarized in table 5.2 can be used to predict the choice of contractual arrangements in any situation. It is assumed that the managers who make the decisions are sufficiently rational and well motivated to choose the contractual arrangement that is most efficient from the point of view of the owners of the firm (the consequences of relaxing this assumption are considered later). It is assumed that the most efficient arrangement is the one with the fewest strategic weaknesses.

In any given situation, not all of the strategic problems discussed in the previous section are important. A strategic problem arises only when one of the characteristics of the situation coincides with one of the characteristics shown in table 5.2. A characteristic of a situation which coincides with one of the characteristics listed in the table is said to be a 'relevant' characteristic of the situation. A particular contractual arrangement encounters a strategic weakness if for some relevant

TABLE 5.3 Example of predicting the choice of contractual arrangements

| | | | Contractual arrangement | | | | | | |
| | | | Outright control | | Joint venture | Industrial co-operation | Subcontracting | Sales franchising | Licensing |
	Weights	Situation	Green field	Merger					
Nature of advantage									
Involves work organization and management	1	+	0	1	1	1	2	1	2
Protection and codification difficult	1								
Further improvements likely from experience	1	+	0	0	1	2	2	2	2
Nature of firm									
Capital is difficult to obtain	3	+	6	6	3	3	3	3	0
Management skills are narrow	1	+	2	2	1	1	0	0	1
Nature of industry									
Output mobile and demand very inelastic	1	+	0	0	1	1	0	2	2
Inputs mobile and supply very inelastic	1								
Quality very variable	1	+	0	1	1	1	2	0	2
Quality difficult to judge by inspection	1								
Perishable or delicate output	1	+	0	0	0	0	2	2	0
Monopolized distribution channel	1	+	0	0	1	1	2	2	0
Economies of scope in marketing	1	+	2	2	1	1	2	0	1
Nature of countries (and industry)									
Large difference in production environment	1	+	2	0	0	0	0	2	0
Large difference in marketing environment	1								
Large scope for transfer pricing gains	1	+	0	0	1	1	2	2	2
Host government dislikes foreign control	1								
Political relations make expropriation risk high	1								
Difficult communications	1								
Total	20		12	12	11	12	17	16	12

characteristics it fails to carry a positive sign in table 5.2. This indicates that it does not completely succeed in dealing with the corresponding strategic problem. The weakness is greater when the arrangement carries a negative sign than when it carries a zero. It is assumed, in fact, that the weakness is twice as serious in the first case as in the second. A contractual arrangement incurs a unit penalty point if it carries a zero for a relevant characteristic, and two penalty points if it carries a negative sign.

Some weaknesses are inherently more serious than others, which suggests that they should be 'weighted' more heavily than the rest. The set of weights illustrated in the first column of table 5.3 attaches a greater weight to shortage of capital – which carries a weight of three – than it does to all the other characteristics – each of which carries a weight of unity. Given the weighting system, it is assumed that the overall weakness of a given contractual arrangement in a given situation is measured by the weighted sum of the penalty points incurred in respect of all the relevant characteristics. The contractual arrangement with the lowest total of penalty points is the one chosen. If more than one arrangement has the lowest score, then any one of them may be chosen.

The procedure above may be elucidated by an example. Consider a small firm with little reputation in the capital market, that possesses a patented technology which requires considerable managerial expertise to implement. The firm has the necessary expertise on the technical side, but is weak on the marketing side. The quality of the product is naturally variable, but is easy to assess by inspection. It is also perishable and delicate. Economies of scope in distribution are significant.

The product is mobile and has a highly elastic demand. The inputs, on the other hand, are difficult to transport. In each locality they are in relatively inelastic supply. The firm is contemplating production in a foreign market where production conditions are different to those at home, but where marketing conditions are fairly similar. Because of lack of fiscal harmonization between the two countries there is considerable scope for transfer pricing. However, the host government is fairly sympathetic to foreign control of production and political relations and communications between the two countries are normally good.

The characteristics which are relevant to the situation are indicated by positive signs in the second column of table 5.3. Characteristics which are not relevant are simply ignored. They do not matter because they are not a potential source of weakness in any of the contractual arrangements.

The next stage is to take each contractual arrangement in turn and identify its weaknesses by noting where it carries a zero or negative sign in respect of a relevant characteristic. A score is then entered in the corresponding row and column, equal to the product of the weight and the penalty points earned by the arrangement. The scores are then aggregated across all relevant characteristics to obtain a total score for each arrangement; these total scores are the column totals shown at the bottom of the table. The column totals are then compared to find which contractual arrangement will be chosen.

The calculations for the example reveal that a joint venture arrangement carries the lowest score. The joint 'runners-up' are outright control, industrial co-operation and licensing. Theory therefore predicts that an efficient firm will choose the joint venture option.

In this particular example, the reasons for the choice are fairly clear. Because the firm has little reputation in the capital market, outright ownership of a foreign subsidiary is difficult to achieve. At the very least, a partner should be found who can put up some of the equity. The firm is in the fortunate position that its technical advantage is protected by patent, so that it does not need to worry too much about secrecy. However, it needs to ensure that its management has some influence over the production process in order to keep down costs and maintain quality. This discourages licensing and subcontracting. Since the technology is still immature, in the sense that further developments are likely, a short-term arrangement such as industrial collaboration is unsatisfactory. Since the local marketing environment is fairly similar to that at home the firm has little to gain from franchising; indeed, since it would probably have to franchise a local wholesale monopolist, this would create a serious bilateral monopoly situation. The most effective solution is therefore to collaborate with the wholesaler through a joint venture arrangement.

This application of the theory hinges on two crucial assumptions. The first is that the management of the firm is sufficiently rational to choose the most efficient contractual arrangement. The second is that the theorist attaches the correct weights to each of the characteristics.

Although economic theory postulates rationality, this postulate in fact says little more than that people will behave as if they are optimizing something. In the case of managers, they may be optimizing the owners' profit, or they may be optimizing their own personal satisfactions. Moreover, this optimization is effected using whatever information happens to be available at the time, so that it is quite possible that managers perceive the situation incorrectly. Consequently, it is likely, from the owner's point of view, that managers will make mistakes. Managers that make a succession of mistakes are liable to be dismissed by the owners, however, and owners that do not dismiss incompetent managers will find that their firms fail. The managers of the successful and profitable firms will, on average, make fewer mistakes than the managers of unsuccessful firms. The successful firms will survive, the unsuccessful firms will die out, and the most successful firms will tend to dominate the industry (until their managers become complacent, and the firms start to falter). Theory suggests, therefore, that even when mistakes are made, the managers of firms with a prospect of survival will be approximating, in some sense, to efficient decision making. It also suggests that if the managers of any firm persist in choosing inefficient contractual arrangements, then that firm will fail.

In the example above, the weights allocated to each characteristic reflect nothing more than the author's personal judgement. In order to avoid fudging the theory, it is important that the weights are maintained constant from one case study to the next. It would be possible to establish a number of alternative weighting systems, and to compare their predictions with the evidence over a large number of different cases. However, the choice of the systems would itself be rather arbitrary. The ideal arrangement would be to devise a statistical procedure for estimating the weights by maximizing the explanatory power of the theory over a sample of cases. Such a procedure, however, would require considerable effort to devise, as the mathematics is, superficially at least, quite different from that of standard techniques such as least squares regression. In the meantime, it seems reasonable to recommend that the evidence be interpreted using only simple modifications of the elementary weighting system employed above.

5.5 INTERPRETING RECENT EVIDENCE FROM BUSINESS HISTORIES OF MNEs

This section reviews new evidence on the emergence and growth of MNEs presented by writers connected with the Business History Unit of the London School of Economics and Imperial College, London. Four case studies have been chosen in order to illustrate how new insights can be obtained by applying the economic theory of the MNE to business history. The case studies provide a suitable means of testing the theory, whilst the theory, for its part, helps to inform the interpretation of historical events.

Pilkingtons and the glass industry (Barker, 1960; 1977; 1985). The hypothetical application discussed in section 5.4 was in fact, based upon the Pilkington case. Pilkingtons is a family-controlled firm based in St Helens, Lancashire, with a tradition of technical innovation in large-scale glass manufacture. Pilkington's technical leadership in certain areas of the glass industry was significantly strengthened in the 1950s by the innovation of float glass, which rendered obsolete the plate glass made by its major rivals in Belgium and the United States. The desire of the family to maintain control inhibited significant dilution of the equity, although it is possible that family control could have been maintained through a holding company structure had the management been sufficiently sophisticated to organize this. The family members who headed the management had strengths mainly on the technical side, and their initial attitude to overseas involvement was to develop a global export trade based upon economies of large-scale production at home. At the top management level the company seems to have been rather weak on the marketing side, and reluctant to heed advice from non-family members who were 'at the sharp end' of selling glass overseas.

When the threat of tariffs encouraged production overseas, the company recognized that the transfer of Pilkington's technology abroad involved training overseas production managers in rigorous quality control methods. Since the company itself was still improving the technology through learning by doing, a simple licensing arrangement would neither afford full opportunity for training, nor protect the company's rights to future improvements developed by the licensee. Glass is fairly easily transported by sea (though not over land) and so there would also be problems in regulating competition between Pilkington licensees in third country markets in order to retain Pilkington's global market power.

In some segments of the market – such as toughened glass for windscreens – the company sold in bulk direct to major industrial users, whereas in other market segments wholesale distribution was in the hands of quite powerful monopolistic distributors. Bilateral monopoly was therefore a significant factor. While it would have been excessively demanding for management to have become directly involved in, say, the motor industry merely to secure the market for windscreen glass, it was quite feasible for it to integrate into the distribution of glass. Lack of equity, however, and the absence of marketing expertise, encouraged joint venture operations with indigenous firms instead – Pilkingtons supplying the technology and the local firm the access to the market.

This strategy was pursued in most of Pilkington's major overseas markets. The company ran into difficulties in India, however, because of the government's lack of sympathy with any sort of foreign equity involvement. With the benefit of hindsight, the company's efficient strategy would have been to avoid producing in India at all, since any equity stake would have produced adverse government intervention, and the absence of an equity stake would have allowed an Indian licensee to invade Pilkington's overseas markets, and perhaps also would have ruined its reputation by supplying a low quality product in conjunction with the Pilkington name.

In recent years Pilkington has gradually increased its equity stake in production overseas, but this has been accomplished largely by the reinvestment of overseas earnings generated by the float glass process. The family has retained control of the company and also preserved its conservative financial structure, by continuing to finance new investment largely from retained earnings.

Glaxo Laboratories and the pharmaceutical industry (Davenport-Hines, 1985a). Two main phases in the growth of Glaxo can be distinguished: the inter-war period, during which Glaxo was controlled by members of an 'extended family' – the Nathans – based both in Britain and New Zealand, and trading in diverse food products, with an emphasis on baby foods; and the post-war period, during which it rapidly matured into a managerially controlled company concentrating on pharmaceutical products. During the inter-war period most of the capital was supplied by the family, whereas after 1945 external sources were used to finance an extensive acquisition programme. In the inter-war period Glaxo concentrated on producing and selling products under licence from other firms, whereas in the post-war period it began to develop a range of products of its own.

The environment was different during these periods too. Political instability during the inter-war years discouraged British firms from taking a large equity stake in countries outside the Empire, because of the risk of expropriation in the event of hostilities, whereas in the post-war period equity investment outside the Empire became much less hazardous. New post-war opportunities, however, were often exploited only reluctantly because, in common with other British firms, its inter-war policies meant that Glaxo had little experience of operating in Europe or the US. Indeed Glaxo was often excluded from the US market altogether because of restrictive clauses in its licensing agreements which reserved the US market for the US licensor.

A major feature of pharmaceutical production is that skilful management is needed in order to achieve the rigorous standards of quality required for medical products. This discourages subcontracting. Pharmaceutical products are not too difficult to transport, and new pharmaceutical products typically have very low price elasticities of demand. Control over international marketing strategy is therefore crucial for a pharmaceutical company, and this discourages licensing and franchising.

Differences in the production environment abroad are not normally very significant – except in developing countries, where skilled labour may be in short supply – but differences in the marketing environment may be acute. The organization of local health services and the attitudes of the medical profession often vary between countries. Care needs to be exercised when labelling products in a foreign language, when giving advice on the local products with which medicines can be diluted, and in complying with local requirements concerning the advertising of claims. This normally

TABLE 5.4 Contractual arrangements for Glaxo

		Contractual arrangement						
		Outright control		Joint venture	Industrial co-operation	Subcontracting	Sales franchising	Licensing
Characteristic	Situation	Green field	Merger					
Nature of advantage								
Involves work organization and management	+	0	1	1	1	2	1	2
Protection and codification difficult								
Further improvements likely from experience								
Nature of firm								
Capital is difficult to obtain	(+)	(6)	(6)	(3)	(3)	(3)	(3)	(0)
Management skills are narrow								
Nature of industry								
Output mobile and demand very inelastic	+	0	0	1	1	0	2	2
Inputs mobile and supply very inelastic								
Quality very variable	+	0	1	1	1	2	0	2
Quality difficult to judge by inspection	+	0	0	0	0	2	2	2
Perishable or delicate output	+	0	0	0	0	2	2	0
Monopolized distribution channel								
Economies of scope in marketing								
Nature of countries (and industry)								
Large difference in production environment	+	2	0	0	0	2	0	0
Large difference in marketing environment	+	0	0	2	2	1	1	1
Large scope for transfer pricing gains								
Host government dislikes foreign control								
Political relations make expropriation risk high	(+)	(2)	(2)	(1)	(0)	(1)	(1)	(2)
Difficult communications								
Total (post-war)		2	2	5	5	11	8	9
Total (inter-war)		10	10	9	8	15	12	11

Bracketed entries apply only to the inter-war period.

calls for close collaboration with someone who has local knowledge of the market.

The calculations shown in table 5.4 have been made separately for the inter-war and post-war periods. It is assumed that in the inter-war period the firm, as a family enterprise, experienced capital rationing, whereas in the post-war period, as a managerially controlled enterprise, it did not. It is also assumed that the risk of expropriation was significantly higher in the inter-war period than in the post-war period. Using the weighting previously employed in section 5.4, the calculations indicate that industrial co-operation agreements would be favoured in the inter-war period and outright ownership of foreign subsidiaries favoured in the post-war period. This accords fairly well with the evidence.

The company's relations with its Italian, Greek and US partners during the inter-war period were a combination of joint ventures and industrial collaboration agreements. This accords with the table, which places industrial collaboration agreements first and joint ventures second in order of preference for this period. In the post-war period the company opted mainly for building a network of wholly owned foreign subsidiaries trading under the Glaxo name. The major exception to this strategy was its policy of licensing its most sophisticated products to its US rivals. This directly conflicts with the theory, because according to the table, licensing is an undesirable option under the conditions of both the inter-war and post-war period.

The strategic problems identified by the theory in connection with the licensing option are certainly real enough, as the company's disastrous experiences in Australia in 1912–14 show. The company:

gave a manufacturing agreement to Bacchus Marsh for only a trial period of about two years duration, and by this and other actions made clear to their licensee that they distrusted him. The licensee realised that he lacked the licensor's confidence, lost his incentive to make Glaxo successful, and feared being out of work when the trial period expired. Instead Bacchus Marsh developed prototype new machinery of their own, to make a new product analogous to Glaxo, but outside the Nathan's patents: in 1914 they launched a homogenised version of Glaxo, Lactogen, using advertising techniques, with infant welfare nurses calling on mothers, copied from the Nathans. Lactogen rapidly became Glaxo's main Australian competitor, and was bought by Nestle, who developed it internationally with disastrous consequences for the Nathans. The short-dated license had resulted in a long-term competitor skilled in Glaxo's manufacturing techniques and sales methods (Davenport-Hines, 1985a, p. 13).

The explanation of the company's later decision to license to the US must be sought in the enormous capital requirements for a company which, though large in British terms, was very small compared to its major

TABLE 5.5 Contractual arrangements for Dunlop

	Contractual arrangement							
		Outright control		Joint venture	Indus- trial co- opera- tion	Subcon- tracting	Sales fran- chising	Licens- ing
Characteristic	Situa- tion	Green field	Merger					
Nature of advantage								
Involves work organization and management	+	0	1	1	1	2	1	2
Protection and codification difficult								
Further improvements likely from experience								
Nature of firm								
Capital is difficult to obtain								
Management skills are narrow								
Nature of industry								
Output mobile and demand very inelastic	+	0	0	1	1	0	2	2
Inputs mobile and supply very inelastic								
Quality very variable	+	0	1	1	1	2	0	2
Quality difficult to judge by inspection								
Perishable or delicate output	+	0	0	0	0	2	2	0
Monopolized distribution channel								
Economies of scope in marketing								
Nature of countries (and industry)								
Large difference in production environment	+	2	0	0	0	2	0	0
Large difference in marketing environment								
Large scope for transfer pricing gains								
Host government dislikes foreign control	(+)	(2)	(2)	(1)	(0)	(2)	(2)	(2)
Political relations make expropriation risk high	(+)	(2)	(2)	(1)	(0)	(1)	(1)	(0)
Difficult communications								
Total (pre-1914)		2	2	3	3	8	5	6
Total (inter-war)		6	6	5	3	11	8	8

Bracketed entries apply only to the inter-war period.

US rivals. Another contributory factor may have been that the company did not have a 'full line' of products to market in the US. Finally, the technological and managerial sophistication of its US rivals meant that the licensee need have little concern over the quality of the product they would produce. Nevertheless, it remains the case that the company's US policy appears inefficient from the standpoint of the theory, so that it must either be established that the company has underperformed in the US, or the theory must be modified to take account of the special factors that seem relevant in this case.

Dunlop and the tyre industry (Jones, 1984; 1985a). To explain the early overseas experience of Dunlop is extremely challenging. In the early twentieth century Dunlop held various patents – some of them were its own, and others were held under licence. One of its crucial patents, moreover, was overturned by the courts, whilst other patents could only be upheld abroad if the company agreed to work them in the countries concerned. The company was a multi-product firm, producing both sports equipment sold mainly through the retail trade, and tyres sold both direct to motor and cycle manufacturers and through wholesalers to the motor and cycle repair trades. Between 1892 and 1938 the company operated abroad in nine countries – in Europe, the Empire, the US, Eire and Japan. It also concluded licensing agreements in these and other countries.

A full explanation of Dunlop's overseas involvement would require an analysis broken down both by product and country. It is possible, however, to obtain some insight into Dunlop's behaviour by comparing its overall strategy before 1914 with its overall strategy in the inter-war period. It cannot be assumed, however, that the company selected the efficient strategy in either of these periods, because its returns on overseas operations were significantly below its returns on its British operations – indeed they were well below what the company could have obtained by investing in purely financial assets instead.

The contractual arrangements suitable for the international exploitation of pneumatic tyre patents are analysed in table 5.5. Because of the safety requirements for tyres, management skill in implementing quality control is most important. Economies of scale in tyre production encourage international trade in tyres, even though they are rather bulky to transport. This means that the international co-ordination of pricing policy is important. Rubber products are, of course, perishable if not correctly stored, and so some operational integration of production and distribution is desirable. Successful marketing requires the building up of goodwill with major manufacturers of cycles and motor cars. The different styles of vehicle developed for local conditions in different parts of the world – involving the different qualities of road surface, etc. – called for some differentiation of tyre products to local conditions. Thus knowledge of local market conditions was important and this encouraged some form of involvement with a foreign firm.

Because of the strategic nature of tyres as a component of military vehicles, the political instability characteristic of the inter-war period also carried with it dislike of foreign control of tyre manufacture. The inter-war environment in which Dunlop operated was therefore very different from the pre-war environment. Table 5.5 indicates that in the pre-war period, Dunlop's optimal strategy was to take an equity stake in foreign production sufficient, at least, to give it some measure of control over quality and over pricing policy. A green field investment would give the company the strongest direct control, but an acquisition or joint venture would give it greater local marketing expertise, at the expense of a reduction in control. Whatever form was chosen, however, equity involvement was clearly preferable to non-equity involvement.

The company's factory in the US, which it owned outright between 1892 and 1898, appears to have been highly successful, and although the company then sold out it had become, by that time, 'the most important maker of bicycle and vehicle tyres in America'. In retrospect, the parent company's decision to sell out was remarkably shortsighted, and it spent the next thirty years in vain attempts to re-enter the market. In France, by contrast, the company entered into a licensing arrangement which, although it involved an equity stake, did not give the parent any effective control – it was essentially an arrangement for relating royalty to the profitability of the licensee. The French licensee 'failed to diversify its product range on the lines of the British company, and exercised poor quality control over its products'. A report produced by the British company in 1912 remarked that 'our manufacture was absolutely discredited in France' (Jones, 1985a, p. 9). A similar problem was encountered with the company's German partner. In an attempt to rectify the situation, the French operation was acquired outright in 1909 and the German operation in 1910.

In the inter-war years the company's optimal strategy was to avoid outright ownership of a subsidiary and instead enter into an industrial co-operation agreement (or possibly a joint venture) with a local partner. Anxious to avoid the mistakes of the pre-war period, however, the company opted for heavy equity involvement in overseas activities. In doing so, it appears to have ignored the probable consequence of being a foreign producer of a strategic product in politically hostile countries. In the 1930s the company's operations in both Germany and Japan became 'hostage' to government military policies.

It also seems to have ignored the importance of local contacts in establishing links with major motor manufacturers. In France, where such links had been forged by its pre-war operations, Dunlop did well, but in the US, where it re-established itself after a considerable gap in time, it failed to win the custom of major manufacturers.

In 1936 the company's controller of finance estimated that the rate of return of its US and Canadian operations was negative, on the French and German operations 3.9 per cent and 4.6 per cent respectively, and while the rate of return in Japan was 9.2 per cent it was very difficult to repatriate the profits. Given the company's success in its domestic operations – where the highest return of all was obtained – it seems reasonable to impute a significant component of its under-performance overseas to the choice of inappropriate contractual arrangements. The Dunlop case is therefore a good example of how the theory can be used to analyse the reason for the failure of a company's international strategy.

Vickers and the armaments business (Davenport-Hines, 1985; Scott, 1962; Trebilcock, 1977). The armaments business has a number of special features, and it is therefore a good test of a theory to see whether it can explain the contractual arrangements of an armaments manufacturer such as Vickers. Possession of weapons embodying the latest technology is crucial to military success, and national self-sufficiency in the production of key weapons is also of great strategic value. Weaponry is always a high-technology business, therefore, and in modern times armament design is in a continuous state of improvement. Since national governments are the manufacturer's major customers, in each country the manufacturer sells to a local monopsonist – a monopsonist, moreover, with legislative and coercive powers. Since the greatest market for armaments is amongst potential belligerents, the risk of losing foreign assets is acute, since they can be lost either as a result of military requisition, enemy action, or expropriation after conquest. On the other hand, if a company does not sell to belligerents, it does not have the opportunity of seeing its weapons tested in battle conditions, and therefore finds it difficult to optimize the overall performance of its product.

Before 1914 Vickers was a family-controlled public company whose business was regarded as 'high risk' by many investors; the company therefore had limited access to external capital markets. Warfare in this era was a more gentlemanly affair than it became after 1914. Civilian mobilization for war was partial rather than total, patent rights to military technology were well respected, and industrial espionage was not the big business that it has become today. Table 5.6 analyses the choice of contractual arrangements for Vickers when exploiting weapons technology in this environment. It indicates that an industrial co-operation agreement is the most efficient form of foreign involvement, with joint ventures and licensing agreements as 'runners up'.

TABLE 5.6 Contractual arrangements for Vickers before 1914

		Contractual arrangement						
		Outright control		Joint venture	Industrial co-operation	Subcontracting	Sales franchising	Licensing
Characteristic	Situation	Green field	Merger					
Nature of advantage								
Involves work organization and management	+	0	1	1	1	2	1	2
Protection and codification difficult								
Further improvements likely from experience	+	0	0	1	2	2	2	2
Nature of firm								
Capital is difficult to obtain	+	6	6	3	3	3	3	0
Management skills are narrow								
Nature of industry								
Output mobile and demand very inelastic	+	0	0	1	1	0	2	2
Inputs mobile and supply very inelastic								
Quality very variable	+	0	1	1	1	2	0	2
Quality difficult to judge by inspection								
Perishable or delicate output								
Monopolized distribution channel	+	0	0	1	1	2	2	0
Economies of scope in marketing								
Nature of countries (and industry)								
Large difference in production environment	+	2	0	0	0	2	0	0
Large difference in marketing environment	+	0	0	1	1	2	2	2
Large scope for transfer pricing gains	+	2	2	1	0	1	1	1
Host government dislikes foreign control	+	2	2	1	0	1	1	0
Political relations make expropriation risk high								
Difficult communications								
Total		12	12	11	10	17	14	11

It is interesting to note that Vickers, in the years before 1914, sought out overseas markets by offering to establish national arsenals which would allow countries to become self-sufficient in basic weaponry. This was considered an alternative to exporting Vickers weapons manufactured in England, although the most advanced weapons would usually continue to be manufactured in England even when an arsenal had been established abroad. The company's reputation for armament manufacture also meant that, in a number of cases, foreign governments themselves took the initiative in approaching the company. The construction and operation of an arsenal fits easily into the conventional concept of industrial co-operation. It involves an initial short-term commitment to construct the arsenal and commission it as a going concern in conjunction with other partners, mainly indigenous firms. Thereafter, the company has a more limited involvement in providing management services, key components, etc., through renewable short-term contracts. In certain cases a more durable relationship was established, similar to a joint venture, and in other cases a more distant relationship akin to a licensing agreement. With the exception of its North American interests, all of the company's major overseas involvements before 1914 followed this pattern – in Italy, Austro-Hungary, Japan, Spain, Russian, Turkey and France. In Canada, the company's arsenal was wholly-owned, and was not a success, failing dismally to obtain orders from the Canadian government. Industrial co-operation of the kind adopted elsewhere might well have been more successful in Canada.

Typical of the company's international involvement was the agreement with Armstrong Whitworths – another British company – and the Turkish government to construct a naval and commercial dockyard. Vickers and Armstrongs each held 20 per cent of the equity. The agreement, lasting for thirty years, established the Société Impériale Ottoman des Docks. The two British companies agreed to provide management and supervision, and to recruit English workpeople where necessary. They would build a floating dock, improve existing facilities, and erect a model village for the employees. Work that could not be done on site would be exported from England. Construction work was to be carried out to a specific timetable, and Turkish personnel were to be trained so that the docks could, in due course, be handed back to the Turkish government as a going concern.

The outbreak of World War I terminated negotiations over this agreement, but it is an interesting example of the early use of an industrial co-operation agreement of a fairly sophisticated kind. Modern commentators who describe such agreements as a 'new form' of international involvement would benefit considerably from the historical perspective on the subject that this Vickers case study provides. Despite the peculiarities of the armaments industry, therefore, it may be concluded that the theory and methodology developed in this paper are still of relevance to the industry.

5.6　CONCLUSIONS, AND IMPLICATIONS FOR FUTURE RESEARCH

While the four case studies reviewed in the previous section cannot be regarded as an adequate sample, since they are not selected at random and the sample size is very small, they clearly suggest that 'compromise' contractual arrangements such as joint ventures and industrial collaboration agreements have much more to recommend them than might at first appear. The contractual arrangements at either end of the spectrum – namely control of a green field subsidiary, and licensing to an independent indigenous firm – each have very obvious advantages in certain cases, but these advantages are very often outweighed by even greater drawbacks. Analysis of contractual arrangements that emphasize a simple polarized choice between 'equity' and 'non-equity' arrangements fails to highlight this. Similarly, an analysis which regards a single strategic issue as being of overriding importance – such as the safeguarding of intellectual property through secrecy – cannot do justice to the way that the strengths and weaknesses of each arrangement must be traded off against each other. It is only when *all* of the different contractual arrangements are simultaneously evaluated by considering *all* of the strategic issues that the great strength of the compromise arrangements becomes apparent.

If it is accepted that the case studies presented above provide preliminary vindication of the method, then it is natural to suggest a number of ways in which the application of the method can be extended – apart from the obvious suggestion that more case studies of the previous type should be examined.

First, the concept of comparing the strategies adopted by the same firm over different time periods could be extended by considering earlier periods, say 1850–70, and later periods, say 1973 to date. In some cases differences in strategy over time may be explicable in terms of changes in the political climate, or in the state of international communications which are common to all firms over the period. In other cases the differences may emerge as the firm evolves through phases of growth which are specific to the firm itself (Corley, 1985).

It could be hypothesized, for example, that in the early stages of growth the firm's management has only a narrow range of skills and the firm lacks reputation in the capital market. Theory suggests that in this phase the firm will opt for low equity involvement such as licensing or joint venture rather than heavy equity involvement, such as outright control. The management may, however, be able to learn from monitoring the experience of its affiliate and thereby increase the diversity of its skills. It may also acquire reputation in the capital market as the success of its operations becomes widely known. Theory indicates that the company will then tend to switch to heavier equity involvement. Thus the licensing or joint venture strategy may represent only a temporary phase in the overseas operations of a successful firm.

Secondly, differences in the same firm's strategy in different host countries could be considered, focusing upon overseas involvements initiated at about the same time. The theory clearly predicts that contractual arrangements are liable to differ between neighbouring countries and distant countries, between countries within an empire and those outside it, and between countries at an early stage of development and those which are more mature.

Thirdly, pair-wise comparisons between firms entering the same host country at the same time could be made. If the firms were from the same country, then differences in contractual arrangements would naturally be explained by differences in the size or ownership structure of the company – reflecting its ability to borrow capital – and the diversity of its management skills. If the firms were of similar size and possessed of similar skills, but came from different countries, then the differences would be explained in terms of factors specific to the source countries.

It is also possible to suggest certain improvements in technique, which would give greater flexibility in the application of the theory. Some of the factors that are particularly prominent in any given situation could, for example, be given a 'double-plus' (+ +) status indicating that the scores associated with these factors should be given a double weight. While it is important not to build too much flexibility into the method – since this increases the scope for the analyst to 'fix' the result – the case studies above suggest that some arrangement of this kind would strengthen the ability of the theory to discriminate between arrangements where differences in characteristics are only marginal.

This chapter has considered only one of several motives for international involvement. Nothing has been said about backward integration to secure supplies of raw materials, about export-platform linkages which exploit cheap labour, or about conglomerate operations which achieve risk reductions by exploiting the principles of a mutual fund. The strategic issues that arise in these cases are not exactly the same as those discussed above, although there are some striking parallels none the less. The relevant theories already exist to guide the business historian who is studying these motives, although once again additional effort will be called for to translate the theory into immediately applicable terms.

Finally, it should be noted that interpretation of the case studies offered in this chapter was prepared only after the historical research had been done. This is unsatisfactory on two main counts. First, it means that the historian may have overlooked, or sifted out as low priority, evidence that the economist would regard as crucial. Secondly, the economist may misinterpret what the business historian says by attaching too much weight to illustrative anecdotes, and generally running into all the problems which bedevil the use of secondary sources. What is needed is for the economist and the business historian to collaborate throughout the research process, beginning with the very first step of identifying suitable and rewarding cases to study.

6

The Scope of the Firm
in the Construction Industry

6.1 INTRODUCTION

This chapter applies the theory of internalization to the analysis of diversification and subcontracting decisions in the construction industry. The focus is upon firms that act as main contractors. The object is to explain the range of projects undertaken by the typical firm, the geographical spread of its operations, and its choice between backward integration and subcontracting in respect of subsidiary activities. In this context, the relationship between quality control and vertical integration – analysed in chapter 4 – turns out to be crucial.

The application of the theory highlights eleven important characteristics of the construction industry.

1 The output of a construction firm is usually customized. Standardization of output is much lower in construction than in manufacturing because of the need to adapt the design of structures to the idiosyncratic constraints of the site. Because the product is customized, production normally involves a sequence of short-lived 'one-off' projects.

2 Final output is immobile. Once built, a structure cannot easily be moved to another site. Structures can, however, be designed with alternative uses in mind: the internal division of space within an office building, for example, may be deliberately made flexible by using moveable partitions rather than internal load-bearing walls.

3 Most construction work takes place 'out of doors' and is therefore subject to the vagaries of the weather. This means that the demand for

labour in construction has a significant seasonal element. In this respect, construction is like other weather-related activities such as agriculture and tourism, and unlike most types of factory production.

4 Intermediate inputs are immobile. The division of labour within construction creates many separate tasks within the production process. Different tasks call for different specialist skills, as in the manufacturing industry. But unlike manufacturing, many of these tasks have to be carried out on the same site. This is because their output is embodied continuously and directly into the structure. Subcontractors producing immobile output do not, therefore, work on their own premises, but on the main contractor's premises. They work, moreover, in close proximity to each other. Unlike manufacturing industries, therefore, subcontractors tend to work 'under the eye' of the main contractor and 'under the feet' of the other subcontractors.

5 Construction is labour intensive, and the division of labour creates many activities for which the only input of any significance is labour itself.

6 Some·of the constituent activities cannot be begun until others have been completed. Hence punctuality in the completion of each activity is crucial for the prompt completion of the overall process.

7 Care and attention to detail is vital both for the safety of the finished structure and for the safety of other workers on site.

8 In cases where work can be carried out off site (because the intermediate input is mobile) the off-site process often benefits from both economies of scale and economies of continuous flow. This means that the efficient length of production run off site tends to be very large compared to the on-site demand for the input.

9 Contracting involves both construction and maintenance work. The value of a maintenance contract is typically much smaller than that of a construction contract. Contracting firms can, therefore, if they choose, undertake two quite distinctive types of work.

10 Demand for construction is subject to short-run fluctuations. Like other durable goods, its demand is a derived demand governed by the 'acceleration' principle. Demand for maintenance, on the other hand, is a recurrent demand which is much more stable in the short run.

11 The contracting industry in many countries – and in Britain in particular – is governed by restrictive working practices. The restrictions are enforced by horizontal combinations of people organized as professional associations or trade unions. The restrictions attempt to reserve certain types of work for members of a particular association. They apply at all levels, from the craftsmen and their apprentices working on site to the architects who design the structure and the surveyors who implement the design.

The extensive specialization of construction work creates many different types of firms in the industry. The focus in this chapter is on firms that act as main contractors, and the question addressed concerns how far these main contractors diversify into other activities within the industry. It is not, therefore, a comprehensive study of all forms of integration and diversification in the industry, but only a study of those forms that involve main contracting as one of the components of the firm's operations.

The nature of the main contractor's role is analysed in section 6.2. The rationale of the main contractor is shown to hinge on the advantages of continuity of employment within a management team. Sections 6.3 and 6.4 develop this theme by examining various aspects of continuity of employment within the construction industry as a whole.

The next three sections consider various aspects of subcontracting. It is argued that the need for assured standards of workmanship in the construction industry makes quality control the most important strategic issue in the subcontracting decision. This affects not only the main contractor's choice between subcontracting and backward integration, but also the choice between ordinary subcontracting and labour-only subcontracting, and the choice of methods of remuneration for subcontractors' employees.

Sections 6.8 and 6.9 discuss the scope of the projects undertaken by a main contracting firm. It is argued that both the technical scope and the geographical scope of the firm's operations are a reflection of thé skills of the management team. Although intuitively obvious, this proposition has a number of interesting implications which are far from obvious. It appears, for example, that within the UK, institutional constraints restrict the range of in-house management skills available to main contracting firms. Until recently, for example, architects were discouraged by their professional association from taking full-time employment with a contracting firm. Such restrictions distort firms' operations and are a source of inefficiency in the industry.

Empirical evidence on the scope of UK contracting firms is presented in section 6.10. The overall picture of diversification and integration is consistent with the main hypotheses derived from the theory. There is, however, extraordinary diversity among firms in their patterns of integration and diversification. This suggests that few managers in the UK construction industry think in rational strategic terms about the scope of the firm's operations. This interpretation of the evidence is consistent with the view expressed above, that main contracting firms may be denied some of the skills they require because of institutional constraints within the industry. The main results are summarized in section 6.11.

6.2   THE MAIN CONTRACTOR'S ROLE:
A THEORETICAL APPRAISAL

Most construction projects originate when a client who owns or leases some land wishes to erect a structure on it. The client typically approaches a main contractor who undertakes the project on behalf of the client (see figure 6.1).

In principle, almost all of the main contractor's work can be subcontracted to specialists, and this raises the question of what precisely the role of the main contractor is. Why does the client not contract directly with the specialists he requires? Why does he use the main contractor as intermediary instead? If the main contractor undertakes only a single project then there is, in fact, little reason why the client would use a main contractor. Most of the reasons for using a main contractor stem from the fact that the main contractor undertakes a sequence of projects of which the client's project is only one.

This raises the issue of why the same firm should remain in business long enough to act as main contractor on a sequence of projects for different clients. The answer is to be found in the structure of transaction costs (Casson, 1982a; 1982b). To undertake a project it is necessary to establish contacts with workers and suppliers, to negotiate prices with them, to specify the quality of the inputs required, to monitor the quality actually supplied, and to enforce agreements with them. Each of these activities incurs costs, some proportion of which are fixed costs, independent of the number of projects on which the parties collaborate. This creates a cost incentive for the same parties to collaborate upon a succession of projects. Since most clients commission projects only

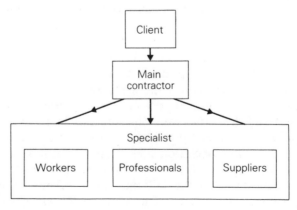

FIGURE 6.1   The main contractor as intermediary

occasionally, the transaction costs savings can only be obtained by channelling the project through a main contractor who contracts regularly with the same workers and suppliers. It is essential to this arrangement that the main contractor remains in business continuously and undertakes projects for a variety of clients.

It can be seen that the major advantage to a client of hiring a main contractor is that the main contractor has previous experience of working with workers and suppliers, which the client lacks. (Even if the client does have some previous experience, the main contractor's experience is likely to be more recent, and therefore his information on workers and suppliers will be more up to date).

The main contractor could, in principle, license his experience to the client by acting as his adviser in the negotiation and enforcement of contracts with workers and suppliers. The client, however, might well have considerable doubts about the quality of the advice he was receiving. To reassure the client, the main contractor would have to bear some of the risks himself, which implies taking some form of equity stake in the project. In some cases main contractors do offer management services to clients, or participate with their clients on a joint-venture or collaborative basis. In most cases, however, particularly where domestic contracting is concerned, the main contractor assumes practically all of the risks by offering to undertake the entire project for an all-in price. The main contractor enters into one contract with the client, and into quite separate contracts with workers and suppliers. The main contractor therefore acts as a pure intermediary. The margin, if any, between the price he quotes and the sum of his opportunity costs is the quasi-rent he derives from knowledge accumulated from his experience on previous projects.

6.3   THE REGULARITY OF EMPLOYMENT IN THE CONSTRUCTION INDUSTRY

Construction sites are geographically dispersed, and idiosyncratic in their configurations. Their geographical dispersal raises the question of whether the main contractor will wish to use the same personnel on each project, since some personnel will live much nearer to one project than they do to another. At the same time, the idiosyncracies mean that some sites call for one type of expertise and others for another. Both of these factors encourage the main contractor to maintain contacts with a variety of different workers and suppliers, who are offered intermittent employment for which they are particularly suitable, rather than with fewer workers and suppliers who are offered continuous employment.

The benefits to the main contractor of offering regular employment are greatest when the fixed components of transaction costs are highest. Suppose, for example, that certain specialists have firm-specific skills which are very costly to acquire, and quickly depreciate if not used. If the specialists are offered only intermittent employment, training costs will escalate because a larger total stock of specialists must be held on call. Certain aspects of project planning, for example, call for a very sophisticated intellectual division of labour between managerial specialists. It is important not only that each manager has the confidence of the main contractor, but that he enjoys the personal confidence of the other managers with whom he works. To build up and maintain this level of confidence it is important to keep the managers together as a team. Turnover of membership significantly reduces the efficiency of team performance (Penrose, 1959). Thus managers engaged in project planning are likely to be offered permanent employment.

By no means all specialists, though, will be permanent members of a team. Some specialists are so highly specialized that it would be difficult for any team of reasonable size to keep them fully employed. Suppose, for example, that the typical specialist is required, on average, to work on half the projects undertaken by the firm, but that the services of one specialist are required on only one-tenth of them. To keep the typical specialist fully employed, it may be necessary to have only twice the number of projects that the individual specialist is engaged upon. But to keep the highly-specialized specialist fully employed, it is necessary to have at least ten times the number of projects that the individual is engaged upon. The resulting size of the team may be so large that diseconomies of bureaucracy set in. This exemplifies the general point that the indivisibility of the specialist worker encourages his services to be shared between different firms.

Another factor encouraging firms to recruit individuals on an intermittent short-term basis is that the non-wage costs of employment arising from pension rights, redundancy payments, etc., are much heavier for full-time workers than part-time workers and tend to increase with the length of continuous service. This affects all employers and not just firms in the construction industry. A firm can often reduce its total labour costs by replacing a permanent and/or full-time staff with a group of temporary and/or part-time workers. Furthermore, the taxation and social security system reduces the net private cost to individuals of spells of unemployment between intermittent jobs. In so far as this encourages individuals to accept temporary work at lower wages than they would otherwise demand, it is an indirect subsidy to contractors who substitute against permanent employees.

It is much easier for a trade union to unionize a work-force that is permanently attached to a firm than to unionize a group of workers who take intermittent employment with various employers. Itinerant workers, who migrate considerable distances between jobs, are particularly difficult to unionize. Once trade unions have gained control of the supply of a particular type of labour, they set wage rates above non-union market rates. This encourages firms to bypass union control by offering short-term employment rather than regular employment, and by discriminating in recruitment in favour of migrant workers.

Trade union power tends to be greater for skilled labour than for unskilled labour, since training opportunities create a barrier to entry into skilled occupations which trade unions can exploit if they gain control of the training process. Also capital/labour substitution in construction appears to be more difficult for highly skilled labour. The cost advantages of using non-union labour are therefore probably much greater where craftsmen are concerned than where unskilled labour is concerned. This gives a main contractor a considerable incentive to use labour-only subcontracting as an alternative to maintaining a permanent staff of craftsmen of his own. Buckley and Enderwick (1985) suggest that many labour conflicts in the construction industry, both in Britain and the US, have centred on the type of contractual arrangement under which craftsmen shall perform work for the main contractor. Trade unions have campaigned long and hard for the 'regularization' of employment, and contractors have, on the whole, strenuously resisted it. The fact that construction work moves around from site to site, and that workers must move around to follow it, provides the main contractor with a natural advantage over a plant-bound manufacturer in undermining trade union monopoly. Because contracting firms have made full use of this advantage, the average number of permanent full-time employees in relation to the value of final output produced, is very low in contracting, relative to most other activities.

6.4   THE INFLUENCE OF CYCLICAL FACTORS
ON THE REGULARITY OF EMPLOYMENT

Construction is vulnerable to cyclical fluctuations in demand because of the durable nature of its output. The need to cope with cyclical fluctuations is an additional factor influencing the regularity of employment.

It is important to note that cyclical fluctuations in construction demand reflect not only fluctuations in *aggregate* demand, but also in the *industrial composition* of that demand. This means that it is advantageous, from a cyclical point of view, if the intermediate products, plant and equipment used in the construction industry are designed so that they have alternative uses to which they can be switched during periods when construction demand is depressed. Flexibility of the inputs to the construction industry insures the owners of the inputs against the worst effects of adverse structural changes in aggregate demand.

The weather, too, causes substantial fluctuations in the industry. While seasonal fluctuations have a much higher frequency than the 7–11 year cycles characteristic of construction demand, their impact on the demand for manual labour is rather similar. Their impact on the demand for management services is much less, however, since managerial activities are more often carried out 'indoors', and certain types of management activity can be easily deferred to take up the slack when there is no manual work to be supervised.

An important implication of cyclical and seasonal fluctuations is that when an input has alternative uses it is inefficient for it to be permanently attached to the construction industry. A similar point applies so far as people working in the industry are concerned. If a worker has general skills that are applicable outside the industry then it is inefficient for him to be permanently attached to the industry. Only if the worker has skills that are specific to the industry, and has little that he can contribute outside it, is it worthwhile for him to remain permanently attached.

In contractual terms, the need for flexibility suggests that wherever possible main contractors will hire in resources on a short-term rather than a long-term basis. The main exception is where the resources concerned have no alternative use outside the construction industry. It applies, for example, to power equipment, vehicles, engineering products and so on; and also to unskilled manual labour. It does not apply, though, to very specialized tools and machinery, or to people with specific professional skills, such as architects or structural engineers. It is for other reasons that these specialists are hired on a short-term basis, as explained in section 6.8 below.

If the construction firm prefers, for other reasons, to hire resources on a long-term basis, or even to own them outright, then it is possible for the firm either to hire out its unused resources to other industries, or to diversify into those industries in order to create a captive market for alternative uses. Both strategies, however, impose great demands on management because they require the firm to manage not only its main construction activity, but subsidiary marketing and production activities as well. Furthermore, if the firm refuses to sell resources to outsiders, then it must harmonize the scale of its main activity and the scales of its subsidiary activities so that an internal balance of the supply and demand for each resource is maintained. The alternative strategies, therefore, are inferior to a policy of short-term hiring, except in fairly unusual circumstances.

If, however, there are operational reasons why the firm should integrate into subsidiary activities – e.g. to guarantee the quality of inputs – then activities which generate products that have uses outside the construction industry may prove particularly attractive. The most attractive of all, from this point of view, is an activity which supplies products to another industry which is completely out of phase with construction over the trade cycle. Industries of this kind are few and far between, however.

It has been established above that the ability to switch a resource to a remunerative use outside the construction industry encourages the use of short-term hiring. In the case of labour resources, the availability of unemployment benefit and supplementary benefit subsidizes a laid-off worker's search for alternative employment and so increases the expected value of his earnings outside construction. This increases the employer's incentive to offer, and the worker's incentive to accept, short-term hiring, along the lines explained earlier.

Maintenance work involves some of the same skills that are required for new construction, although fewer of them. Nevertheless, maintenance work is particularly attractive as an adjunct to new construction work because it helps to compensate for cycles in new construction demand. In a recession, customers who defer orders for new construction may well decide to improve or recondition existing assets instead. This creates a demand for maintenance and 'small works' which tends to vary counter-cyclically with demand. Diversification into maintenance, therefore, provides the firm not only with an additional outlet for its skills, but also affords a hedge against cycles in construction demand.

6.5 SUBCONTRACTING: THE SIGNIFICANCE OF QUALITY CONTROL

This section considers the extent to which a main contractor will subcontract work to other firms rather than undertake the work himself. To fix ideas, it is useful to postulate a particular structure for the division of labour in a construction project. One possible structure is illustrated in figure 6.2. It involves eight separate groups of activities organized into six sequential stages. The activities are grouped in such a way that two pairs of the groups can be carried on simultaneously if necessary. Each group of activities in turn affords certain opportunities for backward integration, some of which are indicated schematically in figure 6.3. In some cases it is possible to go back even further than indicated in the figure; for example, the firm could integrate back from the utilization of plant and equipment into its manufacture and/or its repair.

A recent survey of the theory of vertical integration (Casson, 1984) identifies several factors which could, in principle, affect the extent of subcontracting in the construction industry. The factor of greatest

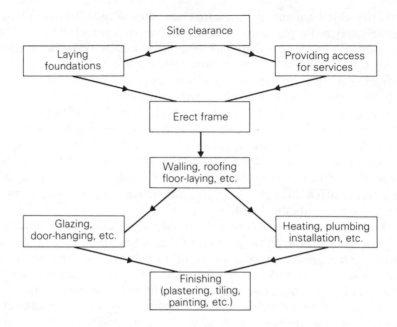

FIGURE 6.2   A simple example of the division of labour in building construction, involving eight groups of subsidiary activities

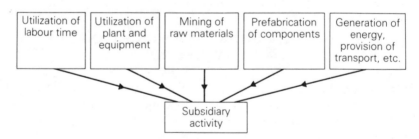

FIGURE 6.3   Five main avenues of backward integration from a subsidiary activity

importance in the construction industry appears to be quality control. It was emphasized in chapter 4 that the quality of a product usually depends upon the exercise of care and attention in production. In some cases it is possible to assess quality simply by inspecting the finished product. In other cases this is not so easy, and the only guarantee of quality comes from supervising and monitoring the process of production itself.

   The main contractor assumes overall responsibility for the quality of the construction project, and he must in turn maintain quality on the separate activities that comprise it. Some activities may be absolutely crucial for the safety of the finished product, and it is these activities that require special attention to quality control. Erecting a load-bearing frame, for example, is more crucial than hanging doors, and electrical wiring is more crucial than decorating. So far as safety of personnel is concerned, there are considerable externalities between people on site, and some tasks carry a high level of responsibility for the safety of others. Operating cranes and hoists, for example, is more crucial for other people's well-being than operating a pneumatic drill, while setting up scaffolding is more crucial than laying bricks.

In most industries, concern over quality control discourages subcontracting. This is partly because the subcontractor's production normally takes place on private premises off site, and the subcontractor is unwilling to allow outside supervision or monitoring because his trade secrets may be threatened as a result. In construction, however, much of the work is carried out on site, and so is relatively easy for the main contractor to monitor. The contractor does not have to put separate representatives into each subcontractor's plant, but can exploit economies of scale by having one representative visit several different subcontractors all on the same site. It is not usually viable for a subcontractor to insist that he is not monitored. To begin with, he may be in danger from, or a danger to, other people on the site. Secondly, he normally works in such close proximity to other people that he has little chance of protecting his trade secrets from every single person no matter what precautions he takes. Since subcontractors are so easy to monitor, therefore, subcontracting is relatively easy in the construction industry even though considerable importance attaches to quality control. Subcontracting is easiest of all for those activities that have few safety implications.

An important aspect of overall quality of service in construction is punctuality. It is often the case that one activity cannot be started until another activity has been completed, and to avoid delays accumulating it is essential that each activity is started as soon as the prerequisites have been finished. Subcontractors must therefore be kept on the alert to begin work as soon as they are required. This calls, in effect, for contingent forward contracts between the main contractor and his subcontractors. Because such contracts are difficult to enforce, there needs to be a high degree of trust between the two parties involved. When a main contractor cannot find a subcontractor he can trust to be punctual, he has a strong incentive to carry out the work himself.

Not all inputs to construction have to be supplied on site. Many metal and ceramic products are fabricated off site, whilst basic materials such as bricks, cement, stone and rubble are supplied from outside. Only in exceptional cases would quality control appear to necessitate the contractor's supervision of the off-site production process. One exception, for example, would be industrial system building. Moreover an efficient scale of off-site production will normally require many construction projects to keep it fully occupied. Unless the construction firm expects to undertake a sufficiently large number of projects with sufficient regularity, it will be unable to generate sufficient demand internally to utilize the capacity of an off-site production subsidiary. This is a particular problem if the output of the off-site facility is costly to transport, because it could then be necessary for the company to undertake a large number of projects in the immediate vicinity of the facility. If it fails to do this, then it must either produce the input at uneconomic cost, or undertake the marketing of surplus output to other construction firms. Given the demanding nature of construction project management, noted earlier, the diversion of management attention to the marketing of the output of subsidiary operations may adversely affect the general efficiency with which the enterprise, as a whole, is managed.

In certain cases, however, there may be significant advantages in owning off-site facilities. Major structural projects often require significant quantities of concrete and aggregates. When such inputs constitute a large proportion of the total cost of a project, the main contractor may wish to obtain assurances about the price and availability of these supplies at the time he tenders for the project. Such assurances, however, are often difficult to obtain. If there were future markets for concrete and aggregates, the risks of an adverse change in prices could be laid off by buying suitable claims, but in practice these markets do not exist. The only way of guaranteeing the cost of the supplies is therefore to integrate backwards into these activities. Even if the main contractor does not actually use his own supplies, but relies upon independent suppliers instead, he is still hedged against the risk of a rise in prices since any capital loss incurred in purchasing the inputs from an independent supplier will be offset by a capital gain from selling the supplies he owns to other main contractors.

Sometimes, though, there is a distinct advantage to the main contractor in using his own supplies, even if independent supplies are closer to the site than his own are. Concrete production and the mining of aggregates both afford economies of scale and, in conjunction with relatively high transport costs, these can create an element of natural monopoly in local markets. If the project in which the main contractor is engaged is a large one, which dominates local demand for inputs, then a bilateral monopoly situation is created. Under these conditions, it may be advantageous for the main contractor to integrate backwards by acquisition of the concrete and aggregates activities – at least for the duration of the major project.

Natural monopolies of inputs could also lead to distortions of input proportions in the construction project, due to substitution by the main contractor against over-priced monopolized inputs. Backward integration can avoid efficiency losses caused in this way. In practice, substitution possibilities seem to be fairly limited in most construction projects, and so such considerations are probably of little importance.

The discussion suggests that, on the whole, where inputs account for only a small proportion of the total costs of the typical project, the main contractor is unlikely to diversify into off-site production. If he does diversify, it will be into the production of intermediate inputs which are crucial for the quality (and especially the safety) of the finished product, are easy to transport, and can be efficiently produced on a small scale with few economies of continuous flow. Where projects make extensive use of inputs such as concrete and aggregates, however, backward integration into these activities is quite likely, especially if the contractor is typically engaged in large projects.

6.6 LABOUR-ONLY SUBCONTRACTING

The main difference between ordinary subcontracting and labour-only subcontracting is that in the first case the subcontractor supplies the other inputs, whereas in the second case the main contractor supplies them instead. This difference is significant because both the responsibility for selecting the *quality* of the other inputs, and the financial liability for *wastage* of them, are allocated differently. They reside in the first case with the subcontractor and in the second case with the main contractor.

In some cases it is possible that poor quality inputs will increase the amount of labour required to generate a given quantity of output. But often the main effect of poor quality inputs is not to increase the subcontractor's labour requirements but simply to produce a poor quality of output. If the main contractor has difficulty in monitoring the quality of the output, then the subcontractor has an incentive to employ low quality inputs.

One solution is for the main contractor to stipulate the quality of the inputs. This could be effected by incorporating a restrictive clause into the subcontracting agreement. To be dependable, however, the contract would have to provide for the main contractor to monitor the quality of the inputs. One of the simplest ways of effecting this is for the main contractor to supply the inputs himself.

The main contractor can either sell the inputs to the subcontractor, or retain ownership of the inputs whilst the subcontractor works with them. The care and attention exercised by the subcontractor may affect the productivity of the inputs, in the sense that lack of attention may result in wastage. The subcontractor's incentive to tolerate wastage is much lower if he owns the other inputs himself than if the main contractor owns them instead. It is, therefore, in the main contractor's interests to arrange to sell the inputs to him. This arrangement is analogous to the 'putting out' system that prevailed in the textile industry before the advent of factories.

The subcontractor may, however, object to having to purchase stipulated inputs from a tied source. One solution is for the main contractor to supply the inputs free, but to meter the wastage and charge only for wasted materials. This arrangement provides the subcontractor with a strong incentive to control wastage, but can be administratively quite complex. Otherwise the main contractor is faced with one of two courses of action. He can either retain ownership of the inputs himself, and rely on close supervision of the subcontractor to avoid wastage. Alternatively, he can allow the subcontractor to purchase his own materials, and do the best he can to control quality, subject to this limitation.

For reasons already noted, when the subcontractor works on site it is relatively easy for the main contractor to monitor him. In this case wastage is relatively easy to control. This suggests that where quality of output is a major concern, and the subcontractor works on site, labour-only subcontracting will be preferred.

If quality is not important, then it is almost certainly administratively inefficient for the main contractor to undertake procurement of inputs on the subcontractor's behalf. The main exception is where there are indivisibilities in the inputs and the subcontractor is working on site. In such cases it may be efficient for several subcontractors to share the same input. Otherwise when quality control is not important and the subcontractor works off site, ordinary subcontracting will be preferred.

The intermediate cases – where quality control is important but the subcontractor works off site, and where quality control is unimportant, but the subcontractor works on site – are highly marginal, and it may be of little consequence to the main contractor which subcontracting arrangement is used.

The case where quality is important and the subcontractor works on site is most common in practice, and, on this basis, labour-only subcontracting will tend to predominate within the construction industry. Because the main contractor is responsible for providing materials under this arrangement, it encourages the main contractor to consider backward integration into the production of these materials. In a sample of contracting firms, therefore, there may well be a correlation between the use of labour-only subcontracting and backward integration into materials supply.

6.7   THE EMPLOYMENT CONTRACT:
CHOOSING BETWEEN TIME RATES AND PIECE-WORK

The employer's choice between time rates and piece-work represents a special case of the more general issues raised in sections 6.5 and 6.6. When the quality of an employee's work is difficult for the employer to monitor, the piece-work payment encourages the employee to maximize the quantity of output by sacrificing the quality. Payment of a time rate of wages removes some of the incentive to reduce quality since it fails to reward any increase in quantity that a reduction in quality would permit. At a fairly superficial level, therefore, it is possible to interpret the choice between piece-work and time rates in terms of the employer's trade-off between quantity and quality.

There are one or two special situations in which it is as difficult to meter the quantity of an employee's work as it is to measure the quality. In such cases a piece-work system may not be viable since any attempt to measure quantity would be extremely *ad hoc*. It could lead to quite arbitrary differentials in rewards between different employees, or between the same employee at different times.

In most cases though, it is much more difficult to monitor quality than to meter quantity. This suggests that time rate payment will be preferred wherever quality of workmanship is crucial. It was noted above, however, that it is relatively easier to monitor the quality of work when it is carried out on site than when it is carried out off site. The hazards of the piece-work system are therefore greater off site than on site. Thus while the emphasis on quality of workmanship discourages piece-work remuneration in general, piece-work may still be preferred for some types of on-site work where quality is basically easy to control.

It has been noted in earlier sections that because the main contractor bears ultimate responsibility for the quality of the completed project, he has more direct interest in quality control than do the subcontractors whom he employs. This suggests that, from the main contractor's point of view, subcontractors may have a bias towards employing workers on a piece-work basis. This problem is likely to be particularly acute where labour-only subcontracting is concerned, because it was noted in section 6.5 that labour-only subcontracting is likely to arise from the main contractor's concern over quality control (though not exclusively so). It would be paradoxical if the main contractor's efforts to maintain quality by controlling the supply of non-labour inputs were vitiated by careless workmanship, stimulated by the subcontractor's use of a piece-work payment system.

This suggests that from the main contractor's point of view, subcontracting has the potential disadvantage that he loses effective control of the payment system. For jobs where quality is crucial, therefore, subcontracting may only occur if the subcontractor is willing to give an undertaking to remunerate his workers on a time rate rather than a piece-work basis. If a subcontractor is unwilling to give such an undertaking, or if the main contractor does not trust him to implement it, then the main contractor may undertake the work himself. In either case, the outcome is that where the quality of workmanship is crucial, labour is remunerated on a time rate basis.

6.8   THE SCOPE OF THE PROJECTS UNDERTAKEN BY A CONTRACTING FIRM

It was noted in section 6.3 that the management team of a contracting firm will consist of those individuals whose services would be the most difficult to hire on an intermittent short-term basis. A team of this kind may build up skills which are specific not to any individual member but to the team itself. To keep the team together, whilst utilizing it efficiently, it is necessary for the main contractor to keep the members fully occupied. This means that the firm must undertake a diversity of projects. This diversity can be revealed in several different dimensions, including (a) the geographical location of the project; (b) the type of client involved: public authority, private manufacturer, home-owner, etc.; (c) the type of technology required: structural engineering, materials engineering, earthmoving, fluid control, etc.; (d) the size and complexity of the project, as reflected in the type of management skills required.

Which type of diversity the firm opts for will reflect the team-specific knowledge it possesses. If the firm has special knowledge of the commercial requirements in a locality, or the geology of a particular region, it will concentrate upon projects in a particular geographical area. Within this area it will achieve diversity by working for various clients using various technologies on various sizes of project. The firm may, however, have particular weaknesses, as well as a particular strength, and these may debar it from certain types of diversification. Thus a firm with very limited project planning skills may only undertake small projects within its chosen area.

Similarly, if the firm has privileged access to a technology then it will concentrate on projects that embody this technology. It will apply the same technology at various locations, for various types of client, and for projects of various sizes. If the firm has special insight into the needs of a particular type of client, it will undertake projects for such clients at a variety of locations, using various technologies on projects of various sizes. If the firm has special project management skills, then it will specialize on projects of a particular size and complexity, using various technologies for various clients at various locations.

The firm's special skills may be only intermittently required on each project. This means that to keep team members fully employed, it is necessary to have several projects in progress simultaneously. This is more true of certain types of expertise than others. Technological expertise is required mainly at the design stage of the project, whereas project management expertise is more likely to be required throughout. This implies that, other things being equal, a main contractor specialized upon a technology will be simultaneously involved with more projects than will a main contractor specialized upon a particular type of project management.

A factor of special significance for the construction industry is that some professional associations – such as the Royal Institute of British Architects – discourage their members, who are key specialists in the industry, from becoming employees of contracting firms, or taking a financial interest in them (although recently these restrictions have been eased significantly). The power of these institutions rests upon their role as training and accrediting agencies for the specialist personnel. The reasons for their restrictions appear to be social rather than economic – a desire to enhance the status of the profession by presenting its members as 'pure' and free from contamination with the low status 'dirty jobs' on the site itself. It is difficult to see how these restrictions directly promote the pecuniary interests of the membership.

An important consequence of these restrictions is that the skills of architects and similar professionals remain specific to the individuals rather than to the main contractor. Although a main contractor can establish close links with these professionals, some of the economies of teamwork are almost certainly foregone. This is a potential source of inefficiency in the contracting process.

Because certain types of professional skill cannot be team specific, the firm-specific skills of main contractors are rather limited compared to the firm-specific skills that are found, say, amongst manufacturing firms that employ large numbers of research scientists. The skills of the successful main contractor have much more to do with liaising between independent specialists than with possession of special in-house expertise itself. The principal source of firm-specific expertise amongst main contractors is probably their managerial experience in planning and costing projects, and their close contacts with subcontractors and suppliers.

Finally, it should be noted that the rather limited extent of firm-specific skills in the construction industry may have wider implications than just the scope of main contractors' operations. It is widely agreed that technological advance in construction since 1945 has been slow relative to many other industries. Although there have been some advances in industrial building systems, most of the technical progress has concerned interior or auxiliary fittings, such as heating and ventilating equipment, and transportation equipment, such as earth-movers. The industry has also been widely criticized for the design and quality of residential and office buildings erected during the 1960s and early 1970s. The rigid division of labour between specialists, referred to above, which dichotomizes the conceptualization and implementation of designs, may be partly responsible both for the slow rate of technological progress and for the failure of designs to measure up to clients' needs.

6.9   INTERNATIONAL DIVERSIFICATION OF CONTRACTING OPERATIONS

It was suggested in the previous section that the special expertise of a typical construction firm lies in management rather than technology. Construction management calls for the techniques of the system analyst and the operational researcher – to determine, for example, the 'critical path' of constituent activities. It also calls for judgement in determining the most appropriate subcontracting arangements and the most appropriate contract of employment for each type of work.

So far as marketing is concerned, the customization of output means that the firm is more likely to require skill in projecting a general image of reliability and excellence of workmanship than in promoting a specific product. Financial expertise is also valuable to the construction firm because of the volatile nature of the cash flows involved, and the importance of tax considerations.

The geographical scope of the firm's operations will be determined by how far the firm's special skills can be transferred. In general, the further they are transferred from headquarters, the greater will be the transmission costs incurred, and hence the smaller will be the firm's advantage over less sophisticated local competitors. Costs of transmission depend not only upon physical distance, but also upon 'psychic' distance as reflected in legal, cultural, linguistic and other differences between the places concerned. Theory demonstrates that the geographical boundary of the firm's operations is set at the margin where the value of the firm's reputation and know-how (measured relative to local competitors) is just offset by the transmission costs to the locality.

Some types of corporate advantage can be more easily transmitted than others. Specific techniques of project management are fairly easy to transmit. They may be formalized in a company operating manual, and a representative can be despatched from headquarters to instruct local site managers in its contents. Judgement respecting the most appropriate subcontracting policy is more difficult to transmit. The theory of subcontracting does not, in its present stage of development, provide simple hard-and-fast rules. The reliability of subcontractors may vary from place to place, so that an activity that should be subcontracted in one location would instead be carried out by the main contractor at another location. Similar difficulties arise regarding the most suitable contract of employment in different localities. Differences in the legal systems may also be important in this respect. Generally speaking, a cautious firm will undertake less subcontracting away from the head office than it will close to it, because it is likely to have less knowledge of – and therefore more doubts about – the quality of work of subcontractors based near the site. A firm with local knowledge may therefore be able to compete successfully against an alien firm with superior project management techniques because it is able to organize its subcontracting and employment more efficiently.

Cultural differences invariably hamper the alien firm. A local culture with strong militaristic values, for example, may allow site management to be highly centralized because the work-force is extremely well disciplined, whilst a democratic or anarchic culture may call for much greater decentralization of site management. The alien firm's relative unfamiliarity with the local culture hampers its choice of the appropriate degree of decentralization.

When a site is under different fiscal jurisdiction from the headquarters, systems of taxation may differ and so financial strategy may have to be adapted to local conditions.

It would appear that while the special skills of a construction firm may be fairly easy to transmit to different sites *within the same country*, some of the skills will be difficult to transfer *between* countries because of differences in law – which affect taxation and contracts of employment – and in language and culture – which may inhibit effective on-site management. The main exceptions are the technical skills of project management, since these are universal, precise and therefore easy to translate.

It is possible for a firm to transfer its skills internationally, whilst avoiding some of the legal and cultural problems of operating abroad, by using a management contract in place of direct control of construction operations. The risks relating to tax, employment policy and subcontracting policy are then borne (at least in part) by others, and the firm receives a more assured reward for its know-how. The obvious advantage of this strategy suggests that whilst construction firms may own a portfolio of projects within their own country, their international operations will be mainly confined to management contracts with indigenous foreign firms.

Table 6.1 Operations of major UK contracting firms

Operations	Costain	Galliford	Aberdeen Construction Group	French Kier Holdings	London & Northern Group	George Wimpey	Taylor Woodrow	John Laing	Fairclough Construction Group	Marchwiel	Robert M. Douglas Holdings	Trafalgar House	John Mowlem	Rush & Tompkins Group	Walter Lawrence	Y. J. Lovell (Holdings)	F. J. C. Lilley	A. Monk & Company	William Press Group	J. B. Holdings	Newarthill	Tilbury Group	HAT Group	Hewden-Stuart Plant	Higgs & Hill	Belway	Crest Nicholson	Allied Plant Group	William Leech	Barratt Developments	Wilson (Connolly) Holdings	Fairview Estates	Bryant Holdings	William Whittingham (Holdings)	Comben Group	Total
Building																																				
Housebuilding	*	*	*	*	*	*	*	*	*	*	*	*		*	*	*	*	*				*			*	*			*	*	*		*	*	*	26
Offices	*	*	*	*	*	*	*		*	*	*	*	*	*	*	*	*				*	*			*						*					18
Industrial	*	*	*	*	*	*	*		*	*	*		*	*	*	*	*				*	*			*											19
Public buildings				*			*								*	*	*	*																		10
Shops			*	*										*	*																					8
Renovation/ maintenance	*											*		*	*							*	*		*	*					*					9
Civil engineering																																				
Roads	*	*	*	*	*	*		*	*	*	*	*	*	*			*	*				*														16
Bridges		*	*						*		*		*	*				*				*														8
Tunnelling				*						*			*		*		*					*		*												7
Pipelines/mains														*			*	*	*			*														5
Marine engineering				*		*			*	*	*		*	*			*	*																		10

Sewage and land drainage	*	*				*		*							9
Power stations	*			*	*	*		*	*						6
Oil and gas related works	*		*	*	*	*		*	*	*					9
Airports/airfields	*	*		*	*	*					*				3
Water and oil storage	*										*				3
Industrial	*		*	*			*	*	*						7
General contract and other	*		*						*	*				*	4
Mines	*	*		*	*				*				*		3
Concrete															
Ready mixed	*	*		*		*						*			4
Pre-cast products	*	*	*		*	*									6
Blocks/slabs/bricks	*	*													3
Pipes	*			*					*	*					1
Cutting & repairs	*			*											2
Mining, dredging & aggregates															
Dredging	*			*											2
Open-cast mining	*	*	*	*	*	*			*						7
Granite		*							*						1
Sand & gravel pits	*	*											*		4

(continued)

Table 6.1 *(continued)*

Operations	Costain	Galliford	Aberdeen Construction Group	French Kier Holdings	London & Northern Group	George Wimpey	Taylor Woodrow	John Laing	Fairclough Construction Group	Marchwiel	Robert M. Douglas Holdings	Trafalgar House	John Mowlem	Rush & Tompkins Group	Walter Lawrence	Y. J. Lovell (Holdings)	F. J. C. Lilley	A. Monk & Company	William Press Group	J. B. Holdings	Newarthill	Tilbury Group	HAT Group	Hewden–Stuart Plant	Higgs & Hill	Bellway	Crest Nicholson	Allied Plant Group	William Leech	Barratt Developments	Wilson (Connolly) Holdings	Fairview Estates	Bryant Holdings	William Whittingham (Holdings)	Comben Group	Total
Slate quarry										*																										1
Aggregate/ stone and other			*			*		*		*		*								*	*	*														8
Interior work																																				
Heating/ ventilation		*			*																	*	*													4
Plumbing		*			*											*						*	*					*								6
Electrical work		*			*																	*	*					*								5
Decoration		*																	*							*										3
Double glazing and glass					*																		*													2
Joinery	*				*																		*													3
Floors											*							*					*													3
Ceilings											*																									1
Kitchen units																										*			*							2
Damp proofing																													*							1

Cavity wall insulation	*	1
Lighting		1
Refurbishment & fitting	*	1
Plant hire		
Fork lift trucks	*	2
Earth moving equipment	* * *	3
Small tools	* * *	3
General plant hire	* * * * * * * *	12
Aerial work platforms	* *	1
Servicing	* *	2
Equipment for testing materials	*	1
Other specialist contracting		
Piling	* * * * *	5
Road haulage	* * *	3
Road surfacing	* * * * * *	6
Heavy lifting	* *	2
Structural steel work	*	2
Land reclamation and landscaping	=	1

(continued)

Table 6.1 (continued)

Operations	Costain	Galliford	Aberdeen Construction Group	French Kier Holdings	London & Northern Group	George Wimpey	Taylor Woodrow	John Laing	Fairclough Construction Group	Marchwiel	Robert M. Douglas Holdings	Trafalgar House	John Mowlem	Rush & Tompkins Group	Walter Lawrence	Y. J. Lovell (Holdings)	F. J. C. Lilley	A. Monk & Company	William Press Group	J. B. Holdings	Newarthill	Tilbury Group	HAT Group	Hewden–Stuart Plant	Higgs & Hill	Bellway	Crest Nicholson	Allied Plant Group	William Leech	Barratt Developments	Wilson (Connolly) Holdings	Fairview Estates	Bryant Holdings	William Whittingham (Holdings)	Comben Group	Total
Baulk extraction & demolition		*																																		1
Earth moving					*																															1
Roofing & cladding											*																									1
Materials handling									*																											1
Pressure testing		*																																		1
Shot blasting																												*								1
Pressure grouting		*						*																												2
Joint sealing		*																*																		2
Basement sealing								*																												1
Sports surfacing																											*									1

Plant installations	*										1
Scaffolding and formwork	*		*								3
Industrial building systems											
Pipework	*							*	*		3
Other	*							*	*	*	1
Other builders equipment											
Materials & clothing		*		*							2
Builder's merchants	*	*	*		*			*	*		5
Timber trading	*	*	*		*			*	*		5
Manufacturing											
Pump and generating equipment				*				*		*	2
Builders materials	*		*	*	*	*		*	*		8
Plant	*		*								2
Tools	*				*						2
Precision control products		*									1
Control panel systems	*										1

(continued)

Table 6.1 *(continued)*

Operations	Costain	Galliford	Aberdeen Construction Group	French Kier Holdings	London & Northern Group	George Wimpey	Taylor Woodrow	John Laing	Fairclough Construction Group	Marchweil	Robert M. Douglas Holdings	Trafalgar House	John Mowlem	Rush & Tompkins Group	Walter Lawrence	Y. J. Lovell (Holdings)	F. J. C. Lilley	A. Monk & Company	William Press Group	J. B. Holdings	Newarthill	Tilbury Group	HAT Group	Hewden–Stuart Plant	Higgs & Hill	Bellway	Crest Nicholson	Allied Plant Group	William Leech	Barratt Developments	Wilson (Connolly) Holdings	Fairview Estates	Bryant Holdings	William Whitingham (Holdings)	Comben Group	Total
Drilling equipment	*							*					*																							3
Other fabrications			*					*				*																								3
Site investigation equipment																								*												1
Vehicle cabs	*																																			1
Road suction sweepers																				*																1
Automotive & marine components															*																					1
Cutlery															*																					1
Vehicle body builders					*																															1
Air conditioning																			*																	1

Transformers, TVs & radar												1
Laboratory/ electronic equipment								*				2
Other	*			*					*			4
Property development												
Residential	*	*	*	*	*		*	*	*			8
Offices	*	*	*	*	*	*	*	*	*	*		19
Industrial	*	*	*	*	*		*	*	*	*		12
Shops	*	*	*	*	*		*	*	*	*		8
Leisure facilities		*			*				*	*		4
Private hospitals				*								1
Professional services												
Computer services	*		*									3
Structural design services	*			*								2
Geotechnical services	*	*		*								3
Managerial services	*		*	*	*	*	*	*				7
Site investigation	*						*					2

(continued)

Table 6.1 (continued)

Operations	Costain	Galliford	Aberdeen Construction Group	French Kier Holdings	London & Northern Group	George Wimpey	Taylor Woodrow	John Laing	Fairclough Construction Group	Marchweil	Robert M. Douglas Holdings	Trafalgar House	John Mowlem	Rush & Tompkins Group	Walter Lawrence	Y. J. Lovell (Holdings)	F. J. C. Lilley	A. Monk & Company	William Press Group	J. B. Holdings	Newarthill	Tilbury Group	HAT Group	Hewden-Stuart Plant	Higgs & Hill	Bellway	Crest Nicholson	Allied Plant Group	William Leech	Barratt Developments	Wilson (Connolly) Holdings	Fairview Estates	Bryant Holdings	William Whittingham (Holdings)	Comben Group	Total
Inspection & testing	*						*												*																	3
Other							*												*																	2
Miscellaneous																																				
Motor distributor					*		*			*										*																4
Leisure	*																										*		*					*		4
Aviation												*									*															2
Shipping												*																								1
Newspapers												*																								1
Printing							*																													1
Waste & sewage disposal						*							*																							2
Boat building		*																																		1
Industrial services														*									*	*												3

Petrol service station			*		1
Insurance broking	*				1
Wholesale jewellery				*	1
Peat harvesters		*			1
Marketing of hydraulic systems			*		1
Steel reclamation		*		*	1
Optical products				*	1
Promotion services		*			1
Supplier of batteries		*			1

TABLE 6.2   Classification of main contractors according to the type of work
undertaken

Builders and civil engineers	Builders mainly	Civil engineers mainly	Plant hire	Property development
Costain	London & Northern	Laing	HAT	Fairview
Galliford	Douglas	Press	Hewden–Stuart	Crest Nicholson
Aberdeen	Lawrence	JB	Allied plant	
French Kier	Lovell			
Wimpey	Tilbury			
Taylor Woodrow	Higgs & Hill			
Fairclough	Bellway			
Trafalgar House	Barratt			
Mowlem	Wilson			
Rush & Tompkins	Bryant			
Lilley	Whittingham			
Monk	Comben			
Newarthill	Leech			
Marchweil				

6.10   EMPIRICAL EVIDENCE ON UK CONTRACTING FIRMS

A comprehensive test of the hypotheses derived from internalization theory is beyond the scope of this chapter. Tentative support for some of the main ideas can, however, be obtained from information of the scope of firm's operations contained in *Savory Miln's Building Book*, 1982 (private publication). The relevant information is summarized in table 6.1. It relates to 35 large contracting firms based in the UK. The table distinguishes 19 different types of contracting work, grouped under two main headings: building, and civil engineering. It also identifies 104 activities related to main contracting into which one or more of the firms has integrated.

The tabulation indicates that five main types of firm are covered by Savory Miln's survey. Fourteen firms are involved in both building and civil engineering, thirteen firms are engaged mainly in building, three mainly in civil engineering, three in plant hire and two in property development. The firms in each category are identified in table 6.2.

Table 6.3 Summary of the operations of UK contracting firms

Operations	Costain	Galliford	Aberdeen Construction Group	French Kier Holdings	London & Northern Group	George Wimpey	Taylor Woodrow	John Laing	Fairclough Construction Group	Marchweil	Robert M. Douglas Holdings	Trafalgar House	John Mowlem	Rush & Tompkins Group	Walter Lawrence	Y. J. Lovell (Holdings)	F. J. C. Lilley	A. Monk & Company	William Press Group	J. B. Holdings	Newarthill	Tilbury Group	HAT Group	Hewden-Stuart Plant	Higgs & Hill	Bellway	Crest Nicholson	Allied Plant Group	William Leech	Barratt Developments	Wilson (Connolly) Holdings	Fairview Estates	Bryant Holdings	William Whittingham (Holdings)	Comben Group	Total
Building	4	6	5	5	3	4	4	3	3	3	3	3	4	5	5	3	4	4	2	1	3	3	1		4	2			1	1	3		1	1	1	89
Civil engineering	6	5	5	8	2	4	1	3	6	6	6	3	6	4	1		6	8	4	4	2	2	1		2	1			1	1				1	1	90
Concrete	1	2	3	2	1		1	2	1		1									1					1											16
Mining, dredging & aggregates	2	3	3	2		2	2	1	1	3				1			1	1		1	2	2	6		3	2		2								23
Interior work	1	4		1	5		1	1			2	1				2		1		1		3	1	3				2	2							33
Plant hire	1	3			1	1	1	2	1		3			2	1	2			1			1	1	1		1		1	2							24
Other specialist contracting	2	7	2	2	2	2	1	3	2		4	1	1	1	1	1	1	1	1	1	1	1	4	1		1	1	3								43
Other builders equipment	1		1		2	1	1		1					2	1	2							1	1												12
Manufacturing	4	2	2	2	2	1	1	3	1			3	2	1	3	3	3	1	4	2				2		2										36
Property development	2	1	1	3		4	3		2	2	1	1	1	3	3	5	3	1			2	1	1		3	1	1			2	3	2	4	1		52
Professional services	6	1					1				1		1		1	1			3			1			1				1			3				22
Miscellaneous	2	1	1	3	3	1	4		1	1	3	3	1	1				1		2	1	1	1	1		3			1		1	5	3	1	1	28
Total	31	30	23	23	21	20	20	18	17	16	16	16	15	15	15	15	14	13	13	12	12	12	11	11	10	9	7	6	6	5	5	5	4	3	3	1

Summary measures of the overall structure of integration are presented in table 6.3.

Because of the way that the firms in the survey were identified, it is doubtful if the tabulation can be used to draw inferences about the diversification of main contracting firms by the type of work they undertake. The table is, however, more informative with respect to backward integration undertaken by the main contractors.

The main activities to attract integration by firms involved in either building or civil engineering are pre-cast concrete products, open-cast mining, aggregates, general plant hire, piling, road surfacing, timber trading, builder's materials, various forms of property development and managerial services.

All five of the firms integrated into pre-cast concrete products are large firms involved in both building and civil engineering. This is consistent with the view that a very large and diversified range of products is necessary in order to fully utilize an in-house concrete fabricating facility of efficient size. Likewise all seven of the firms integrated into open-cast mining are involved in both building and civil engineering. Integration into aggregates involves eight firms, each of which is involved in either road or energy engineering. In some cases there is a clear link between the various activities undertaken by the same firm. Thus all of the five firms integrated into timber trading are also involved in house and office building. In other cases the links are more tenuous; for example, only four of the six firms undertaking road surfacing are involved in road engineering as well.

The nature and extent of diversification varies considerably between firms. Costain and Galliford are much more highly diversified than any of the other firms. Yet although they are both engaged in a similar number of activities, the nature of these activities is very different. Galliford is virtually the only building and civil engineering firm that is heavily involved in specialist contracting; Costain, in common with other firms, does very little of this kind of work. Costain, on the other hand, is heavily involved in providing professional services, whereas Galliford is not.

Galliford, London and Northern group, and Tilbury do some of their own interior work, but most firms do very little of this for themselves. A number of firms offer general plant hire services, but specialist firms such as HAT and Hewden–Stuart Plant do this as well.

The overall picture is that the level of vertical integration within the contracting industry is very low. Not even the most diversified firms could be said, in any sense, to be self-sufficient in either supplies of all their major materials, or in specialist contracting and interior work. This corroborates one of the main hypotheses deduced from the theory. There is some evidence that where a number of firms have integrated backwards into the same activity, that activity is one of particular importance for the overall costing of the projects on which they work. A diversity of types of project also seems to be associated, albeit loosely, with backward integration into activities such as concrete fabrication and aggregates, where there are liable to be economies of scale.

Having said this, however, it is difficult to detect an obvious logic in the diversification strategies of many of the firms included in the survey. The overall impression is that the managements of many of the firms do not think strategically about the diversification issue, and that the observed patterns of integration have emerged in some cases more by accident or inertia than by deliberate forethought. For example, activities acquired as a result of the take-over of another company may not have been divested even though they do not fit in with the major interests of the acquiring firm.

6.11 SUMMARY AND CONCLUSIONS

The construction industry is of interest to the economic theorist principally because of the customized nature of the product, which means that the production process consists of a sequence of one-off projects. Other factors of interest are the immobility of the product and the amplitude of fluctuations in demand. Other writers have drawn attention to these characteristics (see especially Hillebrandt, 1985) and have considered their relevance to subcontracting decision in the construction industry (Ball, 1980; Clark, 1980). The transaction economics approach offers additional insights, however, which cannot be so easily obtained from other approaches to the subject. The main predictions obtained by applying transaction economics to the construction industry are summarized below.

The type of knowledge the firm possesses determines the scope of its activities across different sectors of the construction industry. Most firms will undertake maintenance work as well as new construction, as this partially insulates them against the effect of cyclical fluctuations in demand for new construction.

Punctuality, safety and high-quality workmanship are all important in construction work. Despite this, subcontracting is fairly straightforward in construction because much of the work is carried out on site, and so it is easy to monitor the subcontractor's work. Much of the work that is carried out off site affords economies of scale and/or continuity of flow, and it is therefore efficient to subcontract this work too, though for quite different reasons.

When quality control is important, and the work is to be done on site, labour-only subcontracting will normally be preferred to ordinary subcontracting. Conversely, in the few cases where quality control is not important, and the work is to be done off site, ordinary subcontracting will normally be preferred. The main exceptions to these results occur for inputs such as concrete and aggregates, which account for a significant proportion of the costs of certain types of construction work. Exceptions also occur when it is efficient for several on-site contractors to share the same input, or for different inputs to be agglomerated for transport in bulk to the site. In these cases, the main contractor may undertake to supply the materials himself.

When quality control is crucial, both main contractors and subcontractors will normally remunerate workers on a time rate basis. Indeed, the main contractor may only award the work to a subcontractor if he agrees to remunerate his workers on this basis. For certain types of on-site work, however, where supervision of the worker is easy, piece-work may be acceptable instead. When quality control is unimportant, and output is easy to meter, piece-work will be definitely preferred.

The cyclical nature of demand in the construction industry, together with seasonal effects caused by the weather, encourages workers to be hired on a short-term basis, independently of whether piece-work or time rates are involved.

The range of skills available to the management teams of main contractors is constrained by professional practices which discourage the recruitment of certain types of specialist as full-time employees. This in turn affects the range of different activities undertaken by the typical contracting firm, and may also adversely affect the efficiency with which construction projects are carried out.

Management skills which are culturally specific are difficult to transfer overseas while technical skills are much easier to transfer. It is often most appropriate to transfer technical skills overseas through consultancy agreements and other arm's length contractual arrangements.

A survey of the scope of the operations of large UK contracting firms confirms the broad implications of the theory, but indicates considerable diversity in the nature and extent of backward integration amongst firms carrying out similar types of projects. This suggests that management strategies in the UK construction industry are not particularly well thought out in respect of the scope of the firm.

7

Vertical Integration
in Shipping

7.1 INTRODUCTION

There are two main reasons why an inquiry into vertical integration (VI) in the shipping industry is particularly timely. First, during the current world recession, many multinationals are rationalizing their production internationally so that some stages of production are concentrated in one country and other stages in another. As a result, a significant proportion of intermediate product trade is now intra-firm trade between affiliates of the same company. Given that a multinational owns and controls upstream and downstream activities in different countries, the question of its attitude to the 'gap in control' over transportation naturally arises. Are potential economies of VI between adjacent stages of production sacrificed if an independent carrier is responsible for transport of the intermediate product between them? To what extent will a vertically integrated multinational producer wish to 'close the gap' between upstream and downstream activities by integrating into shipping as well? If – as is often the case – it is uneconomic to integrate into shipping, do there exist alternative contractual arrangements which will give the multinational many of the benefits of VI but without the costs?

Secondly, recent changes in the shipping industry connected with containerization, greater state involvement and the partial break-up of the conference system make VI within the shipping industry a subject of intrinsic interest, irrespective of its wider implications. Do the new technologies associated with containerization lend themselves more or less readily than did the old technologies to exploitation through VI? If greater state involvement in the shipping industry makes it more difficult for cross-traders and non-state owned companies to secure cargoes on the open market, will this encourage integration between production and shipping as a defensive mechanism to assure the continuation of freight business on a long-term basis? Finally, does the weak form of *horizontal* integration that is effected through the conference system either substitute for, or complement, *vertical* integration within the industry? If horizontal and vertical integration are indeed related in some way, is the weakening of horizontal links through the breakup of the conference system likely to have repurcussions on the level of VI?

It would be unreasonable to claim that this exploratory study can fully answer these questions. Nevertheless, the empirical evidence reported below indicates certain regularities in the pattern of VI both within the shipping industry itself and between shipping and other industries. These regularities are consistent with the modern economic theory of the MNE. Furthermore they suggest that some of the factors identified by the theory are of far greater importance than others. It is therefore possible to identify a small number of aspects of VI on which future research on the shipping industry should focus.

Section 7.2 outlines, in general terms, the main incentives and disincentives of VI identified by the theory of the firm. Section 7.3 presents empirical evidence on how the extent of integration into shipping varies across industries. The evidence relates not only to contemporary industries, but also to instances of integration reported in the literature of business and economic history. The evidence indicates that on the whole the level of integration between shipping and the industries that generate cargo is very low. Section 7.4 examines the contractual arrangements that prevail in those sectors of the shipping industry where integration is absent. Section 7.5 discusses the pattern of integration revealed by a sample inquiry into UK shipping firms in 1984. The conclusions are summarized in section 7.6.

7.2　MOTIVES FOR INTEGRATION BETWEEN SHIPPING AND PRODUCTION

VI between production and transport occurs when the same firm directly controls both a production process and the shipping of one or more of its inputs or outputs. VI between production and transport has received surprisingly little attention from economists. The most detailed analysis of the subject is due to Oi and Hurter (1965), but their work is concerned with road transport rather than with shipping.

The relationship between production and shipping is illustrated by the stylized vertical sequence shown in figure 7.1. In the context of this scheme,

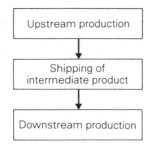

FIGURE 7.1 A vertical sequence involving shipping

the terms 'production' and 'intermediate product' need to be interpreted widely. 'Upstream production' may include mining and agriculture as well as manufacturing, while 'downstream production' may include wholesaling and retailing activities. Correspondingly, the 'intermediate product' may be at any stage of processing from a raw material to a finished product awaiting distribution.

The economics of integrating shipping with production depend upon whether or not the adjacent stages of production are themselves integrated. To simplify subsequent analysis, it is assumed that upstream and downstream production are already integrated and that the only question is whether shipping of the intermediate product should be subcontracted or provided by the producer himself. The question, in other words, is whether the producer should fill the 'transportation gap' in his sequence of operations.

The theory of VI summarized in earlier chapters identifies a number of situations which encourage VI and other situations which discourage it (see also Casson, 1984). Adapting the analysis to shipping activities indicates various *hypothetical* situations in which VI should be prominent. The *practical* importance of these situations is considered in section 7.3 below.

(*a*) Government regulation of the market for shipping services tends to encourage VI. If, as a result of government actions on such matters as flag discrimination, freight rates are too high, then a producer can reduce the cost of shipping services by owning and operating his own ships. Although his shipping division may have to charge his production division a notionally high price, the true opportunity cost of shipping services is nevertheless reduced. If government fixes a maximum price of shipping services too low (in order, say, to subsidize domestic exports) then independent shipping lines may contract their operations, and thereby cause a shortage of cargo capacity. A producer that is self-sufficient in shipping can avoid the rationing of cargo space since his internally generated traffic naturally carries first priority. All taxes, quotas, manning restrictions, inspection requirements, etc. which are applied only to shipping services offered for hire may be avoided by integrating ship ownership with cargo generation.

(*b*) Natural monopoly power on a shipping route tends to encourage VI in the absence of sophisticated pricing arrangements. Because of economies of vessel size, the annual carrying capacity of a vessel on a given route may be quite large relative to the annual volume of traffic. Under certain conditions this creates a natural monopoly situation which the company can exploit by raising the price of shipping services. But if a uniform monopoly price is charged then the company is liable to drive away marginal traffic. To exploit the monopoly effectively it is necessary to charge discriminatory prices based upon what each category of traffic will bear and, within each category, upon what each successive unit of traffic will bear. This is quite compatible with overall economic efficiency provided that marginal units of traffic are charged at marginal cost, and intra-marginal units are never charged at more than the customer is willing to pay.

Economies of VI arise when it is difficult to implement price discrimination. It may then be advantageous for the shipping company to integrate into those activities which generate marginal cargoes in order to avoid losing traffc when a uniform monopoly price is set. Generally speaking, this involves integrating into those activities which generate traffic whose derived demand for shipping services is most price-elastic. Following Bennathan and Walters (1969), such traffic is characterized by highly elastic final demand, a high proportion of transport costs in total costs, and easy substitution at the margin between shipping and other forms of transport.

(*c*) Opportunities for transfer pricing encourage VI. By operating a shipping division out of a tax haven, and overinvoicing production divisions for intra-firm supplies of shipping services, an integrated company can reduce its global tax liability below what equivalent arm's length operations would incur. The advantages of transfer pricing are greater, the greater are the differentials between the marginal rates of profit taxation in different countries. Transfer pricing can also be used to avoid exchange controls and capital export restraints by disguising capital transfers as internal payments for overpriced shipping services.

(*d*) The possibility of deterring entry may encourage a monopolist to undertake VI. A producer seeking to create a monopoly (or a group of producers seeking to establish a cartel) could strengthen their position if they owned a shipping line that monopolized the route that took their products to market. Conversely, a shipping line seeking to strengthen its monopoly might integrate backwards into a monopolistic production facility. By increasing the number of stages at which a potential rival must enter, the entrant's capital requirements, and his cost of capital, are likely to be increased. This raises the limit price which can be charged for the delivered product, so that the profits of the combined production and transport operations are increased under integrated monopoly.

(e) High fixed costs, inelastic short-run capacity limits, and rigid structural interdependence between constituent activities within a plant, all encourage integration into shipping. The main reason is that these technological factors all make for economies of continuity of flow in production. They may apply either to upstream production, or downstream production or both. To avoid interruptions to production, assured continuity in the supply of shipping is crucially important. In principle, continuity of supplies can be assured by negotiating long-term contracts, but in practice such contracts are difficult to enforce. Unless the contract is underpinned by mutual goodwill, there is always a risk that someone will renege. This risk is particularly acute in international transactions because of the limitations of international law.

The volume of litigation in shipping is certainly high, but it should be noted that contracts usually provide that any disputes should be resolved under the law of a particular country (often the UK) and it is sometimes fairly easy to obtain the assistance of courts in other countries for the enforcement of judgements. Large firms can diversify some of their enforcement risks because of the number of different commodities and different shipping routes with which they are involved. Recent institutional developments, such as the BIFFEX futures market in shipping services, have reduced some of the other risks associated with long-term contracts by allowing both sides to hedge against unforeseen changes in cargo rates.

It is difficult to assure continuity through a sequence of short-term contracts because the producer is vulnerable to a renegotiation of the price instigated by the shipping firm. It is relatively easy for the shipping firm to threaten to cut off the producer's supplies at short notice unless he concedes a higher price for shipping services.

It is worth noting, however, that this vulnerability is often mutual, because ship operation itself is characterized by high fixed costs and inelastic short-run capacity limits. This point is explored further in section 7.4 below.

(*f*) 'Small numbers' bargaining with non-recoverable set up costs encourages VI. Small numbers bargaining typically arises when the intermediate product requires highly specific upstream plant to produce it, highly specific downstream plant to use it, and highly specific vessels to transport it. This makes it difficult for the upstream producer to switch at short notice to another downstream producer, or to another shipping company. Likewise it is difficult for the downstream producer and for the shipping company to switch to other clients. In the short run, therefore, barriers to entry into each activity mean that each party has only a limited number of other parties with whom he can deal.

Non-recoverable set-up costs arise because of the difficulty of switching specific equipment to alternative uses. The costs incurred in meeting the specific requirements of the industry cannot be recovered if the equipment has to be redeployed in another industry instead. Each party, once they have entered, confronts a barrier to exit. While the barriers to entry are responsible for creating a short-run bargaining situation, the barriers to exit make each party very vulnerable to threats from the others. It is difficult for any party to refuse an unfavourable offer from the others because the credibility of a counter-threat to leave the industry is undermined.

The solution to this bargaining problem is for all the parties to agree terms *before* they have committed themselves to investment in specific plant. By negotiating before commitment they are bargaining in a competitive environment which includes all potential entrants, and they are immune to threats induced by barriers to exit. But how can any of the parties be sure that the others will not renege on the bargain once a specific investment has been made? The surest way to avoid this risk is for the various parties to financially consolidate their interests before any commitment is made. In other words, investment in upstream production, downstream production and transportation facilities is effected by a single integrated company.

(*g*) The introduction of a new technology into production or shipping encourages VI. The benefits of the new technology may spill over to other stages within the vertical sequence. Alternatively, the successful introduction of the technology may call for expenditure at other stages of production by firms who do not stand to benefit from it directly. These technological externalities can, in principle, be resolved through arm's length contracts. But it may be simpler to financially consolidate the activities before the new technology is introduced.

(*h*) Difficulty in controlling the quality of shipping services encourages VI. Some products are particularly difficult to transport and are liable to damage. Their handling requires special expertise and considerable care. When a shipping company is carrying goods on its own account (see section 7.4) it has a direct pecuniary incentive to exercise care. But where the shipping company is a subcontractor handling another producer's good, the producer may wish to monitor and control the handling himself. Integration between production and shipping gives the producer the requisite degree of control.

Perishable products are also sensitive to delays in shipment. An important aspect of quality of service in this case is that sailing times are closely synchronized with upstream and downstream production schedules. Perishability is particularly important when it is combined with short-run volatility in demand or supply. When a product is perishable it is difficult to accommodate short-run fluctuations by holding precautionary inventory and so when fluctuations occur it is necessary to rearrange transportation. For example, if production plans have to be revised because of unforeseen breakdowns either upstream or downstream, then a solution may be found by revising sailing times at short notice.

The problems of co-ordinating production and shipping can be solved, in principle, by a sophisticated subcontracting arrangement which specifies rights and responsibilities under a range of different contingencies, and so provides appropriate incentives in each case. Greater flexibility with less formality can be achieved, however, by bringing the shipping operation under the producer's control.

(*i*) Differences in the efficient scale of operation at adjacent stages discourage VI. When technological factors mean that the minimum efficient scale of operation at one stage is well above the maximum efficient scale of operation at an adjacent stage then a single large facility at the first stage must be coupled to several small facilities at the second stage.

The problem of reconciling efficiency of scale at the adjacent stages becomes particularly acute when efficient scales are not integer multiples of one another. For example, if a vessel with annual carrying capacity of 350,000 tons is sourced from upstream plants with an annual capacity of 100,000 tons each, then either three plants are fully utilized and the vessel operates at below capacity, or four plants are operated at below capacity in order to fully utilize the vessel. To achieve full capacity working in both production and shipping it is necessary to produce at an annual rate equal to the lowest common multiple of the capacities: in this case 700,000 tons is produced by seven plants and carried in two vessels.

The problem can be avoided if it is possible to open up the market at the margin to balance supply and demand through arm's length trade. Thus the company could either operate three of its own plants and hire out 50,000 tons of its vessel's capacity to third parties, or operate four plants and allocate 50,000 tons of intermediate product to independent vessels. The difficulties with this strategy are twofold. First the company's policy of internalizing shipping services may increase the costs of using the external market to a prohibitive level. Secondly, opening up the market undermines any strategy of seeking to strengthen monopoly power along the lines indicated in (*d*). If the company cannot open up the intermediate product market then its management must assume responsibility for multi-plant operation, quite possibly with several plants upstream and downstream and several vessels in operation between them. This is likely to create diseconomies of bureaucracy within the management team.

If production or transportation equipment is versatile then part of the problem identified above can be avoided by arranging for plants to produce a variety of products, or for vessels to carry a variety of products. This, however, only transforms the problem rather than solves it. For the versatile use of equipment increases the diversity of the activities that must be managed, and stretches the expertise of the management team to its limits.

(*j*) Existence of joint products discourages VI. Integration into an activity which generates joint products creates the problem of arranging for the profitable disposal of the product that is not required by the integrated operations. One solution is to widen the scope of the firm even further by integrating into the activities which utilize the by-product, but this encounters the problems of diversity mentioned above. The existence of joint products is, in fact, a characteristic of transportation activities, including shipping. In the case of outward and return journeys on a single route, for example, transport services on the two legs of the round trip are in joint supply. In certain cases it may be easy for a producer who has integrated into shipping to obtain a return cargo for his vessel. But often suitable return cargoes are difficult to find. Efficient operation may require the rostering of vessels on triangular voyages or even on round the world trips. To achieve full integration between shipping and cargo generation on every leg of the trip would involve extremely wide and finely balanced global production by the company. To avoid the management problems associated with this strategy, it may be preferable to hire shipping services from an independent line.

7.3 DISCRIMINATING BETWEEN ALTERNATIVE MOTIVES

Evidence on the extent of VI between production and shipping is extremely sketchy, but the following generalizations seem to be valid.

1 The extent of integration has been very small throughout the world economy during the last century. Integration between manufacturing and shipping is particularly unusual: the main instance occurs in the paper and pulp industry.

2 In agriculture and minerals, most integration into shipping involves the carriage of just one (or at most a few) commodities per vessel. The commodities are generally shipped in large consignments from a single port. This applies particularly to bananas and other tropical fruits which are grown on large plantations. It also applies to chilled meat, palm oil, oil, bauxite, iron ores, coal, nitrates, etc.

3 Within agriculture, it is in the carriage of refrigerated products that integration is most conspicuous, e.g. the United Fruit Company's 'white fleet' used in the banana trade and the Vestey family's 'Blue Star' fleet which transports chilled Argentinian and Australian beef to Britain. (It is noteworthy that the Blue Star fleet services independent producers too, and operates a container service through a consortium.)

4 Within the mineral sector, it is the oil industry that is most heavily integrated into shipping. Although oil companies' vessels account for only about 30 per cent of world oil tonnage, this percentage is high relative to that in other industries. Recently, though, the proportion of world tanker tonnage owned by the oil companies has noticeably diminished. During the time when ships were coal-fired, integration between coal mining and shipping was also significant, although there appears to have been little day-to-day integration of the operations. The cross-investments between companies appear to have been more a matter of trade investments and hedging rather than vertical integration *per se*. There is also some integration between domestic gas distribution and the shipping of liquified natural gas.

5 Within the same industry, integration into shipping may occur on some routes and not on others. For example, the export of chilled lamb from New Zealand to Britain involves very little integration compared to the export of beef from Argentina.

Shipping Technology

The lack of integration between production and shipping is readily explained by factors (*i*) and (*j*) above.

Ship operation is characterized by major economies of scale. Both capital cost and fuel requirements per cubic capacity decrease as the size of vessel increases. On the other hand, the vessel's manoeuvrability, the convenience of stowage and the number of ports that can be used all diminish with size beyond a certain point. The size of vessel at which these disadvantages become important is normally very large relative to the volume of traffic that is likely to be generated by any one plant, however. This means that to keep a vessel of efficient size fully utilized a producer would either have to replicate plants within the hinterland of a given port, increase the number of ports of call on each voyage, or design the vessel as a general carrier and diversify his activities over a range of industries. All of these strategies are liable to incur diseconomies in the management of production. Another alternative is to sell space on the vessel to other producers. This has the disadvantage that the producer has to diversify into the marketing of shipping services.

It has already been noted that shipping generates joint products. This creates a problem in finding a return cargo on each trip. The more specialized the vessel, the more difficult it normally is to find a return cargo. This provides an incentive to utilize general purpose vessels when return cargoes are available. On the other hand, there is no advantage to a general purpose vessel in this respect if no return cargo of any type is available.

Economies of Scale in Production

The conditions most favourable to integration are when the producer can keep a fleet of efficient-sized single-purpose vessels fully utilized on one leg of a journey, and when there are no return cargoes available of any kind. This requires that economies of scale in production generate a sufficient volume of intermediate product trade from a single origin to a single destination to support sailings of sufficient frequency to avoid stockpiling of the product at port for too long. It also requires that the freight should originate from an isolated port that neither imports nor exports other cargoes in significant quantities.

It is interesting to note that in the paper and pulp industry, referred to above, both lumbering and pulping involve significant economies of scale. The industry operates a few very large plants in isolated locations where the possibilities of alternative cargoes are fairly remote. Bowater's isolated Corner Brook pulp mill in Newfoundland, for example, was serviced in the 1930s by two steamships specially designed for the transport of its products to North America and Europe (Reader, 1981, p. 148). In the post-war period the company operated a fleet of nine vessels, though at one time the fleet was managed on their behalf by British and Commonwealth. Subsequently the fleet was disposed of and shipping was subcontracted to companies such as Furness Withy.

Similar principles apply to the export of tropical agricultural products from isolated plantations in 'banana republics' of Central America. The poverty of the banana republics means that few return cargoes are available to them from the consuming countries. Scale economies are important both in the plantations (Ellis, 1978; Read, 1983) and in the physical distribution to consumers in North America and Europe. The importance of scale in distribution is highlighted by the fact that when Sir Alfred Jones began importing Canary Island bananas in Elder Dempster Line ships at Liverpool, he gave away the bananas to costermongers in order to build up a market among consumers throughout the North of England (Davies, 1978, p. 67).

Tea, on the other hand, has historically been exported from colonies which import significant quantities of manufactured products, and has been shipped through ports which have a substantial entrepôt trade. The availability of return cargoes has encouraged the use of general purpose vessels, and this has, in turn, almost certainly discouraged VI.

Quality Control and Technology

A key factor that often seems to tip the balance in favour of integration into shipping is quality control. Some products require considerable care and attention in transport. Lever Brothers created their subsidiary Bromport Steamship Company in 1916 to transport palm oil and ground nut oil from West Africa to Britain, partly because they were dissatisfied with the arrangements offered by Elder Dempster Line for the shipment of oil in wooden casks and barrels. The casks were expensive and prone to leaking. Lever Brothers chartered a tank steamer and applied different heating systems to the different tanks in order to find out by experiment which was most suitable (Pedler, 1974, pp. 176–7). They then acquired their own vessels and operated them in opposition to Elder Dempster Line. This operation was a precursor of the Palm Line which Lever Brothers subsequently operated in West Africa.

Oil is a highly inflammable product. In the early days of the oil industry accidents were very common. Henriques (1960, p. 68) notes that when the first shipload of Pennsylvania oil in barrels was shipped to Europe the crew deserted out of fear of being burnt in their bunks, and had to be replaced by a crew of dead-drunk seamen recruited from the wharf-side bars. An early fleet of sixteen tankers used in the export of Russian oil was almost completely eliminated by a succession of explosions caused by lightning strikes, imperfect cleaning of tanks, etc. The first major oil companies introduced important technical advances into their fleets. The first tanker to use the skin of the ship as the wall of the tank was introduced by Anglo-American, the British subsidiary of Standard Oil. The early tankers of the Shell Transport and Trading Company were the first to be allowed through the Suez Canal, on account of the novel safety features they incorporated, including expansion tanks and special cleaning apparatus (Henriques, 1960, p. 90).

In the agricultural sector the most important aspect of quality control is connected with the perishability of the product. This calls not only for special shipboard facilities, but also for very strict scheduling. Bananas and chilled meat, for example, can only be kept in transit a few weeks at most. Indeed, until the advent of refrigeration, long distance trade in these products was practically impossible. Careful synchronization of production and shipping is necessary. In the banana industry the cutting of stems on the plantation is often timed to anticipate the arrival of a vessel for loading in port. Furthermore, ships are sometimes diverted at sea from one destination to another as the supply situation changes at various ports from day to day.

The role of the oil companies in pioneering technical developments in shipping suggests that problems in allocating the costs and benefits of new technology may have been important in encouraging VI. The same remarks apply to Lever's pioneering work in the transport of vegetable oil. The fact that the shipping companies would have been required to make substantial investments in tankers for which there would have been, at the time, a limited number of alternative uses, suggests that 'small numbers bargaining' may also have been a factor in the situation. It should be noted, however, that more recent innovations, such as the supertanker, were pioneered by independent shipowners.

Unlike the situation in the oil industry, where the producers were pioneers of the new tanker technology, there is little evidence that the agri-business firms were pioneers in shipboard refrigeration, although they were quick to adopt the technology on their ships once it became available.

Capital Intensity

In the oil industry an additional factor encouraging integration is the combination of high fixed costs and rigid capacity limits in the refining process. Oil refining is a capital-intensive activity whose profitability depends crucially upon operating the refinery at full capacity (McLean and Haigh, 1954). Reducing the rate of throughput, or shutting down the refinery altogether, because of temporary shortage of crude oil, is very expensive. To reduce the risk of a logistical failure in crude supplies, the refinery is fed from storage tanks, normally located (along with the refinery) at the port to which the crude oil is shipped. In the short run, these tanks have a definite capacity limit. It is essential that ships do not arrive at port too early, when the tanks are still full from the previous shipment, because the ships will then be held up in port waiting to discharge. Nor must they arrive too late, when the tanks are already empty and the refinery has had to shut down.

Similar considerations apply to the loading of oil from tanks at the oil field. In some oil fields, however, where the oil is pumped up rather than allowed to gush out, it is possible to vary the output of oil at a moderate cost. Thus while the accurate timing of shipments is crucial to successful refinery operations, its importance at the oil field depends upon the method of extraction used.

Integration between shipping and coal mining cannot easily be explained in terms of the co-ordination of the mining and transport of coal. Rather, it is explained by the desire of owners of steam-powered vessels to secure supplies of high-quality steam coal on a long-term basis. Once these supplies had been secured, however, the company's own vessels might well be used to transport the coal to overseas bunkers, and possibly to develop an export trade for the supply of other shipping companies as well. This was certainly the pattern followed in Elder Dempster Line's acquisition of two collieries in Glamorgan (Davies, 1978, p. 60).

Industrial Concentration

Differences in the extent of integration into shipping on different routes may be explained by differences in industrial concentration in the same industry in different countries. In national industries with a high degree of concentration, integration into shipping may be employed as a barrier to entry, forcing potential entrants to acquire their own shipping, and thereby increasing their capital requirements. It is interesting, for example, that following the formation of Colonel North's Chilean nitrate cartel in the 1890s, one of the first actions of the cartel was to lay down its own vessels. The carriage of nitrate poses no difficulties, and indeed the ships were of a conventional – indeed traditional – design, so that the other motives for integration discussed above could not possibly apply (Greenhill, 1977, p. 148).

The desire to consolidate a monopoly position may also be a factor in the Vestey family's decision to integrate into the shipping of Argentinian meat to Britain in the 1920s. This case is less clear cut, because of the operational economies that were undoubtedly present. However, the same tendency was not present in the shipping of New Zealand meat to Britain. Crossley and Greenhill (1977, p. 301) note that in 1902, when the three pioneer meat packing firms in Argentina were moving towards combination, New Zealand had as many as 25 independent plants and Australia 16.

The role of industrial concentration in promoting integration into shipping has also been stressed by Kindleberger (1984b) who claims, on the basis of further case study evidence, that once one firm has integrated into shipping, its rivals may feel obliged to follow suit in order to protect themselves. It is possible, for example, that independent shipping companies may find it difficult to survive after the loss of one of their major customers, and may be tempted to raise prices in order to cover their fixed costs on a reduced volume of traffic. Rival firms must therefore integrate into shipping to avoid a scarcity of shipping capacity.

Direct evidence on the use of transfer pricing by shipping companies is difficult to obtain. There is no doubt, however, that shipping operations are well adapted to tax avoidance, not only because of the possibility of transfer pricing on intra-firm supplies of transport services, but also because of the high level of fixed costs and the possibility of arbitrarily allocating them to operations centred in practically any port at which the ship may occasionally call. The fact that many shipping subsidiaries are based in tax havens appears to corroborate this. It is also well known that the Vestey's highly profitable integrated operations avoided UK tax liability for over 30 years. This does not explain the incidence of integration across industries, but it may explain why shipping operations are often included in the portfolios of conglomerate companies, whose operations do not have any obvious link with freight generation.

The anecdotal evidence presented in this section suggests that the pattern of integration between production and shipping is explained mainly by factors (*c*)–(*j*). Factors (*a*) and (*b*), involving regulation of the shipping industry and the avoidance of monopolistic price distortions, appear to be of little importance. The most important positive incentives to integration are the desire to maintain continuity of flow in production (factor (*e*)) and quality control of the transport of perishable products (factor (*h*)). The major disincentives are the enormous scale of ships relative to the volume of cargo generated by a typical manufacturing plant – which call for general carriers rather than purpose-built vessels – and the difficulty of internally generating a return cargo.

7.4 ALTERNATIVES TO VERTICAL INTEGRATION

One of the most conspicuous features of the shipping industry is the range and versatility of the contractual arrangements that are involved. This feature of the industry can be explained quite naturally by the attempts of various parties to obtain the benefits of VI without the costs.

A major dilemma in the shipping industry concerns how to achieve effective synchronization of production and shipping when shipping services are provided by general-purpose vessels which must meet the needs of many different customers. A quality of service comparable to that available under VI can be achieved if the general-purpose carrier operates frequent scheduled services whose timetables are advertised well in advance and whose ships are well-equipped and normally sail with a margin of spare capacity. The advertising of timetables allows individual producers to plan their production schedules around sailing times so that, provided sailings are punctual, production can be organized much as it would under integration.

High standards of shipboard equipment help to reduce damage in transit and prevent deterioration of perishable products. Budgeting for spare capacity obviates the need for the producer to reserve cargo space well in advance. In this way, the liner system provides the quality of service to everyone that they could expect to obtain from their own fleet of purpose-built vessels. Because of economies of scale in the vessels, the liner system provides it more cheaply than they could provide it themselves.

It was noted under (e) in section 7.2 that the shipping industry is characterized by high fixed costs and rigid capacity limits. This poses a problem which is particularly acute in the case of the liner system. The commitment to sail at advertised times puts the shipping firm at a strategic disadvantage, because it encourages customers to hold back their cargoes to the last minute in order to negotiate a lower rate. Customers anticipate a low rate because they can see that as the departure time approaches and a margin of spare capacity remains, most of the costs of the voyage are sunk, and so the opportunity cost of taking the marginal consignment is very low.

Two responses are possible. One is to encourage customers to take a long-term view by establishing loyalty discounts for customers who do not hold back their cargo or switch it to rival ships. This is effective mainly in respect of producers who regularly trade over the route. For occasional customers the problem remains, however, and is particularly acute if other ships are loading in port at the same time or are about to depart soon afterwards. The obvious solution in this case is collusion. The regular shipping firms on the route agree to maintain prices at no less than long-run average cost, and to fight outsiders who attempt to undercut them. The historical fact that conferences normally combine rate fixing with loyalty agreements, and function mainly in the liner trade, supports the view that the conference system has evolved principally to solve the problem of maintaining rates for scheduled sailings.

Conferences have also used their power to enforce tariffs which discriminate between different categories of cargo on a basis which is related to the product's elasticity of derived demand for shipping (Deakin with Seward, 1973). The conference arrangement therefore obviates some of the problems of enforcing price discrimination, which were noted under (b) of section 7.2. This confirms the view, implicit in earlier remarks, that horizontal integration between conference members is an effective substitute in many respects for vertical integration between production and shipping.

Another problem in the shipping industry is that of generating return cargoes. As noted under (j) in section 7.2, it is a special case of the general problem that transportation activities normally generate joint products. Careful scheduling of services and ingenious rostering of vessels – perhaps involving complicated round trips – increase the chances of achieving full utilization of cargo space on all legs of a voyage. The operation of vessels in organized 'pools', and 'rationalization' within the certain conferences, both contribute to a greater efficiency of this kind.

Another feature of the shipping industry is that there is a well-developed charter market. This enables companies to hire vessels through brokers on either a time basis or a voyage basis. Chartering means that effective control over a vessel can be purchased on a short-term basis without acquiring ownership of the vessel on a long-term basis. The owner of a vessel that is regularly chartered out essentially specializes in bearing long-term risks concerning appreciation in the capital value of the vessel, and lays off to the charterers the short-term risks of finding a profitable use for it. The firm that charters a vessel can achieve all the operational economies of integration between production and shipping for the time that the vessel remains under its control.

There is also a market in ship management services, which allows the charterer to hire the expertise necessary to operate the ship whilst it is under his control. When a vessel is hired for a specific voyage, the company may take out an option to change the destination (within limits) whilst the vessel is at sea.

The combination of the charter market and the management services market provides producers with the flexibility to integrate temporarily into shipping as and when conditions warrant it.

There is also flexibility in the shipping industry regarding the contractual arrangements under which freight is carried in the absence of VI. An independent shipping firm can either carry customers' consignments on a fee-paying basis, or convey goods on its own account. In the first case the consignment is the property of someone else – normally, though not invariably, the seller of the consignment – whereas in the second case it is the property of the shipping firm itself. Given no VI, the consignment in the second case is purchased at the port of origin and resold at the destination; the shipping firm, though not integrated *vertically* into production, is integrated into merchanting instead.

Two or three centuries ago it was very common for merchanting and shipping to be integrated, but with the advent of the liner trade in the early nineteenth century its importance diminished. Today, tramp shippers may well top up fee-paying business with products carried on their own account. The advantage is fairly obvious; it is a useful way of increasing the utilization of cargo space when there is a shortfall in fee-paying traffic at the quoted tariff. The main disadvantages are threefold.

First, it is risky for a shipowner to purchase a product whose quality it is difficult to inspect before loading at port. This discourages the shipping of products that have already been packaged and sealed before they reach port, and whose quality is difficult to assess from a small sample. However, if the product has been checked and graded by a reputable intermediary, then the quality control problem is overcome.

Secondly, it is risky for the shipowner to buy for resale a product which has been produced with the specifications of a particular customer in mind, since he is likely to be at a bargaining disadvantage when the product is landed at its destination. Thus only products with a wide resale market are likely to be shipped on own account.

Finally, even if there are many buyers, the market price at the destination may fluctuate considerably, exposing the shipowner to speculative risks. In certain cases, however, it may be possible to lay off these risks by selling the product forward, perhaps on an organized futures market. Such markets are quite common where the first two conditions are met, namely a wide resale market and easily graded products. Typical of such products are coffee, wheat, vegetable oils, rubber and oil. In practice, there are a number of shipping companies which specialize in shipping such products in bulk on their own account.

Before the days of oil, it seems to have been quite usual for steam ships to carry coal on their own account. Trade in high quality steam coal made sense on a number of grounds. Since coal had to be loaded as fuel for the ship, and had to be checked for quality in this respect, it was relatively simple to carry extra in the hold. Secondly, there was a ready market for coal overseas, because of the widespread need for bunkering. Finally, if coal had not been loaded, then in some cases the ship would have had to travel in ballast.

7.5 INTEGRATION STRATEGIES OF MAJOR UK SHIPPING COMPANIES

This section re-examines integration between production and shipping from the point of view of the shipping firm. Unlike section 7.3, which examined the evidence from the point of view of the producing industry, this section presents evidence on the strategies of integration pursued by shipping firms.

Table 7.1 presents the results of a sample inquiry, conducted in 1984, into the operations of major shipping companies. It is a revised version of a table presented in Casson, Barry and Horner (1985). The sample is stratified: it includes most of the major companies, but only a relatively small proportion of the minor ones. The sample is not random. It is truncated by a lower limit of £1 million turnover in 1982, and is biased towards companies on which information is most readily available. Information on company activities has been collected from published statements of account, trade magazines, consulting reports and personal

TABLE 7.1 Principal activities of a sample of shipping companies operating in or controlled from the UK

Type of Shipping / Shipping Services	Very large					Large									Medium-size											Small			Total
	Canadian Pacific	Inchcape[b]	P & O[a]	Trafalgar House	Louis Dreyfus	Ocean Transport & Trading[a]	Hunting Group[a]	British & Commonwealth[c]	J. Swire & Son[d]	Furness Withy	Ellerman Lines	Hill Samuel[e]	Van Ommeren[a]	Andrew Weir	Brostrum UK	Walter Runciman	Evans & Reid	Lyle Shipping[a]	Common Brothers[a]	Reardon Smith	J. Fisher & Sons	Turnbull Scott	London & Overseas[a]	Eggar Forrester[a]	The Charente SS Co.[a]	F. Bolton Group[a]	Commodore Shipping[a]	Burnett SS Co.[a]	
Type of Shipping																													
Passenger	✓	✓	✓	✓		✓		✓	✓	✓		✓	✓	✓	✓	✓			✓		✓				✓				8
Cargo	✓	✓	✓	✓		✓	✓	✓	✓	✓	✓	✓	✓	✓	✓	✓			✓		✓	✓	✓		✓				14
Container	✓	✓	✓	✓	✓	✓	✓	✓	✓	✓		✓	✓	✓	✓	✓					✓	✓	✓		✓		✓		19
Bulk carriers			✓		✓	✓		✓		✓		✓	✓	✓							✓				✓				18
Tankers		✓	✓	✓		✓	✓	✓		✓		✓	✓		✓	✓	✓	✓	✓	✓	✓				✓			✓	16
Hovercraft			✓																										1
Fishing vessels						✓																✓							1
Shipping Services																													
Management	✓	✓	✓	✓	✓	✓	✓	✓	✓	✓	✓	✓	✓	✓	✓	✓	✓	✓	✓	✓	✓	✓	✓		✓	✓		✓	20
Agents	✓	✓	✓	✓	✓	✓	✓		✓	✓	✓	✓	✓	✓	✓	✓	✓				✓	✓			✓	✓	✓		20
Charterers	✓	✓	✓		✓	✓	✓	✓					✓	✓	✓						✓			✓	✓				17
Freight forwarders	✓	✓	✓			✓	✓				✓	✓	✓	✓	✓	✓					✓				✓				12
Stevedores	✓	✓	✓			✓	✓						✓		✓						✓								10
Warehousing	✓		✓			✓	✓					✓	✓	✓		✓					✓								9
Ship broking		✓	✓		✓	✓	✓					✓	✓	✓	✓	✓		✓	✓	✓	✓				✓	✓			16
Tugs and barges			✓			✓	✓		✓			✓				✓					✓				✓	✓			8

Port facilities	10
Marine services	14
Off-shore supply	8
Marine engineers	8
Financial Services	
Insurance broking	17
Underwriting	9
Investment management	15
Banking	3
Finance	8
Building society	1
Service Industry	
Hotels	8
Travel agents	13
Computer services	8
Telecommunications	3
Waste disposal	3
Weather forecasting	1
Transport & Trading	
Road hauliers	12
Rail transport	1
Aviation	9
Aircraft services	8
Distribution	10
General trading	8
Commodity trading	5
Energy dist. & traders	6
Motor vehicle trading	3
Timber	4
Plant hirer	2
Office equipment	2
Auctioneers	1

(continued)

TABLE 7.1 (continued)

	Very large					Large																				Small			Total
	Canadian Pacific	Inchcape[b]	P & O[a]	Trafalgar House	Louis Dreyfus	Ocean Transport & Trading[a]	Hunting Group[a]	British & Commonwealth[c]	J. Swire & Son[d]	Furness Withy	Ellerman Lines	Hill Samuel[e]	Van Ommeren[a]	Andrew Weir	Brostrum UK	Walter Runciman	Evans & Reid	Lyle Shipping[a]	Common Brothers[a]	Reardon Smith	J. Fisher & Sons	Turnbull Scott	London & Overseas[a]	Eggar Forrester[a]	The Charente SS Co.[a]	F. Bolton Group[a]	Commodore Shipping[a]	Burnet SS Co.[a]	
Land																													
Agriculture	✓	✓	✓										✓																4
Property investment	✓	✓	✓	✓		✓	✓	✓									✓					✓							9
Property developers		✓	✓				✓	✓									✓				✓			✓					6
Estate agents																	✓												1
Industrial																													
Engineering	✓	✓		✓		✓	✓	✓	✓	✓						✓		✓	✓					✓					11
Oil exploration	✓	✓	✓			✓	✓	✓	✓	✓							✓		✓										9
Mining	✓	✓																											2
Chemicals		✓		✓		✓		✓					✓					✓											5
Brewers		✓																											1
Fish processing																								✓					1
Rubber & plastics		✓				✓								✓										✓					4
Boat builder						✓								✓															2
Oil diving									✓																				1

[a] The entries for this company have not been confirmed by officials of the company.

[b] Inchcape is involved in container shipping not as a principal, but only as an agent. Their tanker fleet comprises only small product carriers operating in the Gulf and the Pacific.

[c] British and Commonwealth participates with Ocean and P & O in OCL.

[d] Swire's operations are mainly confined to the Far East.

[e] Hill Samuel, through Lambert Brothers, provides a wide range of services but does not own, and rarely controls, vessels. Many of its major functions are carried on overseas, especially in Hong Kong and Japan.

contacts in the shipping industry. In over half the cases, the information has been confirmed by officials or directors of the companies concerned. No distinction is drawn between vessels operated on long-term charter and those owned outright. Unless otherwise stated the activities of all majority-owned affiliates are included in the list of activities for each company. No information has been collected on the extent of day-to-day operational integration between activities. In many cases the activities may operate quite independently in the short run, as separate assets in the portfolio of .a holding company.

The most important result obtained from the table is that there is little connection between the type of vessel which is operated and ownership of activities which generate freight for that type of vessel.

If integration into freight-generating activities were an important aspect of shipping company strategy, it would be expected that the owners of bulk carriers would be heavily integrated into agriculture and minerals, the owners of cargo liners would be integrated into a diverse range of manufacturing industries, and so on. There is very little evidence of such a pattern in the table. In particular, the owners of general cargo vessels are not significantly more diversified into freight-generating activities than are other shipping firms.

It is quite possible, of course, that where integration is significant, the company is actually classified to another industry and is no longer regarded as a shipping firm. This is unlikely to be the case, however, in respect of general cargo vessels, since the common denominator in the range of productive activities would be the transport of goods in the same vessels over the same route.

Shipping companies which have little systematic involvement in generating their own freight are obliged to either market the services of their ships, or to charter their ships to others. Many shipping companies perform these activities themselves. The table shows that, of the 28 companies listed, 20 are involved as shipping agents, 17 as charterers and 16 as shipbrokers, and practically all the companies perform at least one of these functions. The companies are certainly more heavily integrated into the marketing of shipping than they are into freight-generating activities.

The owners of passenger vessels are particularly strongly integrated into the marketing services identified above. The table shows that all these passenger shipping firms also operate general cargo vessels, container ships and bulk carriers. This ties in with the fact that, historically, passenger liner operation has been one of the most sophisticated areas of shipping management. The marketing and organizational skills developed in this area have subsequently been transferred to other sections of the industry, through both diversification of ship ownership and integration into shipping services.

The smaller firms offer a narrower range of services than do the large firms, and also tend to specialize in operating particular types of vessel. Among the medium-size and small firms, for example, it is unusual to operate both general cargo vessels and bulk carriers. This is consistent with the view that within the shipping industry there is functional specialization between the carriage of ship-load consignments, and the carriage of mixed consignments of smaller size.

Efficient marketing of shipping may involve offering the customer a 'package' of services of which shipping is just one component. This is especially true of general purpose vessels dedicated to the carriage of mixed consignments. When a large number of small customers regularly demand a bundle of transport services which are strictly complementary to one another, overall transaction costs can be significantly reduced if the producers of the services arrange to package them beforehand. This can be achieved by one of the producers – say the shipping firm – acting as a middleman and hiring the other services on the customer's behalf. If the overall quality of service is also important, then the middleman may integrate into the complementary activities, so that he can more effectively guarantee quality to the customer.

Quality control over complementary services may explain why passenger shipping lines are integrated into travel agencies and hotels. Integration allows them to offer comprehensive travel facilities of an assured standard to businessmen and tourists. It may also explain why container shipping firms are integrated into road and rail transport. Integration enables them to control the movement of the container from door to door, and to ensure that the customer's perception of the quality of the shipping service is not adversely affected by delays or damage on other parts of the journey.

The extent of integration into warehousing, stevedoring and port facilities is not so great as might be expected. One explanation is that where several different shipping companies operate infrequent or occasional services to a particular port, it is more efficient for them to share the use of warehouses and port facilities, because none of the companies could keep its own facilities fully utilized. Moreover, provided the capacity of the port facilities is adequate, the problem of establishing priorities between companies simultaneously requiring access to the same facility is unlikely to arise. Likewise, where there is an abundant supply of dock labour, there is little point in maintaining an independent team of stevedores.

Integration into port services of this kind appears to be more common among container shipping lines than among the others. Efficient container operation involves a large steady flow of traffic concentrated upon a small number of ports. This alone makes it viable to invest in specialized dockside equipment and in a well-trained labour force to operate it. The need to match up the dockside equipment and the type of vessel, and to synchronize investments in shipping capacity and handling capacity, encourages integration between container shipping and port facilities (Gray, 1984). The availability of steady work, and the importance of retaining skilled labour, encourages container firms to integrate into stevedoring too.

It was noted earlier that the versatility of the container system allows vessels to carry a wider variety of cargoes at little extra cost, and thereby discourages integration into freight-generating activities. At the same time, the intermodal character of container operations encourages integration between shipping and other forms of transport. This suggests, in short, that containerization promotes integration within the transport sector at the expense of integration between transport and other activities.

Many shipping companies are integrated into financial services – particularly insurance broking and investment management. To some extent this may be explained by the highly speculative nature of ship ownership, which attracts to the industry people with considerable general expertise in financial planning. Another possibility is that because of its international scope, shipping is an industry that lends itself to transfer pricing and other techniques of tax avoidance; by integrating ship ownership into a financial portfolio it may therefore be possible to effect considerable reductions in overall tax liability. It should also be noted that during the 1960s several British shipping firms acquired large tax credits in connection with purchases of new vessels, and this encouraged the companies to merge with others, such as those in property development, which had a large liability for tax. This is often cited as one of the motives for the acquisition of Cunard Line by Trafalgar House.

7.6   CONCLUSIONS

The transactions economics approach appears to be quite successful in explaining the nature and extent of VI in the shipping industry. Problems connected with maintaining continuity of flow in production, and with quality control in the transport of perishable products, appear to be crucial in explaining the few cases in which shipping is integrated with a freight-generating activity. By and large, however, such integration is rare, because scale economies encourage the operation of general-purpose vessels whose services are normally marketed, for reasons explained by the theory, on a fee-per-consignment basis. The pattern of integration pursued by shipping companies is better explained by their desire to market a comprehensive range of services of assured quality to arm's length customers, than it is by their desire to integrate into freight generation.

The shipping trade as a whole is organized using a remarkably sophisticated set of contractual arrangements, which give shipowners and producers alike considerable flexibility in obtaining many of the advantages of VI without its costs. These contractual arrangements have evolved over three millenia of recorded history (L. Casson, 1960). No doubt they are capable of further improvement. It may be advantageous, for example, to modify contractual arrangements in the light of the technological advance associated with the container revolution and the development of intermodal transportation systems in general. But theory suggests that existing contractual arrangements make a substantial contribution to the efficiency of the shipping industry, and should not be lightly discarded in favour of untried innovations.

8

Foreign Divestment and Rationalization in the Motor Industry

8.1 INTRODUCTION

Perceptions of divestment amongst businessmen and economists tend to vary with the economic climate. In a steadily growing economy it is usually believed that any firm can achieve success simply through balanced investment across all its operations. Divestment is therefore regarded as *prima facie* evidence of failure. In a stationary or declining economy, however, divestment may be perceived more positively, as either cutting out the 'dead wood' from the firm's operations, or as permitting much needed structural change.

Organized divestment has become quite popular in the past decade, not only amongst businessmen, but amongst political leaders and workers too. Divestment through 'management buy out' is increasingly used to devolve ownership and control to small firms which function in some respects like producer co-operatives (Coyne, 1986). Privatization is a special form of divestment in which the state spins off activities to private industry (Bruce, 1986). In both these cases there are ideological as well as economic forces at work – in particular, disenchantment with the large organizations formed by conglomeration and nationalization, and a strong belief that 'small is beautiful'.

MNEs, too, have been involved in divestments, but here the forces of economic logic appear to have been far stronger than ideologial aspirations. It is, of course, natural that as the number of MNEs increased rapidly after 1945, thereby increasing the total number of foreign subsidiaries, so the number of divestments involving MNEs should increase too. There are, however, reasons to believe that the acceleration of divestment in the past decade reflects more fundamental economic changes which are forcing MNEs to rationalize their operations.

This chapter is specifically concerned with *foreign* divestment, in which a corporation headquartered in a foreign country relinquishes control of the productive activities of a local subsidiary. In this context, 'productive activities' include not only manufacturing but also marketing and distribution.

Early studies of foreign divestment include an analysis by Franko (1971) of factors influencing the survival of international joint ventures, a study by Kitching (1973) of successes and failures amongst US acquisitions in Europe, and an analysis of US divestments by Torneden (1975). Business International (1976), Sachdev (1976) and Chopra, Boddewyn and Torneden (1978) present further case study evidence, and survey the strategic issues from the standpoint of the divesting company.

A wave of foreign divestments in Europe, beginning in 1973, emphasized the need to consider more carefully the social and economic impact of divestment on the host country. Grunberg (1981) has examined Leyland's divestment of the Italian motor manufacturer Innocenti and Litton Industries' closure of its British Imperial Typewriter subsidiary, whilst Hood and Young (1982) and Young, Hood and Hamill (1985) have examined foreign divestments in Scotland by Singer, Hoover, NCR, Honeywell, Goodyear, Timex, Hyster and IBM. More specific studies of the impact of foreign divestment on a local economy are provided by Gaffikin and Nickson (1984) for the West Midlands and Lloyd and Strutt (1983) for the North West.

Van Den Bulcke (1979) examined the case of Belgium and found that during the two years 1975–6 foreign affiliates were responsible for 32 per cent of job losses arising from plant closures and collective dismissals in manufacturing industry – a proportion very similar to their share in total manufacturing employment. However, foreign affiliates were more inclined than their Belgian counterparts to close down smaller plants and to retain large ones, which suggests that foreign affiliates were involved in a more coherent form of rationalization than were indigenous firms. In a more recent study, however, Van Den Bulcke and Halsberghe (1983) noted that this difference between foreign and indigenous firms has since disappeared. This is confirmed in a study of employment losses in the Irish manufacturing industry by McAleese and Counahan (1979), who found no significant differences at all between foreign subsidiaries and indigenous firms.

Figures published by the Industry Department for Scotland indicate that this applies in Scotland too. The Scottish experience suggests that branch plants operated in Scotland by British companies are, if anything, more vulnerable to closure than plants operated by foreign companies. One reason could be that the foreign investors have a strong commitment to their Scottish location as a major centre from which to source the entire European market. Their European operations are already rationalized around a Scottish centre, in contrast to British companies whose operations are not initially rationalized, and for whom the Scottish plants are peripheral. When a British firm is forced to rationalize, therefore, the headquarters plant in England is retained and it is the Scottish plant that is closed down.

While all of these studies make important contributions to knowledge, it is difficult to synthesize their findings because of the very different approaches adopted by the authors. There is little agreement, for example, on the basic issue of how a divestment is to be defined. Some of the authors concentrate on expropriation, whilst others concentrate on voluntary divestments. Some identify divestment with factory closure, whilst others recognize the importance of divestments effected by selling off a subsidiary as a going concern.

There is still less agreement upon the criteria by which the success or failure of a divestment is to be evaluated. Some authors consider only the point of view of the divesting firm, whilst others concentrate upon national or local interests – as interpreted from their own particular political point of view. When adopting the corporate point of view, some authors implicitly assume that divestment is a reflection of failure, whilst others are also prepared to regard it as a creative response to changing circumstances. It seems, therefore, that some clarification of the issues is required if new insights are to be obtained into the divestment process.

The remainder of this chapter is organized into three main parts. Sections 8.2 and 8.3 discuss fundamental issues in the analysis of divestment, and derive some general policy implications. This part represents a self-contained introduction to the subject. Sections 8.4–8.6 consider the nature of rationalization and restructuring in the motor industry, whilst sections 8.7–8.10 present a case study of the divestment and rationalization process. The conclusions are summarized in section 8.11.

The case study chosen is the divestment of Chrysler's European operations to Peugeot in 1978. This case has already been discussed by both Grunberg, and Hood and Young, although their emphasis is different from the present study. Grunberg focuses upon the negotiations between Chrysler and the British government in 1975, while Hood and Young focus upon Peugeot's closure of Chrysler's major Scottish factory in 1981.

The object of the case study is to illustrate some of the general points made about divestment and rationalization in the first half of the chapter. The study does not describe in detail the machinery of the corporate decision-making process. Rather, it is a case study of the way that economic circumstances dictated a particular rational response by the managements of the two companies to changes in trading conditions in their industry. In describing the response as rational, it is assumed that both managements had well-defined objectives, and attempted to choose the appropriate means to fulfil them. It is recognized, however, that managements were responding to the situation as it was perceived at the time, and not as it might now be perceived with the benefit of hindsight. It should be clear, therefore, that this case study is informed by the insights of economic theory rather than by insights gained from the study of organizational behaviour.

8.2   DIVESTMENT: BASIC CONCEPTS

There is an important distinction between divestment of ownership and divestment of control. It is well known that the acquisition of majority equity ownership in another company is normally sufficient to acquire control of it, and that an increase in equity investment from a majority holding to a 100 per cent holding may be of only marginal consequence. Conversely, a divestment which reduces ownership from 100 per cent to 51 per cent may have little consequence for control, whereas a divestment from 51 per cent to 49 per cent may – if the remaining shares are held by a single owner – cause effective loss of control. In the analysis that follows, the emphasis is upon control. Divestment is identified with any reduction in ownership of a subsidiary which effects a significant or total reduction in control.

The focus of this study is upon *voluntary* divestment. Involuntary divestment effected by nationalization or expropriation, or by damage to assets arising from natural causes, is ignored. The impact of expropriation on foreign divestment was quite significant during the 1960s and 1970s in certain developing countries – particularly in Africa – though for the time being the threat of further large-scale expropriations appears to have receded.

Voluntary divestment may represent either 'equilibrium adjustment' or 'error correction'. In the case of equilibrium adjustment, the firm divests as a rational response to changed circumstances. A change in technology, for example, may reduce economies of vertical integration and encourage a downstream plant to be spun off as an independent firm. Error-correction divestment involves the firm divesting an activity that it should never have invested in to begin with. In this case it is not circumstances themselves which have changed, but only management's perception of them. With the benefit of hindsight, for example, the management may realize that the economies of vertical integration it anticipated were illusory. It therefore divests a downstream activity that should not have been acquired in the first place.

Although the distinction between equilibrium adjustment and error correction applies to both investment and divestment decisions, it is of particular relevance to divestment. This is because of a fundamental asymmetry: namely, that in the absence of 'short selling', a firm cannot divest an asset before it has invested in it, whereas it must invest in it before it can divest it. This does not mean that error correction is more common amongst divestments than amongst investments, but only that it is more transparent when it occurs. Cases where a company invests and then quickly divests the same activity, taking a loss, are prima-facie evidence of error-correcting behaviour.

A further distinction that needs to be made is between the short-run and long-run determinants of the divestment decision. This is particularly important where error-correcting divestment is involved. As a consequence of a previous error, the firm's profitability may be low, and so divestment may occur in the context of a cash flow crisis (see chapter 2). A purely short-run analysis may therefore suggest that a liquidity crisis is a major reason for the divestment. A long-run analysis, however, would identify the earlier mistaken decision which has led to the liquidity crisis as the fundamental cause of the divestment.

There is a third type of voluntary divestment, which is not considered in detail in this chapter. This is divestment stimulated by a change in the time preferences of investors, which leads them to prefer companies generating dividend streams which are high in the short run to those generating streams which are high in the long run. The sudden appearance of a short term bias in investor preferences may encourage companies to liquidate investments in order to boost current dividend streams. An example of this effect is the recent Bowater demerger (Wright, 1986), in which the British and North American divisions of the enterprise had very different patterns of cash flow. One of these was particularly attractive to British investors, who typically reveal a short-term bias in their preferences, whilst the other was particularly attractive to North American investors, many of whom appear to have a long-term bias in their preferences. The demerger allowed investors to specialize their investments in the type of activity most suited to their time preferences.

In practice, managers are involved in a continuous learning process in a continuously changing environment, and for this reason both the first type of 'equilibrium adjustment' divestment and the second type of 'error correction' divestment normally proceed simultaneously. It is therefore often difficult, in a particular situation, to disentangle one from the other. Indeed, short-run and long-run effects are sometimes difficult to disentangle too.

The case study presented in this chapter illustrates the way in which these various aspects of divestment are intertwined. Changes in Chrysler's environment called for structural adjustments by the company which the management fully recognized it needed to make. But because of an earlier error of judgement in acquiring loss-making assets, it lacked the profits to finance the adjustment. The effects of failing to adjust became cumulatively worse, and in the end the company was forced to divest as the result of a cash flow crisis.

8.3   THE DETERMINANTS OF DIVESTMENT

When analysing the determinants of divestment, it is useful to consider whether a decision to divest can be regarded simply as the 'reverse' of a decision to invest (Boddewyn, 1983a; 1983b). If the analysis is confined to equilibrium adjustment then the analogy works quite well, as explained below.

There are two ways of divesting control:

1 closure of the facility, and
2 sale of the facility as a going concern to another company.

It is also useful to distinguish different types of sale:

— sale to a company with which one continues to trade;
— sale to a company with which one plans to have no further connection whatsoever;
— sale to an existing rival; and
— sale to a new company that will become a rival.

TABLE 8.1   Parallels between strategic options in investment and divestment

Investment	Divestment
Establishment of a 'green field' facility	Closure of a facility
Acquisition as a going concern of:	Sale of the facility as a going concern to:
a company with which one has previously traded at arm's length	a company with which one will trade with at arm's length
a company with which one has no previous connection	a company with which one plans to have no further connection
a facility that previously belonged to a rival	an existing rival
a rival company in its entirety	a new company that will become a rival

Each of these types of divestment has an investment analogue, as indicated in table 8.1. It is appropriate to consider the determinants of these types of investment, and then in each case to turn the argument around to consider how the same factors affect divestment.

(1) Closure as the Opposite of Green Field Investment

The closure of a facility is the opposite of a 'green field' investment (on green field investment, see chapter 5). Before a green field investment is made, the land involved is allocated to a quite different use; conversely, when closure is effected, the land that was used reverts to an alternative use.

The most obvious motive for building a green field facility is that no satisfactory alternative facility is available elsewhere. This may be because the facility is unique or because alternative facilities exist but are defective. If other facilities exist, the defects must be irreversible in the sense that they cannot be remedied except at prohibitive cost.

Turning this around, the circumstances most likely to lead to closure of a facility are either that the facility was unique, but due to a change in circumstances it is no longer required, or that the facility is now irreversibly defective relative to other facilities currently available. The most likely defects are summarized below.

(*a*) The facility may be in the wrong location.

1 The geographical distribution of customers may have changed, with the result that production is now remote from the centre of the market. A facility supplying *consumer* goods may find that international differences in population growth and income growth have caused the market to grow fastest in countries that are a long distance away. A facility supplying *raw materials, components, semi-processed products, business services or producer durables* may find that its downstream customers have relocated, so that rival suppliers are now much nearer to them than they were before.
2 The geographical pattern of input availability may have changed. Since capital is relatively mobile, it is changes in the availability of labour and natural resources that are crucial in this respect. Exhaustion of mineral deposits, deforestation, erosion of top soil, and many other factors can induce the closure of mines, plantations, and other resource-based production facilities. The discovery of new natural resources elsewhere, or technological innovation which makes it feasible to exploit such resources for the first time, can have a similar effect. Improvements in the training of foreign labour can raise productivity at other locations so that the cost advantage of using the domestic labour force is lost.

3 Tariff and non-tariff barriers may have altered. Tariffs on many final products were reduced under the General Agreement on Tariffs and Trade, although in many industries where intermediate products are tradable, the effective rates of protection on the final stages of processing have remained relatively high. Early stages of processing are therefore more susceptible to international competition that final stages. The recent introduction of 'value added' tariffs has stimulated off-shore processing, much of which takes place in newly industrializing countries (Casson and associates, 1986). In many industries the main obstacles to trade are now non-tariff barriers such as government discrimination against purchasing imports, artificially strict quality controls on imports and voluntary restraints negotiated with exporting countries. The net effect, however, is that many mature industrialized countries have lost the protection their industries enjoyed in the inter-war and early post-war period.

4 Transport costs may have changed. The past 25 years have witnessed significant developments in transport technology, including the innovation of extra-large highly automated bulk carrier ships, the construction of comprehensive motorway networks and the increasing carriage of high-value freight by air. Perhaps the single most important influence on the location of manufacturing industries, however, has been the development of inter-modal transportation using containers (see chapter 7). Because of scale economies in handling containers, inter-modal traffic tends to be concentrated upon a few major trunk routes. Manufacturers located in older industrial districts where roads are congested and local ports are too small to handle bulk traffic may be disadvantaged as a result of this development.

5 Government policies may have changed. Many governments nowadays offer a package of inducements to new investors which include rate rebates, tax holidays, subsidized factory units and energy sources, cheap loans – and even exemption from local labour laws in the case of some 'export processing zones'. These inducements lure industry away from traditional areas, and encourage manufacturers to become 'footloose' – moving their factories around to areas newly designated for industrial development. Unless established firms in mature areas are offered similar subsidies, they suffer competitive cost penalties which may force them to close. Producers in certain countries may also be subject to price controls, production quotas, anti-pollution measures, employment taxes etc., from which producers in other countries are exempt, and which further penalize their operations.

(*b*) The facility may have the wrong capital infrastructure.

1 Technical progress may have rendered the design obsolete. It may be

difficult to replace old plant with new on a piecemeal basis. If continuity of production is important then it may be necessary to build an entirely new facility and then close the old one down.

2 Changes in relative prices may alter the appropriate input or output mix. If production utilizes highly specific dedicated machinery then it may be difficult to adjust the equipment to meet new needs. The cost of retooling or rebuilding may be prohibitive. Thus the new input or output mix must be obtained from a new plant, and the old one closed down.

3 New opportunities may arise for exploiting economies of scale. Standardization of technology in the 'mature product' phase of the product life cycle affords economies of scale (Vernon, 1979; B. D. Brown, 1978). Overall growth of the market, and greater integration of local markets through reductions in transport costs and tariffs, encourage the vigorous exploitation of these economies of scale. Other things being equal, overall market growth encourages the use of a similar number of plants of larger scale while integration of markets encourages concentration of production upon fewer plants. During the last few years, it has been argued, an increasing number of products have reached maturity, and this, together with reductions in transport costs and tariffs, has encouraged firms to abandon small-scale plants which are no longer of an economic size to manufacture standardized products.

(*c*) The facility may have the wrong management and working practices. In some cases it may be viable to improve managerial efficiency and labour relations by a change of leadership in the company. A company may be 'turned around' by improving self-motivation and incentives at all levels of the organization. But in some cases inefficient traditions may be so entrenched within the company – and perhaps also within the local community from which the employees are drawn – that only wholesale recruitment of a new management and work-force with a different social background will suffice. This is often best done by constructing an entirely new facility in another location and closing the old facility down.

(*d*) The facility may be the marginal plant in an industry faced with falling demand. During the recent recession overall demand in several major markets has declined. Reductions in demand encourage the closure of high-cost plants. Thus a plant which may be viable in buoyant demand conditions may not be viable in depressed conditions. If management believes that the recession is temporary then the plant may be 'moth-balled' and the work-force laid off awaiting recall. If, however, the recession is expected to be permanent, then closure will be effected instead.

(2)   Divestment as the Reverse of Acquisition

Divestment of a facility to a trading partner is the reverse of the acquisition of a facility from a trading partner. An acquisition of this kind is most naturally explained by economies of vertical integration. As noted in previous chapters, these economies represent the net economies achieved by replacing arm's length contracts between an upstream and downstream facility by managerial control. Divestment is explained by economies of vertical *disintegration*. Vertical disintegration involves replacing an intermediate product market which is internal to the firm with a similar market external to the firm. This is effected by spinning off either the upstream or downstream activity as an independent firm.

Disintegration is induced by changes in the environment which either reduce the benefits or increase the costs of internal trade. The analysis in the earlier chapters of this book suggests that the most important factors are likely to be as follows.

1   The relaxation of government interference in arm's length trade in the intermediate product encourages disintegration. If, for example, statutory price controls were abolished in the intermediate product market, a firm might become just as willing to buy from, or sell to, an independent firm as to one of its own subsidiaries.
2   Fiscal harmonization between countries may eliminate the benefits from transfer pricing. Therefore in the interests of administrative economy a firm might prefer to deal at arm's length with a facility that was previously a subsidiary. This effect could be produced by the equalization of the marginal rates of taxation between two countries, or by the abolition of exchange controls which had impeded international capital movements.
3   A reduction in barriers to entry into either the upstream or downstream activity may render arm's length trade more competitive. A reduction in barriers to entry could occur for several reasons, such as the introduction of a new technology affording lower returns to scale, the expiry of a patent, and so on. The adjustment of the arm's length price towards a competitive level eliminates potential distortion of the downstream input mix, or the upstream output mix, and avoids the consequent waste of resources. When barriers to entry are eliminated at both adjacent stages, the problems of bilateral monopoly in the intermediate product market, and of multiple monopolistic mark-ups of the final output price, are also avoided. Thus in various ways the reduction in barriers to entry promotes arm's length trade.
4   Improved methods of quality control in upstream production, or

improvements in quality testing of inputs at the downstream stage, may reduce the incentive for the downstream producer to monitor production in the upstream plant. Since the problems of confidentiality created by this form of monitoring are often resolved through vertical integration, the reduction of these problems is an incentive to arm's length trade.

5 The maturing of the technology and the division of labour within the industry means that there is less need for centralized coordination of investments at the upstream and downstream stages. This encourages the vertical disintegration of production.

6 A reduction in the range and diversity of skills within the management team – due, for example, to the retirement of the founder of the company, or the loss of other key employees – may mean that the day-to-day management of both upstream and downstream activities becomes too onerous a task. This encourages the substitution of arm's length negotiations between two smaller management teams for integrated bureaucratic control.

(3) Transfer of Managerial Resources

The acquisition of a facility with which one has had no previous connection may be explained as a transfer of managerial resources. The acquiring firm has surplus managerial capacity, whilst the management of the acquisition is under considerable pressure, possibly because of the unexpected rapid growth of the company. Another possibility is that the acquiring company is simply adding greater diversity to its portfolio of assets in order to reduce its risks. It is behaving, in other words, according to the same principles as a mutual fund.

Turning this argument around, the divestment of a facility may be explained by excessive pressure on the managerial resources of the divesting firm. Perhaps the company has had an unexpected success with one of its subsidiaries, and wishes to divest a slower-growing subsidiary in order to concentrate on making the best of the most promising opportunity. Alternatively, the company may have found that its management skills are much more specific than it at first believed, so that divestment represents the correction of an initial error caused by overconfidence. The company may be facing a capital constraint which forces it to divest one activity in order to finance the acquisition of another. A further possibility is that the management has overestimated the potential gains from portfolio diversification.

(4) Making Better Use of a Facility

The acquisition of a facility that previously belonged to a rival suggests that the new owner can make better use of the facility than could the rival firm. The main reason for this is that the acquiring firm has a proprietary advantage – such as new technology or new marketing ideas – which can be transferred to the rival firm. This implies, amongst other things, that the deficiencies of the rival are reversible – unlike the deficiencies considered under (1) above.

Putting this argument into reverse indicates that divestment to a rival is most likely to occur when either the divesting firm has lost a proprietary advantage it once possessed, or its rival has acquired an advantage that the divesting firm does not possess. In each case, it suggests that the rival firm is more progressive: its management is more entrepreneurial, its research is more imaginative, its marketing is more aggressive, and so on. Divestment to a rival may therefore be regarded, in the broadest possible terms, as a symptom of entrepreneurial failure.

(5)   Replacing Competition with Monopoly

Acquisition of a rival company in its entirety is most likely to be motivated by a desire to replace competition with monopoly. The converse case – the divestment of a facility to a new company that will become a rival – reduces monopoly power in the industry. It is conceivable that the divesting firm intends to tacitly collude with its new rival, but there can be no guarantee that the rival will take up the offer or, if it does so, that it will wish to continue the arrangement indefinitely. Theory suggests, and experience seems to confirm, that divestment which creates a new rival will normally be undertaken only under duress – for example, under the threat of prosecution for violations of competition law. Since the focus of this chapter is on voluntary rather than coercive divestment, this type of divestment will not be considered any further.

A key implication of this analysis is that divestment cannot be considered in isolation from investment. Divestment and investment are quite likely to occur in parallel. The closure of a divested facility, for example, may be associated with green field investment in a new facility involving new technology and/or a more appropriate location. In a firm with limited managerial resources, or facing capital rationing, divestment of one facility may be necessary to liberate resources for investment in another facility. In all these cases, therefore, divestment is one facet of a process of adjustment: investment and divestment are just two sides of the same coin.

The only situation in which divestment is purely one-sided is when final demand is contracting and marginal plants are liquidated without any new plants being built. Many writers on divestment adopt this rather one-sided view of the subject. When the cases they discuss concern recession-induced closure this is unobjectionable, but in other cases the resulting impression can be misleading.

8.4   PRODUCTION, MANAGEMENT AND MARKETING IN THE MOTOR INDUSTRY

The next three sections apply the theory of divestment to the motor industry, with particular emphasis on developments in the European motor industry. Considerable effort is made to place current events in an historical perspective. This section considers the influence of technology and product demand on management problems in the motor industry. The next section considers the emergence of pressure to rationalize within the European industry during the 1970s, illustrating the general points using British experience. The final section considers the management structure and rationalization programme pursued by the European market leader – Ford of Europe.

The motor car is built by the assembly of many diverse components: the internal combustion engine, mechanically engineered transmission and suspension, pressed steel bodies, synthetic rubber tyres, electrical and electronic components, plastic trim, and so on. Each component is produced to fine tolerances to allow spare parts to be interchanged. Mass production was introduced into the motor industry by Henry Ford, who adapted techniques from the Chicago meat packing trade to generate the moving track assembly line now widely used for mass production in manufacturing industry. Ford also used the techniques of scientific management pioneered by F. W. Taylor – in particular, time and motion study – to determine the optimal speed of the track.

The problem of organizing a continuous supply of components was one of a number of factors that encouraged General Motors president, Alfred P. Sloan, Jr., to apply multi-divisional organization to his company. Although the multi-divisional concept originated with E. I. du Pont Nemours, a large US chemical conglomerate, which at the time had a stake in General Motors, its application in General Motors proved extremely influential (see, for example, Chandler, 1962; Rae, 1965, and the numerous references given therein).

Quite recently, the Japanese have formed 'quality circles' amongst their key employees to improve component reliability (see chapter 4) and have exploited the 'just in time' production concept to reduce component inventories by promoting punctuality amongst their suppliers. Many motor manufacturers are now introducing robots to undertake welding, wheel assembly, paint spraying, etc.; the pioneers include Volkswagen at Wolfsburg in West Germany and Nissan in Japan.

The variety of components used in the motor industry means that many different types of manufacturing process are found. Body panels, for example, are pressed from sheet steel using high-volume dies which can produce 5–10 million stampings before replacement. Maxcy (1981, p. 201) estimates that the presses into which the dies are inserted can produce up to 2 million pressings a year, which means that minimum cost production of body panels requires a rate of output of 2 million units per annum sustained over 2½–5 years. For further information on cost structures in the motor industry see Rhys (1977).

It has been estimated that the minimum efficient scale (m.e.s.) in the casting of engine blocks is 100,000 units per annum, in the machining and assembly of the power train (engine and transmission) 500,000 units per annum, and in final assembly 200,000 units per annum.

The importance of economies of scale means that the profitability of motor production depends crucially upon the intensity of demand for the product. At given prices, the higher is the volume of sales, the greater is the margin of profit on each unit sold. In the early motor industry some of the most sophisticated vehicles were produced in France, but they were usually custom-made and sold only to a limited number of wealthy people.

Henry Ford was one of the first to create a mass market for motor vehicles amongst middle- and low-income families. Demand was particularly strong in rural areas, such as the mid-western states of the US. In inter-war and early post-war Europe there were two main segments of the motor market: the mass production sector dominated by Citroën, Volkswagen, Fiat and Ford (UK), and the luxury sector dominated by smaller British and Italian firms.

Within the last 25 years a third segment of the motor vehicle market has emerged. Narrowing after-tax income differentials, higher oil prices, the trend towards hypermarket shopping and the increasing availability of motorways have created a large demand for medium-size five-door vehicles which offer low running costs but provide some differentiation in styling.

The multi-component character of the motor vehicle can be exploited to meet some of the needs of this market. Superficial differentiation of the product can be achieved by substituting one type of component for another in the final assembly process. By developing a standardized range of components, the same basic vehicle can be offered with different sizes of engine, with manual or automatic transmission, with different levels of trim, and with or without power-steering, turbochargers, electronic displays, and so on.

The introduction of robots on the assembly line has eliminated many of the delays which were caused by retooling production using manual labour. Thus when robots are used the capacity of the assembly line effectively determines, not the efficient output of a single model, but the efficient output of the entire range. This has tended to reduce the importance of economies of scale in assembly (see Altshuler et al., 1984). On the other hand, the high capital cost of robots means that the cost penalties of operating the assembly line at below its rated capacity are much greater than before.

Because so many differentiations of the motor vehicle are possible, the choice of model tends to reflect the lifestyle of the owner. This allows skilful marketing to exploit the consumer's social aspirations by suggesting that a particular model will allow him to achieve his desired lifestyle. The versatility of the motor vehicle also calls for marketing skill in explaining to the customer the precise range of functions that any particular model can perform.

One of the crucial issues in marketing is how far the manufacturer should market the model rather than the range. This is related to a wider issue of the advantage of selling a 'full line' under a single brand name or 'badge'. The badge is a symbol of the quality of product: Ford, for example, is widely associated with mechanical reliability, Volkswagen for durability, Volvo for safety, Citroën with technical sophistication, and so on. Customers for motor vehicles progress through a life cycle during which the pattern of their movements and the size of their family change. By marketing the badge rather than the model, the manufacturer can attract customers for life, who will trade up and down the model range, confident that each of the models shares with the others the quality that they value most. When promoting the badge, it is important that the range includes a model at the bottom end with which the young customer can begin. It is less important to have a model in the extreme luxury category, since few customers are likely ever to earn sufficient income to afford one, except perhaps at the very end of their life cycle. On the other hand, although the volume of production may be low, luxury models can carry a high margin of profit, and their sophisticated image may help to raise the sales of other models in the range.

Novelty is a major aspect in attracting customers, and the annual sales of most models peak fairly early during their life. Because of the large number of different components involved, however, it is difficult to introduce an all-new vehicle, and many new models are, in fact, restyled versions of older models with updated specifications, effected by modifying a few components. R and D is thus an ongoing process in which information from salesmen and from service engineers about deficiencies in the performance of existing components are continuously fed back to prompt further improvements. Likewise marketing is an ongoing process in which much of the emphasis is placed on explaining to consumers the advantages of the latest specification changes, or drawing their attention to new styling.

8.5   THE PRESSURE FOR RATIONALIZATION

The cost structure of the motor industry indicates that component production should be concentrated upon a small number of very large plants in order to fully exploit economies of scale. To justify large-scale production it may be necessary for the same component to be used in several different models in the range. If the sales of the range are fairly modest, the producer may buy in the components from a specialist who supplies a number of different firms in the same industry. The specialist producer enjoys economies of scale which he may be able to pass on to his customers in lower prices. The disadvantage of this arrangement is that economies of vertical integration are lost.

Because of the variety of different components involved, it may be advantageous to produce different components in different locations. Sophisticated components can be produced where skilled labour is abundant, larger and heavier components where raw materials and energy are cheap, and so on. Production of components such as engines and transmissions, which afford substantial economies of scale, should be concentrated on the fewest plants. Components that are difficult or costly to transport should be produced close to the assembly line. The assembly line itself needs to be located somewhere near the 'centre of gravity' of the major sources of component supply and the major centres of consumer demand.

In inter-war Europe, economic nationalism encouraged high protective tariffs to stimulate domestic motor production for military and strategic reasons. It was not until the postwar period, with the formation of the European Community and the improvement of infrastructure through motorways and container handling systems, etc. that production could be specialized internationally to fully exploit economies of scale (Foreman-Peck, 1986).

In Britain the industrial heritage of protectionism was a large number of relatively small plants, most of which survived the war intact. Most of them needed to be enlarged and modernized, or closed down altogether in favour of new plants on green field sites. Only the highly integrated operations centred on Ford's Dagenham plant approximated to an efficient scale (although Ford did not buy control of the body-works at Dagenham until the late 1950s).

Restructuring along these lines was, however, inhibited by regional policy, which encouraged investment in declining peripheral regions remote from the major metropolitan markets of Europe. In Britain a system of industrial development certificates was introduced to restrict investment outside designated development areas. Companies that wished to rationalize by building new factories were often obliged to locate them in areas far away from the rest of their operations (Young with Lowe, 1974). The Regional Employment Premium subsidized payroll costs in designated areas. Moreover, companies that had high-cost plants already located in the regions were under political pressure not to close them down. The designation of development areas became a party political issue, particularly when the areas seeking designation contained marginal parliamentary constituencies. In the early 1970s for example, when the Scottish National Party was challenging many traditional Labour seats, a substantial budget was available for attracting companies to Scotland and discouraging those already there from closing down.

Employment protection policy also discouraged rationalization. Government was reluctant to see high-cost production units closed down. It preferred to avoid bankruptcies and liquidations by arranging the take-over of unprofitable firms. After a take-over or merger, the new management would often find itself preoccupied with the short-run problems of the 'lame ducks' it had acquired. The short-run losses incurred by the weaker operating divisions of the company also absorbed funds which could otherwise have been used to finance restructuring and long-term growth.

The British government's Redundancy Payments Act of 1966 reflects another aspect of employment protection which discouraged rationalization. It encouraged employers with high-cost plants to run them down through natural wastage rather than to shut them down and make all their employees redundant. The pace of rationalization was almost certainly slowed down as a result.

The delay in rationalizing production led to growing problems in the British motor industry. These were exacerbated by the OPEC oil price rises beginning in 1973, which escalated British wage costs, because the incomes policy in force at the time linked wage rates to the cost of living. In Japan, however, productivity improvements continued apace and import penetration by their low-price high-quality vehicles reached such a point that several countries, including Britain, negotiated voluntary export restraints. The British market was particularly vulnerable because of the absence of non-tariff import barriers of the kind found in France and Italy. It has also been suggested that the British market was particularly vulnerable because of the way that high-cost local manufacturers remained in business under the Ford 'price umbrella' – an umbrella that raised Ford prices in Britain up to 20 per cent above the prices of equivalent Ford models in continental Europe.

TABLE 8.2   Leading car market shares in Europe

Company	Percentage					
	1979	1980	1981	1982	1983	1984
Ford	12.0	11.1	12.3	12.4	12.6	13.0
Fiat	10.0	11.8	12.7	12.5	12.3	12.9
VW	12.2	11.8	12.6	11.8	11.7	12.0
Peugeot	17.1	14.6	13.2	12.4	11.8	11.7
General Motors	9.6	8.7	8.4	9.7	11.2	11.2
Renault	13.5	14.9	14.0	14.7	12.8	11.0
Japan (total)	7.3	9.8	9.2	8.9	9.4	9.6
Other	18.3	17.3	17.6	17.6	18.2	18.6
Total	100.0	100.0	100.0	100.0	100.0	100.0

Source: Ford of Europe.

8.6   THE FUTURE OF RATIONALIZATION IN EUROPE: SOME LESSONS FROM FORD

In 1984 Ford of Europe had the largest share of the European car market (see table 8.2). Ford is one of the 'big six' firms shown in the table which dominate volume car production in Europe. Despite their volume, however, these producers have, in the aggregate, been consistently unprofitable in the last five years. The somewhat smaller and more specialized manufacturers such as BMW, Mercedes–Benz, Volvo and Saab have enjoyed a much better record of profitability.

The low profitability of volume car production is a reflection of over-capacity in the industry – estimated to be at least 15 per cent. Private manufacturers such as Ford and General Motors blame this situation on the reluctance of state-owned or state-supported manufacturers to eliminate unprofitable operations. Companies such as Fiat, Renault and Peugeot price very aggressively in order to maintain volume, it is alleged, and rely on their status as 'national champions' to cover any losses they make with government grants or loans. There are signs, however, that the situation is changing: the top management at Renault has been replaced, for example, and the company's policy of avoiding compulsory redundancies has been abandoned. Nevertheless, for reasons explained below, excess capacity in Europe is unlikely to fall in the foreseeable future unless major closures are implemented.

Ford of Europe is widely recognized in the industry for the sophistication of its marketing and management, and in particular for the way that it has rationalized its European operations. Ford began manufacturing in Europe in 1911. Ford of Europe was formed in 1967 to co-ordinate its various European operations. In 1985 Ford of Europe had 22 manufacturing locations, with major industrial complexes in Britain and West Germany and large plants in Spain, Belgium and France. It also has research, development and testing facilities in Britain, West Germany and Belgium, and a national sales company in each of 15 European countries.

Rationalization at Ford means that many of its plants specialize in producing just a narrow range of components. The company's plants in South Wales, for example, produce mainly transmissions and related components for use in assembly operations elsewhere. Relative to other manufacturers, Ford is self-sufficient in a wide range of components, and actively promotes sales of Ford components to other manufacturers. The European Power Products Division, for example, sells 1.6 litre and 2.5 litre diesel engines, fast burn–lean burn petrol engines and transmissions, to other producers. The Diversified Products Operation is involved in both vertical and conglomerate diversification. Its operations include the processing of raw materials, the manufacture of aluminium radiators and climate control equipment, and the development of electronic products. In these fields, too, the company plans to develop its role as a supplier of components to other manufacturers.

Despite its relative strength compared to European competitors, the company recognizes that its trading position in Europe is far from secure. The demand for cars in Europe grew at only 0.6 per cent per annum in 1980–4, and the company's projected growth for 1985–90 is 1.6 per cent per annum – a slight improvement, but well below the rates anticipated in a number of markets outside of Europe (see table 8.3). With fairly static demand, and pressure for productivity improvements, the company's European workforce has shrunk from about 140,000 in 1979 to about 100,000 in 1985. Most of the adjustment has been effected by voluntary redundancies and early retirements, without the closure of any of the major

TABLE 8.3 Growth of European car sales (per cent per annum)

Period	Growth rate
1960–9	7.7
1970–9	2.4
1980–4	0.6
1985–90 OECD forecast	0.8
1985–90 Ford forecast	1.6

Source: Ford of Europe figures.

facilities. Given the importance of economies of scale at the plant level, however, it is doubtful if further contraction can be effected without a major closure. It is likely, though, that the company would prefer not to implement a closure of this kind. Although the company would never admit it, it would probably prefer to use the threat of closure to negotiate subsidies (or some form of import protection) from European governments or, better still, from the European Community itself.

Japanese competition poses a major threat to the European motor industry. The European industry is suffering from Japanese competition not only in Europe itself, but in third country markets where, of course, governments are unlikely to intervene to discourage Japanese imports in the way they have done in certain European countries. Ford estimates that Japanese manufacturers have a landed unit cost advantage of over $500 in West Germany and up to $1500 in some of Europe's traditional export markets. This is ascribed, not to any difference in capital per worker, but to differences in the work rate on the shop-floor. Bob Lutz, chairman of Ford of Europe, claims that in 1984 it took about 72 hours of labour to produce a Ford car in the United Kingdom, 35 hours to produce the same car in West Germany, and 18–20 hours to produce an equivalent car in Japan. Although there are some differences in the extent of vertical integration between Europe and Japan, it is estimated that after allowing for this, productivity in Japan is at least double that in Britain.

Ford is attempting to introduce a Japanese-style management philosophy into its European operations in a modest sort of way. In 1983 the company commissioned an 'insight' team to evaluate the Ford system of product development. The team compared the development of the Mazda 626 and the Ford Sierra – two cars aimed at the same buyers, built in similar volumes and introduced at similar times. It was found that Ford spent more than twice the man hours on development of their car. The team ascribed this to the fact that Ford's development involved too many narrowly specialized groups who felt themselves to be in direct competition with one another. They have now introduced a programme management concept to harmonize the goals of the specialists by introducing greater flexibility into the system.

The company is also looking to the Japanese philosophy to promote more harmonious industrial relations. It cites with approval the way that the threat of import competition in the US led, five years ago, to a new accord between the United Automobile Workers Union and the manufacturers, and Ford is looking for a similar accord with labour in Europe.

The nature of the Japanese challenge to Europe is, however, changing. Japanese manufacturers are now establishing a manufacturing presence in Europe through either wholly-owned green field investment, joint ventures, or licensing agreements. The crucial issue here is the local content of the assembled vehicle. At the moment this is relatively low, and if it is increased it seems likely that it will be done by subcontracting to local suppliers who supply only the Japanese and are heavily dependent upon them. This certainly appears to be existing practice in Japan. A switch within Europe, therefore, from European-owned to Japanese-owned assembly could have serious implications for existing European component suppliers. Downstream investments by Japanese firms in assembly could eventually lead to upstream divestments by European component manufacturers. If, on the other hand, Japanese manufacturers are willing to modify their component sourcing strategies by patronizing established European component producers, then the transfer of Japanese technology to Europe could well make a substantial contribution to overall competitiveness in the industry.

An improvement in European competitiveness would be reflected in increased penetration of overseas markets. The problem of relatively stagnant European demand could then be overcome by an improvement of the export trade. It is doubtful if Europe has the skills to compete with Japan in the volume production of small cars, but in the medium and large luxury categories – which are amongst the most profitable – its potential competitive position is quite strong.

In the past decade, the most profitable European manufacturers have tended to be those with the greatest penetration of the US market. The high value of the US dollar makes US sales very attractive to European producers, although the costs of meeting US emission and safety standards are very substantial too. Volkswagen is the only European manufacturer to have penetrated the US small car market in a big way, but several producers of larger cars – BMW, Mercedes–Benz, Volvo, for example – have enjoyed considerable success with larger luxury vehicles. Ford is now trying to emulate this success by establishing a prestige franchise – Merkur – to sell vehicles such as the Sierra XR4Ti to the compact luxury segment of the US market.

It is evident that rationalization is an ongoing process, and is likely to remain so for the foreseeable future. Within Europe, Ford is pursuing a number of specific programmes aimed at improving component quality – involving the introduction of lifetime guarantees on certain repairs effected by authorized dealers – and reducing the complexity of assembly sourcing to improve economies of scale. Between 1984 and 1985 Ford has reduced the number of product derivatives offered in Europe from over 2,500 to under 1,500, although the degree of complexity still remains high, since these figures do not include a large number of optional features offered on particular models.

It is also evident, however, that rationalization can no longer be effected on a purely European scale. The sourcing of the US market with European vehicles has already been mentioned. The Scandinavian market is already being sourced with small Ford cars produced in Brazil. It is conceivable that European manufacturers will begin to draw upon component suppliers from Brazil, Korea and Japan. Thus even if the European market were to grow faster than anticipated, the pressures for rationalization would still induce restructuring, and future divestments in the motor industry would still be likely to occur.

8.7 BACKGROUND NARRATIVE TO PEUGEOT'S ACQUISITION OF CHRYSLER (UK)

The highlights of the Chrysler/Peugeot story are well known (see, in particular, Young and Hood, 1977; Bhaskar, 1979; Grunberg, 1981, ch. 5; Maxcy, 1981; Wilks, 1984). Chrysler is one of the 50 largest private manufacturing corporations in the US in terms of sales, and the third largest US motor manufacturer, behind General Motors and Ford. In 1960 its two main rivals both had long-established European operations, but Chrysler did not. From about this time, Chrysler headquarters in Detroit pursued a deliberate policy of diversifying into the European motor industry. Forecasts made at the time suggested that the European car market would continue to grow rapidly, but in retrospect these forecasts were grossly over-optimistic. The chairman of Chrysler, Lynn Townsend, was personally committed to turning Chrysler into a fully-fledged multinational enterprise. Approaches were made to a number of established European firms and this eventually led to acquisitions in Britain, France and Spain. As a late entrant into the European market. Chrysler was unable to negotiate acquisition on favourable terms. It finished up acquiring those companies which its major indigenous competitors had, in many cases, already decided not to acquire.

In 1964 Chrysler took a 30 per cent stake in Rootes Motors, a British family-controlled firm founded in 1898, whose Hillman, Humber and Singer saloons enjoyed a reputation for quality in the medium–large size sector of the market. At the time this minority interest was acquired, Rootes had just entered the small car market with the launch of the Hillman Imp, a rear-engined car which was a close competitor of the Mini. The Imp was manufactured at a new 1.6 million square foot factory at Linwood, near Paisley on Clydeside, some 250 miles north of the main centre of Rootes operations around Coventry.

Sales of the Imp were disappointing and industrial relations at Linwood were poor. In its first full year of operation, Linwood operated at under half capacity. By 1967 Rootes was losing £10.7 million on a turnover of £171 million (Hood and Young, 1982, p. 64). At this time Chrysler increased its stake to 66 per cent of the voting shares. This acquisition of control required the consent of the British government because of an undertaking given by Chrysler in 1964.

A new family saloon, the Hillman Avenger, was launched from the Ryton factory in Coventry but the launch of two other models – the Chrysler 180 and the Chrysler Alpine – was switched to Chrysler's French subsidiary, mainly because of labour problems in Britain. Subsequently production of the 180 was transferred completely to Spain.

At the end of October 1975 the Chairman of the Chrysler Corporation, John J. Riccardo, indicated at a press conference in Detroit that in view of the corporation's adverse financial position, it was considering withdrawing from Britain. Riccardo's statement appears to have taken the British government by surprise. After intensive negotiations, the government agreed to support Chrysler to the tune of a maximum of £162.5 million between 1976 and 1979, while in return the company committed up to £64 million, agreed to the launch of new models and signed a Planning Agreement with the government (United Kingdom, House of Commons, 1976).

Notwithstanding the consultative arrangements called for by the Planning Agreement, it was announced abruptly on 10 August 1978 that Chrysler's European operations would be acquired by the French motor manufacturer PSA Peugeot–Citroën. Chrysler would receive US$230 million and a 15 per cent stake in the French company. It also obtained a seat on the supervisory board of PSA. The Planning Agreement continued in force, and the financial arrangements with the British government were taken over by the French company with certain minor modifications. However, by the time of the acquisition, the joint union–management consultative committees set up under the Planning Agreement were practically moribund, due to lack of interest in them within the company.

Altogether, PSA Peugeot–Citroën acquired control of 11 Chrysler European subsidiaries at this time, including a 99.62 per cent stake in Chrysler France and a 46.51 per cent stake in Chrysler España. It also acquired six import subsidiaries and two property subsidiaries in a separate deal shortly afterwards. The Chrysler Europe operation was renamed Talbot at the end of 1978 and in 1980 the management structure of the Peugeot and Talbot operations was unified. Also in 1980 the name of the Peugeot group was changed to Peugeot SA.

Chrysler's stake in Peugeot was valued on the Chrysler balance sheet at $323.9 million, as compared to a value on the Paris stock exchange on the date of agreement of $202 million. However, Chrysler reported that an independent valuation from a leading European investment banking firm valued the stake at above the balance sheet figure.

The European divestment was one of several undertaken by Chrysler about this time. Also in 1978 Volkswagen acquired a 67 per cent equity stake in Chrysler's Brazilian operation, and Chrysler reduced to 49 per cent its own stake in Chrysler Argentina. In 1979 General Motors agreed to purchase Chrysler's interests in its Colombian subsidiary and to purchase the fixed assets of its Venezuelan subsidiary. Divestments were also undertaken in Peru, Australia and South Africa. By 1980, Mexico was host to the only major Chrysler operation outside North America. The overseas operations divested by Chrysler between 1978 and 1980 had lost the company approximately $40 million in earnings between 1974 and 1977. Losses had been particularly heavy in France during 1977 because of a combination of cost inflation, falling market share and government price controls. In place of the divested operations, Chrysler had established a link with Mitsubishi, and set up an office in Tokyo.

Since the divestment, both the Chrysler parent company and the Peugeot group have been in financial difficulties. Both have been committed to heavy investment expenditures to launch new models. Having lost the confidence of their bankers, and of the private capital market in general, both have been obliged to obtain government underwriting for new loans. Chrysler was guaranteed up to $1.5 billion via a Loan Guarantee Act in 1979. Chrysler has had to make its US models comply with increasingly exacting pollution and safety standards, and adapt them to provide greater fuel efficiency at the same time. Peugeot has been financially stretched by losses incurred by the Citroën operation which it acquired in 1976. Another major acquisition coming only two years later has compounded the financial difficulties. As a result of these two acquisitions Peugeot has suddenly risen to become one of the six largest motor manufacturers in Europe, and its management has had to face the problems of imposing an overall corporate strategy on a diverse group of enterprises, each with their own independent traditions. Chrysler management, on the other hand, has been liberated from concern over its European operations, and has been able to concentrate on re-establishing its position within the US domestic market. Operating profits for Peugeot in 1984 suggest that it may now have turned the corner too.

8.8   THE LOGIC OF THE DIVESTMENT DECISION

The causes of Chrysler's poor performance in Europe are not hard to find. To begin with, Chrysler did not have the same kind of international reputation, marketing skills and technical know-how as did its two main

US rivals. In the 1960s Chrysler's profitability in the US rested upon an exciting range of large high-performance vehicles with a sporting image (Iacocca with Novak, 1985). The models were, however, far too large to appeal to the European consumer. The relatively staid vehicles produced by Rootes and Simca could not easily be promoted using Chrysler's marketing techniques.

The Chrysler management appears to have been overimpressed by optimistic forecasts of the growth of the European car market. As table 8.3 indicates, European car sales grew at an annual rate of 7.7 per cent during the 1960s, but the growth unexpectedly levelled off to only 2.4 per cent during the 1970s. Management may therefore have overvalued the assets it acquired in Europe, and have underestimated the severity of the competitive pressures that would develop in Europe as overcapacity emerged (particularly at the bottom end of the market).

Chrysler management may also have been concerned that its rivals Ford and General Motors could use profits generated in Europe to finance further expansion in the US. By investing in Europe, Chrysler was acquiring the ability to 'spoil' the European market for its rivals, and so indirectly strengthen its own position in the US (see chapter 3).

Management may also have hoped that European operations would generate new products that could be transferred to the US. Chrysler's 'home-grown' products lost their appeal to US consumers during the 1970s. Chrysler's share of the US car market fell from 16.1 per cent in 1970 to a mere 8.6 per cent in 1980. Indeed, it was one of the company's European-designed vehicles that helped the company to make substantial progress in the sub-compact segment of the US market at a time when it was rapidly losing ground in its traditional stronghold, the standard segment of the market. The popularity of the Plymouth Horizon and Dodge Omni allowed the company to increase its share of the sub-compact market from 4.8 per cent to 17.4 per cent between 1975 and 1978, at a time when its share of the standard market fell from 9.6 per cent to 2.7 per cent.

Chrysler US had few skills in the management of vertical integration. Compared to its two rivals, Chrysler relied heavily upon independent suppliers for components. In 1978 the company was using over 30,000 independent suppliers and purchased from them substantially all its requirements for batteries, bearings, bumpers, carburettors, passenger compartment interior trim, radiators, glass, steel, tyres and wheels.

Financially, the company was highly geared, and relied extensively on short-term bank loans. This insecure financial structure meant that the company faced a higher cost of capital than its rivals. It also meant that the company faced a very tight capital constraint when its trading difficulties became public knowledge during 1978.

The company also faced particular difficulties in Britain because of problems that it had inherited from Rootes. It was affected more seriously by the oil price rise than were its major rivals because its engines were relatively old, and therefore less fuel-efficient, and because it was weak in the small-car segment of the market to which consumers were switching.

Chrysler inherited from Rootes the problem that its most modern production facility, Linwood, was bedevilled by poor industrial relations. It also suffered from component supply problems caused by its remoteness from the heart of the UK engineering industry in the West Midlands. Transport costs were high: engines were cast at Linwood, the cylinder blocks were then taken to Coventry to be bored, and complete engines were then transported back to Linwood for installation before the completed vehicles were shipped south for sale. Chrysler was also committed to producing a vehicle – the Hillman Imp – for which there was very little demand. It was extremely difficult to boost sales of the Imp by cutting prices because its main competitor, the Mini, was itself underpriced because of shortcomings in the British Motor Corporation's cost accounting methods and its marketing strategy.

Political pressure and financial inducements had taken Rootes to Linwood in the first place, and the maintenance of employment at Linwood formed an integral part of the 1975 rescue plan. It was hoped that the Linwood plant would generate its own local supply industries, but this never materialized, possibly because the government underestimated the volume of demand needed to take advantage of economies of scale in the supply industries.

The failure of the Imp meant that the company could not generate sufficient internal funds to finance the development of new models. It has already been noted that R and D is an ongoing process. A buoyant demand for current models generates finance for further improvements to the range, helping to boost sales even further. If sales of existing models are low, however, then this virtuous circle becomes a vicious one. When R and D has to be cut back, models get older and their sales decline further; eventually the company faces extinction if there are no new models in the pipeline.

Chrysler management appears to have recognized fairly early that rationalization was required, but the shortage of funds meant that only a very limited programme could be pursued. They followed what must have seemed the obvious strategy of concentrating the production of the few new models they could afford on their French subsidiary, where productivity was much higher, and turning UK production into an assembly operation using mainly French components. From the British government's point of view, of course, this strategy seemed more like adverse discrimination than rationalization.

It is instructive to compare Chrysler's European operations with those of Ford, because Ford pursued the kind of policy that Chrysler needed to emulate (see section 8.6 above). Ford had, however, been much longer established in Europe, and so had more time in which to develop a coherent model range and to rationalize its production. Ford had relied heavily on green field investments to build up its European operations, and so when the 'Ford Europe' division was formed to impose integration, it avoided the problem of dealing with subsidiaries that had previously enjoyed a separate identity (although it did have to buy out certain minority interests). Ford had also by this time built up an effective dealer network offering a high standard of servicing with a uniform scale of charges. Ford's small cars, which until the development of the Cortina/Taunus were the basis of its model range, were all highly successful. In particular, the new Escort, introduced in 1980, was designed as a 'European' car. The success of these models has generated the finance necessary to support the development of the next. It has also spilled over to other models in the range: part of the success of the Granada, for example, may have been due to the fact that it is the obvious choice for the Cortina owners who wish to trade up to a luxury car.

It was clear by 1978 that Chrysler's financial position was so parlous that it had an urgent need to cease its loss-making European operations and to convert fixed assets into hard cash as quickly as possible. By selling out the entire European operation as a going concern, the company avoided redundancy payments and other closure costs which could have been financially crippling for the parent firm. The sell-out strategy also had substantial tax advantages in the US. What is not so clear, at first sight, is why Peugeot was so willing to take over Chrysler's European operations.

Peugeot is essentially a family firm that began operating a steel foundry in 1810, commenced producing bicycles in 1885, automobiles in 1889, and in 1965–6 underwent structural reorganization as part of a programme to become a major European motor producer. In 1976 the company took over the ailing Citroën company, which would otherwise have had to be nationalized (although Peugeot itself received government funds to help it 'turn around' its new subsidiary).

It appears that Peugeot planned to consolidate its position in the European market by becoming one of the very biggest producers. Peugeot management believed that only a small number of very large producers could survive in Europe in the long run, and it hoped that by becoming larger it could increase its own chance of survival.

Peugeot management also believed that it possessed substantial managerial expertise that could be transferred to Chrysler's European operations. The performance of the Citroën company had improved remarkably within two years, but although Peugeot management took much of the credit, it seems likely that Citroën was mainly sharing in a temporary general revival of European motor sales, and very little of its success was due specifically to Peugeot management.

There was clearly a potential to integrate Chrysler and Peugeot production in France, and in particular to exploit economies of scale in component production by designing new cars which used similar parts. There was also the possibility of integrating the marketing of Chrysler and Peugeot models.

Peugeot's acquisition also made sense from the point of view which asserts that US multinationals find it more difficult than European firms to adjust to a social and political climate which favours the gradual run down of an unsuccessful manufacturing facility to precipitate outright closure. There is some evidence that US managements in general find that a run down of production, through natural wastage in the work-force etc., is too expensive both in terms of finance and management time, and so prefer divestment to accepting responsibility for closure. They divest to indigenous companies which have greater expertise in raising funds from host governments. These funds are offered in order to 'save jobs' and avert redundancies. European governments are more willing to support indigenous firms for such purposes than they are to support foreign firms. This is particularly important in the case of France, with its tradition of government antipathy towards US multinationals. The Citroën case had already demonstrated Peugeot's skill in negotiating substantial loans from the French government.

On balance, therefore, it seems that Peugeot's acquisition of Chrysler had more to recommend it than did Chrysler's original investment in Europe. Although Peugeot may have overestimated their management skills, the underlying economic logic was probably sound. The value of Chrysler's European operation was probably higher to Peugeot than it was to Chrysler; though whether it was worth all that Peugeot paid for it remains a moot point.

The fact that Peugeot acquired the whole of Chrysler's European operation, rather than just the French part, may indicate the company's willingness to build upon the very limited intra-European integration that Chrysler had achieved. Alternatively, it may reflect Peugeot's desire to strengthen its dealer network in the UK. The most likely explanation, however, is that it reflects the high level of capital market transactions costs faced by Chrysler in disposing of its activities at short notice. It was noted in chapter 2 that companies divesting in response to a cash crisis may prefer to divest an entire group of activities, even though they might be able to get more for them if they had the time to split them up and sell them off separately. It is more attractive to sell to a single buyer whose price reflects the buyer's expectation that he can sell off peripheral or unprofitable activities later, at his leisure. Chrysler, therefore, divested because it urgently needed the part-cash payment to meet the liquidity crisis of the parent firm, and Peugeot acquired in the knowledge that it could make smaller scale divestments later if required.

8.9　THE PROGRESS OF RATIONALIZATION SINCE 1975

The business strategies pursued by Chrysler and Peugeot in the few years immediately prior to and immediately following the divestment are examined below under seven headings.

Marketing. Demand for Chrysler vehicles in the UK contracted sharply between 1975 and 1982. Table 8.4 shows that the company's share of the market for cars and light vans fell from 8.0 per cent in 1975 to 3.6 per cent in 1982. The ratio of the 1982 market share to the 1975 share is even lower than for BL, for which the corresponding figures are 30.7 per cent and 17.8 per cent. Over the same period Ford increased its market share from 21.5 per cent to 30.5 per cent, and Vauxhall (a General Motors affiliate) from 8.2 per cent to 11.7 per cent. A number of foreign manufacturers performed extremely well over this period, especially BMW, Volvo and Volkswagen, whilst the Japanese producers consolidated their position. The proportion of the UK market supplied by vehicles produced abroad increased from 33.1 per cent to 57.7 per cent. These figures include intra-firm imports of finished vehicles by multinational producers such as Ford, General Motors and, of course, Chrysler–Peugeot.

About three years after the acquisition, leading Chrysler dealers became Peugeot–Talbot dealers, of whom there are now approximately 500 in the UK. There has been no effort to integrate Peugeot and Citroën dealerships, presumably because Citroën products are highly distinctive, attract loyal customers and require special maintenance skills because of their ingenious and unusual engineering. The company has lost many dealerships in the UK since 1975, through defections to competitive franchises, splitting franchises and closing down. In 1980 it became clear that the dealership organization was very weak. Strenuous efforts have been made to improve dealer performance, including the introduction of an 'on the road' pricing policy and the withdrawal of franchise from dealers who perform badly.

Peugeot–Talbot models do not form an integrated range. In the spectrum from small to large vehicles, the Talbot Samba occupies a similar niche to the new Peugeot 205 (and the old Peugeot 104), while the Talbot Solara and Alpine models occupy a similar niche to the Peugeot 305. The Talbot Horizon, however, has a distinctive place as a short, spacious and relatively high performance front-wheel drive hatchback, filling the gap between the 205 and the 305. (The Talbot Sunbeam, a small car emanating

TABLE 8.4   Leading manufacturers' shares of the UK market for cars and light vans, 1975–82

Company	Source of production	Percentage 1975	Percentage 1982
Ford	Various	21.5	30.5
BL	Britain	30.7	17.8
Vauxhall	Various	8.2	11.7
Datsun	Japan	5.3	6.0
VW Audi NSU	W. Germany	4.0	5.9
Renault	France	4.7	4.1
Talbot	Various	8.0	3.6
Volvo/Daf	Sweden (mainly)	1.9	3.3
Fiat	Italy	3.2	2.8
Toyota	Japan	1.7	1.8
Citroën	France	1.8	1.5
BMW	W. Germany	0.6	1.5
Fiat licensees total		0.8	1.5
Lada	USSR	(0.6)	(1.1)
Polski–Fiat	Poland	(0.2)	(0.2)
Zastava	Yugoslavia	(0.0)	(0.2)
Peugeot	France	1.2	1.3
Honda	Japan	0.8	1.0
Mazda	Japan	0.9	1.0
Mercedes–Benz	W. Germany	0.5	0.8
Alfa–Romeo	Italy	0.7	0.6
Saab	Sweden	0.6	0.6
Skoda	Czechoslovakia	0.8	0.6
Colt	Japan	0.3	0.6
Daihatsu	Japan	0.0	0.3
Lancia	Italy	0.0	0.3
Hyundai	Republic of Korea	0.0	0.2
Suzuki	Japan	0.0	0.2
Subaru	Japan	0.0	0.2
Others	Various	1.5	0.3
Total		100.0	100.0
Total imports		33.1	57.7

Source: Society of Motor Manufacturers and Traders, *The Motor Industry of Great Britain*, various issues.

TABLE 8.5   Production of Chrysler–Peugeot vehicles in Britain and France, 1975–82

Model	Production of cars and light vans (1000s per annum)	
	1975	1982
Chrysler UK/Talbot UK		
Imp	8.0	—
Avenger	86.0	—
Hunter	136.0	27.2
Alpine	—	6.3
Solara	—	8.4
Horizon	—	14.2
Total	230.0	56.2
Chrysler France/		
Talbot France		
Simca 1000	71.3	—
Simca 1100	193.2	0.0
Simca 1301	36.1	—
Simca 1501	11.3	—
1307/8	46.7	—
180/2 litre	24.6	—
Samba	—	102.7
Horizon	—	71.3
Alpine	—	10.3
Solara	—	32.1
Tagora	—	3.3
Others	—	14.7
Total	383.2	234.5
Peugeot		
104	114.5	117.9
204	88.2	—
304	93.3	—
305	—	186.5
404	15.8	—
504	239.4	80.7
505	—	145.7
604	10.3	5.7
Total	561.4	536.5

from the 1975 rescue plan, and using many Avenger components, ceased production in 1981.)

The Samba and Solara/Alpine models appear to be sold at a discount relative to their Peugeot counterparts. The current premium for a Peugeot model over its Talbot counterpart is approximately 6 per cent, and this probably reflects the relatively modern engine and transmission, the more sophisticated suspension and general reputation for higher standards of manufacturing quality control. The Horizon has sold extremely well relative to other vehicles in the Talbot range, and at quite high prices – the 1.5 GL 5-speed Horizon was listed in the UK in July 1984 at £5,715, compared to £5,660 for the Peugeot 305 GR.

The top end of the Peugeot–Talbot range is weak. The ageing Peugeot 604 is being phased out, and its potential successor, the Talbot Tagora, has been a disaster ever since its launch in 1981; it ceased production in 1983. Only the Peugeot 505 has adequate sales. This weakness at the top of the range is somewhat ironic in view of the relative strength of the Rootes group in this niche under its Singer and Humber names.

Scale of production. The poor sales performance means that there has been little opportunity to exploit economies of scale in production. Table 8.5 reports the outputs of the major models of Chrysler UK, Chrysler France, Peugeot and Citroën in 1975 and 1982. In 1975 Chrysler had just commenced production of the Alpine, which was highly acclaimed by the motoring press and sold well for the first two years. By 1982, UK production of the Alpine had fallen to 6,500 units. The other major model, the Hunter, was kept in production only because of an export order for kits, supplied from Ryton to a state-owned assembly plant in Iran; it had been withdrawn from the UK market in 1979. The Iranian contract is one of the largest-ever export contracts in the world motor industry and is very important for Britain's reputation as an exporter to the Middle East; the need to avoid its cancellation was a major factor in the Chrysler rescue of 1975.

The scale economies enjoyed by the French operations are greater than those of the British operations because of the relatively high volume of Samba and Horizon production. The figures for Peugeot are even better: the 104, 305 and 505 all achieved outputs of over 100,000 units in 1982. Citroën produces the best-selling Visa, although the proliferation of the less successful Citroën models has caused problems for the Peugeot group.

It is when these production figures are compared with those of Chrysler's rivals that the true magnitude of the problem is revealed. Table 8.6 shows that in 1982, 186,000 Escorts were produced by Ford in the UK, and 281,200 in West Germany; 352,000 Renault 5s, 284,700 Renault 12s and a staggering 494,800 Volkswagen Golfs were produced in the same year.

TABLE 8.6   Changes in the sourcing of the UK market, 1980–2

| Country of production | Registration of cars and light vans (vehicles per annum) | |
	1980	1982
Talbot	90,874	56,196
UK	62,876	31,607
France	25,481	24,534
Eire	1,853	47
Spain	664	6
Others	0	2
Ford	464,706	474,192
UK	247,946	244,140
West Germany	85,091	100,349
Belgium	49,135	66,911
Eire	13,537	10,472
Spain	68,878	52,187
Others	119	133
General Motors	133,078	181,737
UK	82,233	102,573.
West Germany	29,147	30,062
Belgium	20,708	48,862
Others	990	276

Source: L'argus de l'automobile, various issues, and Talbot Motors.

The scale economies available to these producers far outweigh anything that could have been achieved with Chrysler or Talbot models.

Location of production. Between 1975 and 1982 the number of different models produced by Talbot in Europe fell from eleven to eight. Much of this reduction occurred in 1976 when the Hillman Imp, Humber Sceptre and Sunbeam Rapier were all withdrawn; the Talbot Sunbeam, introduced in 1977, was withdrawn in 1981.

Three of the six new models introduced since 1975 were until recently produced only in France or Spain; they are the Samba, Horizon and Tagora. Since 1980 the Horizon has been produced in the UK as well. Two of the new models were produced in both France and Britain – the Alpine and the Solara – and only one, the Talbot Sunbeam, was produced in Britain alone. Many of the components for the Alpine and Solara came from France, so that the British side of the joint manufacturing operations was little more than assembly.

The policy of concentrating production in France appears to have been followed by both Chrysler and Peugeot. It is reflected in a large volume of intra-firm exports from France to Britain. In 1982, 44 per cent of Talbot registrations in Britain were sourced from France (see table 8.6). In the same year, less than 0.1 per cent of Talbot registrations in France were sourced from Britain. If intra-firm trade in components is considered as well, the use of French production to source British operations becomes even more marked.

Table 8.6 shows that in the period 1980–2 both Ford and General Motors also sourced the UK market extensively from continental Europe, although it must be remembered that their European operations were much more extensive than those of Talbot. What is particularly striking, however, is that between 1980 and 1982 the dramatic reduction in Talbot sales in the UK was almost entirely accounted for by the contraction in UK production, consequent mainly on the closure of Linwood in 1981. UK production was halved, while French imports to the UK remained practically unchanged. UK production has now become relatively small within the Peugeot group as a whole (about 100,000 units per annum on average).

Use of common components. Chrysler models, like those of other manufacturers, utilized engines which were interchangeable. Since the Peugeot acquisition, there has also been common use of engines between the Talbot and Peugeot models. The Peugeot 205 uses some of the same engines as the Talbot Samba, and the Tagora SX used a V6 engine that is also fitted to the Peugeot 604. The Peugeot 104 coupés share a body shell with the Citroën LNA and the Talbot Samba.

Other examples of standardization include the use of Avenger and Alpine components in the Talbot Sunbeam, and the use of certain paint colours which are common to Talbot and Peugeot.

Vertical integration. During the 1970s Chrysler UK – like its US parent – was sometimes criticized for relying too heavily upon outside suppliers of components. It was alleged that the company was obliged to pay too high a price for its components, and also had difficulty guaranteeing supplies. However, the m.e.s. for producing many components was much higher than Chrysler's output of finished vehicles, so that in many cases it would have been impossible for the company to produce its own components on an efficient scale. Moreover, the company suffered so many disruptions of production in its own plants that it is difficult to see how internal sources of supply could be more reliable than external ones, especially when the company was able to 'shop around' among competing suppliers for a number of components. It seems likely therefore, that reliance on external suppliers was a rational response to the company's inability to exploit economies of scale.

In Europe, matters are rather different, however, now that Chrysler operations have been incorporated within the automobile division of Peugeot, because the Peugeot group is both larger and more diversified. It is involved, for example, in the cold-rolling of special steels, in the manufacture of transmissions, cycles, motor cycles, electrical and plastic components and armour-plating.

Even a large diversified company, however, may be unable to take full advantage of scale economies in components such as large engines for luxury cars. An alternative to relying on outside suppliers is for the company to undertake joint ventures with its competitors to produce these components, or to enter into a specialization agreement whereby companies can trade or barter components for one another's use. Inter-firm collaboration affords many of the advantages of full integration without some of the costs; it is of growing importance in the world motor industry.

Inter-firm collaboration. Continental European motor producers have for many years been more heavily involved in collaborative arrangements that their British and US counterparts. Fiat, for example, has at one time or another held financial interests in Citroën and Unic (a commercial vehicle manufacturer) in France and NSU in West Germany, and has licensed production of its models to Spain, Yugoslavia, Poland and the USSR. In France, state-owned Renault and privately-owned Peugeot have collaborated on a number of ventures in recent years.

Peugeot is a member of the Joint Research Committee with Renault, Volkswagen, Volvo, Fiat and BL which undertakes research into combustion technology, new materials, computerized engineering and a number of other subjects. Peugeot is involved with Fiat in the development and production of a new one-litre engine for the Fiat Uno and Peugeot 205, and in the production of a new van in Italy. The Peugeot subsidiary, Cycles Peugeot, has an agreement to manufacture motor cycle engines for Honda in Belgium and to assemble a Honda scooter in France for the Belgian market (Automotive Industry Data, 1983). Peugeot and Chrysler also entered into negotiations about industrial collaboration, soon after the acquisition, that explored the possibility of producing small Peugeot cars for the sub-compact market in the US, but so far there has been little to show for this. A recent development is an agreement to produce Peugeot cars in China.

Peugeot and Renault are involved with Volvo in a joint venture, manufacturing engines at Douvrin in France, and also jointly producing automatic transmissions in France. In 1981 Renault purchased a stake in Karrier Motors, a commercial vehicle manufacturer whose British operation was inherited by Peugeot from Chrysler UK, and acquired full control from Peugeot in 1983. The sale of commercial vehicle operations by Peugeot to Renault has a precedent in the disposal of the Berliet commercial vehicle subsidiary of Citroën to Renault when Peugeot acquired control of Citroën. It represents the continuation of a policy, beginning with the Renault acquisition of Saviem in the 1950s, by which heavy commercial vehicle production in France has been concentrated upon Renault. (It is worth noting, however, that Peugeot's original intention was to sell Chrysler's truck operations to Daf.)

The fact that Talbot operations are now beginning to be integrated within the operations of a company which is, in turn, heavily involved in inter-firm collaboration with other motor producers is perhaps one of the most hopeful aspects of the current situation. It suggests that any future Talbot model will be able to incorporate much more modern components than any of its predecessors, and that it will be produced more cheaply because of the more effective exploitation of economies of scale. Only skilful design can, of course, guarantee success. However, some of the conditions necessary for success have now been met, even though these conditions alone are not sufficient to guarantee Talbot's future.

Other aspects. Engineering research and styling has been concentrated on the main facility in Paris, and the Whitley research centre, near Coventry, has been closed down. The UK parts operation has been rehoused on a single floor at Tile Hill, Coventry, from an inefficient multi-floor plant in Birmingham. An interesting aspect of this development is that the Citroën UK parts operation has now been consolidated with that of Peugeot–Talbot. Peugeot has entered into rallying to give its models a more sporting image, and the Peugeot 205 has proved extremely successful in competition.

8.10 FUTURE PROSPECTS FOR PEUGEOT

It has been estimated that there was approximately 15 per cent excess capacity in the Western European motor industry in 1984. Some of this is ageing high-cost plant, kept going in the hope that jobs can be maintained until there is an economic recovery, whilst other is modern highly automated plant, utilized more intensively, but often still with a margin of spare capacity.

The consumer market is highly competitive, particularly in countries such as Belgium which produce very few of their own models. Competition is less intense in France because of the obstruction of Japanese imports by French customs procedures. British conditions are also special because of the high costs of the only major indigenous mass producer, BL, and because the demand for right-hand drive rather than left-hand drive vehicles encourages price discrimination against British consumers. The EC Competition Directorate has recently attempted to discourage producers from using their tied retail outlets to enforce discrimination of this kind.

Many major motor producers incurred losses in Europe in 1983, which was an exceptionally difficult year. Peugeot has been incurring losses continuously since the acquisition of Chrysler Europe, though its performance in 1983 was significantly better than in 1982. In 1983 the company lost FF 2604 million (approximately £250 million). Sales were up over 12 per cent on the previous year, reflecting the successful launch of new models – the Peugeot 205 and the Citroën BX – which enabled the company to increase its share of the French market at the expense of its main rival Renault. Both French companies have, however, been losing ground in Europe to rivals such as Ford. It is also unfortunate for Peugeot in that the impact of its new models has been less than it might have been if the overall market had been more buoyant.

Funding the development of these new models has imposed a considerable burden of debt on the company. Financial restructuring has marginally diluted the interests of the major shareholders (the Peugeot family and their trusts 33.9 per cent, Chrysler Corporation 14.1 per cent and the family-controlled Michelin tyre company 9.0 per cent). Between 1980 and 1983 the company's current liabilities have risen steadily relative to its total assets, and long-term loans have increased substantially. At the end of 1983 the ratio of long-term loans to assets net of current liabilities was 65 per cent, which is very high, at least by British standards. Accounts payable and bills payable have risen from FF 6,123 million in 1980 to FF 13,371 million in 1983. A company in such a shaky financial position would normally find it difficult to increase its credit with suppliers in this way; the company's good standing with its creditors almost certainly reflects their perception that the company's obligations are underwritten by the government.

As already noted, the group's UK operation is now somewhat peripheral to its main activities, and indeed the number of production workers in the UK is currently less than 4,000, and total UK employees number about 6,300. The reduction in employment has been associated with a substantial increase in productivity at the company's main plant at Ryton and with a notable lack of industrial disputes. In 1984 Ryton workers produced a phenomenal 37 cars per man without the use of robots. Coupled with the recent weakness of sterling, this has led UK production costs to fall relative to those in France. In 1983 the automobile division, which is dominated by French operations, had a productivity of 8.3 vehicles per employee per year, compared to 8.7 for Volkswagen and 10.9 for Fiat. These figures need to be interpreted with caution because of the different sizes and sophistication of the vehicles being built, and because of different degrees of vertical integration within the companies concerned. Nevertheless they suggest that productivity in the company's French factories is unimpressive, and it is well known that some of these factories have recently been the scene of serious industrial disputes, especially the Talbot plant at Poissy near Paris and the Citroën plant at Aulnay. It has been estimated that in the UK, labour costs are now approximately £200 per car lower than in France.

The future of the company's Stoke plant, near Coventry, remains uncertain because of its heavy dependence on the continuation of the Iranian contract. A new medium-sized car – the Peugeot 309 – was launched from Ryton early in 1986. It is a medium-sized family saloon that replaces the Horizon and will compete with the Vauxhall Astra, Ford Orion and the BL Maestro. Together with the 205 it forms the basis for a new look Peugeot range that will in due course replace the ageing models in the existing range. There was some controversy between the French and British managers over the decision to badge the car as a Peugeot rather than a Talbot. Badging the car as a Talbot might have helped the company to break back into the UK fleet market, where the 'high profile' business customers still prefer to nominally buy British. It might also help to raise sales of other vehicles in the Talbot range. Badging the car a Peugeot, on the other hand, has probably produced a better initial response from non-fleet buyers.

The major obstacle to even further investment in the UK would appear to be the company's financial dependence on the French government. So long as this dependence persists, political considerations are likely to prevent any substantial long-run 'export of jobs' from France to the UK. It will be interesting to see what marketing and production strategies the company adopts for the Peugeot 305 replacement due to be launched in 1987.

8.11   CONCLUSIONS, AND IMPLICATIONS FOR FUTURE RESEARCH

When evaluated carefully, it can be seen that the Chrysler–Peugeot case study illustrates a number of the points made earlier in the paper. Chrysler's initial investment in Europe represents a managerial error of judgement. It was based, implicitly, upon an overvaluation of the company's own technical and marketing strengths, and probably an overestimation of the future growth of the European car market too. Chrysler's divestment in 1978 may be therefore regarded as an error-correcting reversal of a flawed investment policy.

The divestment decision itself may be judged a success from Chrysler's point of view, in the sense that the company was able to find a buyer with sufficient liquidity to take its entire European operations off its hands. The international capital market worked well – although the role of the French government in supporting the acquisition of the French assets should not be underestimated. The French government clearly took the view that the maintenance of existing jobs in the French motor industry overcame any objection that the acquisition turned volume car production in France into a Peugeot–Renault duopoly.

The fact that Chrysler divested to a European rival is consistent with the view that the company was unable to make the best possible use of its European facilities because of the poor technology and marketing skills within the company.

Peugeot acquired from Chrysler some facilities which were defective – notably the Linwood plant which was in the wrong location and suffered from endemic poor industrial relations. In accordance with the analysis presented in section 8.3, this facility was closed down.

Other facilities were in the right location but were producing too wide a range of products on too small a scale – particularly where components were concerned. The facilities needed to be rationalized so that each produced a smaller range of products on a larger scale. Integration within a larger group is one of the remedies prescribed by the theory, and several component manufacturing facilities have indeed continued operations within the framework of the Peugeot group.

Yet other facilities were simply producing the wrong product. The Talbot range of vehicles was ageing and needed replacement. The most promising replacement vehicle forthcoming since the acquisition was launched from Ryton early in 1986. The Ryton plant is in a suitable location, has a work-force with a good productivity record in recent years, and simply lacks the right product. The future of Peugeot's manufacturing operations in the UK hinges on the sales of this car. The failure of a new volume car began the difficulties of the Rootes group in the 1960s. The failure of the new British Peugeot could signal the end of assembly – and eventually all manufacturing – in the former Rootes plants. Its success, on the other hand, could enable Peugeot to recover the very strong position in the European market that it enjoyed at the time of the Chrysler acquisition.

Although the British government disliked the way that Chrysler management disclosed its problems with its UK operations to its US shareholders before it informed the British government, and although it disliked Chrysler's hard-line bargaining tactics, the government got what it wanted from Chrysler during the 1975 negotiations – namely the preservation of employment at Linwood and the production of new models in the UK. A purely British solution to the UK operations had been ruled out as early as 1967, when the Labour Government failed to find acceptable alternatives to the Chrysler acquisition of Rootes. By the time of the divestment in 1978 it was widely appreciated that BL management could not cope with the acquisition of Chrysler, and that Chrysler would not fit in to the European operations of either Ford or General Motors. Given Chrysler's financial difficulties, therefore, and the government's own reluctance to provide further finance, it was forced to admit that there really was 'no alternative' to the Peugeot take-over if jobs were to be preserved.

It is possible that when a foreign company sells off a plant, there may be a capital outflow which temporarily worsens the host country's balance of payments, or weakens the exchange rate. This applies, however, only when funds are raised in the host country to buy out the foreign firm. In the case of the Chrysler divestment, the capital account of the British balance of payments was largely unaffected because the transfer of funds occurred between France and the US.

It could be argued that it was wrong of Chrysler management to convert into cash, assets whose purchase had been partly subsidized by the UK government through the rescue agreement of three years earlier. This argument does not, however, make very good economics if the assets would in fact be better managed by another company. Moreover, Peugeot agreed to take over Chrysler's outstanding commitments under the rescue plan, and in so far as these obligations reduced the market value of Chrysler's UK assets, the final distribution of rewards may have been quite equitable.

The Chrysler–Peugeot case also demonstrates the magnitude of rationalization problems in the motor industry, and the enormous level of funding that rationalization requires. Peugeot has essentially rationalized on a European basis and, as noted earlier, there is likely to be considerable excess capacity in the European motor industry for some time. It is conceivable that rationalization on a European basis is no longer sufficient to ensure viability, and that the successful companies of the 1990s will be those that have rationalized on a global scale. It is too early, though, to pass judgement on this issue yet.

9

Postscript and Prospect

9.1 INTRODUCTION

The 1980s is an interesting decade for the professional economist to practise in. Fifteen years ago very few people anticipated the major changes which have occurred in the world economy since then. Businessmen have had to rethink many of their attitudes. For example, fifteen years ago very few managers seem to have evaluated the international licensing of technology as a serious option, whereas now many would regard it as an essential element in their overall corporate strategy. Governments too have had to modify their views. The growth of collaborative agreements between firms, for example, resulting from positive attempts to rationalize industries, has obliged governments to rethink their hitherto critical attitudes to cartels and mergers. In economic theory, major rethinking has been going on, most notably in macroeconomics, but also in the fields of industrial organization and the theory of the firm.

This chapter considers what further rethinking needs to be done in order for economists to deepen their understanding of the forces affecting the evolution and growth of large firms – and MNEs in particular. The one thing most inimical to theoretical progress is a complacent view that the 'new theories' that have emerged in the last decade have answered all the salient questions. There are many questions that remain to be answered and, it is argued below, only further synthesis of different strands of thinking will provide satisfactory answers to them.

At a time of far-reaching structural change, it is natural to look back into history for guidance on how previous generations coped – or failed to cope – with similar upheavals. It is, after all, an old adage that one of the best ways to anticipate the future is to understand the past. This means that the economist must interpret the historical record on the growth of firms if he is to make successful predictions about their future. This exercise, however, reveals a number of shortcomings of existing theory which were not apparent in the critical review of the literature presented in Chapter 2. The reason they did not emerge at that earlier stage is that they only become serious when the theory is asked to do more than simply explain the configuration of MNE activities that exists at a single date.

This chapter suggests three new avenues of research. Each lies at the borderline of economics and other social sciences, and therefore calls for a fairly broad-based synthesis of ideas from different intellectual traditions. Each avenue is particularly pertinent to explaining the evolution of the MNE, although its potential implications are far wider than this. The first concerns the reason why, in certain epochs, MNEs of one particular nationality outperform MNEs of other nationalities. The vitality of a firm's home economy seems to affect the success not only of its domestic operations, but its international operations too, and the reasons for this are not entirely clear. In the terminology of chapter 2, the question is why the ownership advantage of the firm seems to be strongly influenced by its nationality, and why particular nations have achieved this ascendancy of ownership advantage at particular stages in their history. It is suggested in section 9.2 that a synthesis of the theory of entrepreneurship and the theory of the MNE is necessary to answer questions of this kind.

Section 9.3 considers relations between the MNE and the nation state, drawing on concepts from the theory of public choice. Particular attention is given to the role of source-country governments in 'protecting' the overseas operations of their MNEs. Finally, section 9.4 considers the still wider issue of the influence of social and cultural factors on the performance of MNEs.

9.2 ENTREPRENEURSHIP AND THE DYNAMICS OF OWNERSHIP ADVANTAGE

It is a commonplace that, where entrepreneurship is concerned, there is a gap in conventional economic theory (Baumol, 1968). Theories of the MNE are no exception to this. The entrepreneur fills the gap labelled 'fixed factor' in the neoclassical theory of the firm. Entrepreneurial ability is analogous to a fixed factor endowment because it sets a limit to the efficient size of the firm. The fact that neoclassical theory reduces the entrepreneur to a mere 'fixed factor' illustrates well the essentially static nature of its approach.

The same criticism may be applied to the 'ownership advantage' approach. Ownership advantage may be interpreted as a measure of the net wealth accruing from past entrepreneurial activity (Buckley, 1983b;

Hirsh, 1976) but it tells us nothing about how this entrepreneurial activity was actually carried on, and offers little clue about the circumstances under which it is likely to continue in the future. Why is it, for example, that in the past five hundred years technological and commercial advantages have passed from Italy to the Netherlands, and then to England, Germany and the United States? Why did US advanced technology appear exactly when it did, and why has it diffused so slowly to developing countries as compared to Western Europe? Why has it diffused much more rapidly to Japan? Current theories are too static to handle issues of this kind.

It is possible to develop a dynamic theory of ownership advantage using the economic theory of the entrepreneur. The theory views the economy as an evolutionary system (Nelson and Winter, 1982) whose future is very uncertain, so that decisions have to be made on the basis of mere speculations about their consequences. Even the *probable* consequences of decisions cannot be estimated objectively: there are often insufficient precedents with which to estimate the relative frequencies of different outcomes (Knight, 1921). People therefore hold different opinions about what is the best policy to pursue. Decisions upon which opinions differ may be termed judgemental decisions, and a person who specializes in taking judgemental decisions is defined as an entrepreneur (Casson, 1982a). The entrepreneur is important because at turning points in the evolutionary process it is his judgement which most often prevails.

There is one aspect of this theory that is particularly relevant to the MNE, and that is the idea that the most crucial entrepreneurial judgements take place on 'the frontier'.

Schumpeter (1934) defines the entrepreneur as someone who innovates by carrying out 'new combinations'. Leibenstein (1978) emphasizes judgement in identifying 'gaps' to be filled, and Penrose (1959) judgement in finding 'interstices' to explore. Kirzner (1973, 1979) emphasizes the importance of alertness to opportunity. This activity of exploring new opportunities takes place on the frontiers of knowledge. Other activity takes place on the territorial frontier: voyages of discovery to new lands, for example, or expeditions to prospect for mineral deposits. In historical terms, the exploitation of the frontiers of technology and territory seem to have gone hand in hand. In eighteenth- and nineteenth-century Britain, the industrial revolution at home was accompanied by the commercial exploitation of new colonial territories abroad. In the late nineteenth-century United States, the exploitation of the mid-Western frontier was paralleled by inventive activity in the Eastern states. Several other examples could be given from earlier periods.

The historical parallel between territorial and technological frontiers is matched by a theoretical parallel. It is a feature of any frontier that the environment in which people operate is not properly mapped out or fully understood. Since people do not have a proper model of the 'frontier territory', it is difficult for them to make choices which are 'optimal' in the usual sense of that word (Simon, 1983). People may not know exactly where the frontier is, nor how far it extends, nor how many rival 'prospectors' there are and where exactly they are 'located'. It is difficult for people to plan rationally under these circumstances, and even more difficult to imagine how any kind of equilibrium distribution of frontier activity could emerge.

Another feature of frontiers is that property rights are usually ambiguous and ill-defined. As the frontier moves forward, the law moves along behind. It usually consolidates the position that has already been attained. The theory of the entrepreneur analyses the kind of situation that frontiersmen – working in a legal vacuum – are likely to generate. Where people on the frontier are drawn from a unified social group, they will tend to appropriate the frontier in accordance with custom. Custom cannot, however, anticipate all eventualities. It may dictate, for example, that priority of discovery confers ownership, but fail to indicate just how much of a newly discovered territory may be fairly appropriated. Custom may recognize the rights of individuals to keep newly discovered information secret, but may equally recognize the rights of others to extract the information by subterfuge, if they can.

Where there is a mixture of social groups on the frontier, it is more likely that force and not custom will govern appropriability, and that the strongest group will consolidate its position through the laws that it finally imposes upon the others.

There is reason to believe that the nature of the frontier has undergone further significant change in the last twenty years or so. Many Western nations still seem to equate the knowledge frontier with the embodiment of advanced technology in new products. Such thinking may be misleading, however. The knowledge frontier may now have more to do with the management of international production and distribution systems for high-quality low-priced goods built to fairly standard specifications. World markets in computers, for example, are saturated with entrepreneurs seeking monopoly rents from new products and finding that these rents are increasingly short-lived as each new product is rendered obsolete by its successor. Because of their short life, new products must be produced immediately in large volumes if their fixed costs are to be spread over a reasonable length of production run. The key to such an exercise lies in the successful overall management of a production system, and this skill is not specific to the launching of new products. The same skills can be applied to mature products, and can produce rents simply from an overall cost advantage. Novelty of the product will, of course, continue to be a source of rents in the future, but the magnitude of these rents may have been overestimated in the past, and led to a mis-direction of entrepreneurial effort. Reliable performance, and low price made possible by scale economies, may have been sacrificed too much by producers for the sake of novelty of design.

Successful frontier activity requires a combination of skills: the ability to identify profit opportunities, the judgement to evaluate them and the tactical awareness to exploit them properly.

The identification of profit opportunities involves synthesizing information from diverse sources. Identifying a potential innovation, for example, requires the entrepreneur not only to make contact with the inventor, but also to know something about the activities which the invention may displace. Skill in making social contacts is invaluable in obtaining information of this kind, and to exercise this skill it is often important for the entrepreneur to gain entry to the right social group.

Judgement is required because imponderables always have a crucial effect on the profitability of an innovation. There are diminishing returns to collecting 'objective' information: sooner or later the entrepreneur must rely upon subjective assessments. Entrepreneurs who have acquired a varied background – through travel or migration, for example – are most likely to develop judgement of this kind.

Tactical awareness is important in securing exclusive rights to the opportunity, and thereby appropriating the maximum reward from it. Dynamic considerations suggest that a particularly successful appropriation strategy is likely to be the 'pre-emptive strike'. Once a discovery is made, the entrepreneur quickly extracts all the economically relevant information from what he has found, and uses it to guide him towards further discoveries before others learn of his find and draw similar conclusions for themselves. An entrepreneur with a good 'track record' may attract a following of potential imitators, and may have to resort to diversionary tactics to put them 'off the scent'. At the same time he will attempt to consolidate his position by erecting 'barriers to entry' – which in this context could be anything from physical defences to announcements of threatened reprisals against imitators. Where resources are difficult to defend, the entrepreneur may attempt to monopolize more easily defensible resources which are complementary to them, e.g. if the entrepreneur has discovered a new technology, he may attempt to monopolize the raw material sources on which the exploitation of the technology depends.

The theory of the entrepreneur makes it possible to identify the kind of skills which favour business success. The 'frontier' concept indicates that these skills are most likely to belong to the social extrovert, the migrant and the military officer. This in turn provides a link with the kind of cultural values most likely to encourage entrepreneurship (Redlich, 1956).

Cultures which promote entrepreneurship are most likely to prove viable in the long run. Cultural differences may explain, for example, why foreign entrepreneurs often persistently identify opportunities that are missed by indigenous entrepreneurs. The foreign culture may accord higher status to the skills that make for entrepreneurial success. Even when the indigenous population is inventive, it may be foreign entrepreneurs who adopt the inventions and appropriate the economic rewards. Cultural differences may also explain why in some countries indigenous entrepreneurs are so much slower to learn from foreign example than in others. The very narrow background of the indigenous entrepreneurs in some countries may make the practices of the foreign entrepreneurs seem quite alien to them: their inclination is to resist the innovations, rather than to imitate them.

9.3   THE MNE AND THE NATION STATE

In current economic theories of the MNE the *multinational* aspect receives much less attention than the *enterprise* aspect. An extreme position on this is taken by Williamson (1981), who discusses the theory of the MNE as though it were merely a special case of the theory of the firm.

It was, in fact, political concern about the threat to national sovereignty that sparked off post-war interest in the MNE (Servan-Schreiber, 1968; Vernon, 1971). Economic theories of the MNE assume a fixed configuration of nation states. Taking the nation state for granted, they inquire into the viability of the enterprise. This is the thrust of the Hymer–Kindleberger approach: given the costs of operating across national borders, what are the economic advantages of doing so? But this question can be turned around the other way. Given the economic advantages of operating on a global scale, what is the rationale for continuing to split up the world into different nation states? Is the nation state really viable in a world where the barriers to organization over distance have been substantially reduced by jet travel and modern telecommunications?

To answer this question it is necessary to inquire into the economic functions of the nation state. Four main functions may be distinguished: legislation, adjudication, protection and executive government. Legislation involves making laws which specify which individuals and institutions are entitled to hold property, and establishes general principles for the allocation of rights between them. Casuistry is normally needed to interpret the law in specific cases. Adjudication involves applying the law in situations where conflict has arisen. Adjudication involves both casuistry and the weighing of evidence. Protection involves upholding rights on behalf of individuals and institutions. Protection against fellow citizens is effected by policing and deterrent sentencing. Protection against aliens is effected by national defence, though if deterrence fails and rights are violated, there may be recourse to war. Executive government involves exercising rights which have been reserved for the state and are delegated to members of the government.

Government is financed mainly through taxation, though other sources of revenue are available: fines, the sale of licenses, state trading profits, tariff revenues, seignorage on currency issues, capital gains from devaluation of the national debt, and so on.

With the world split up into different nation states, each claiming sovereignty over some particular territory, an individual entrepreneur may, within limits, choose the state from which he takes citizenship. Although he is likely to be born a citizen of one particular country, he does not necessarily have to remain a citizen of that country if economic incentives suggest otherwise. The same point applies to a legal entity such as a firm. Differences in legislation mean that the privileges offered to firms – joint stock organization, limited liability and, above all, rights to confidentiality – may differ between states. A firm registered under one jurisdiction may change to another by arranging to be taken over by a holding company registered elsewhere. Companies such as Shell and Unilever maintain dual nationality, whilst it is reported that before the outbreak of World War II the Nestlé Company of Switzerland had arranged a scheme of triple nationality so that its property would be secure whoever won the threatened war. An early example of an MNE that changed its nationality is given by Jones (1985b).

With both individuals and firms having a choice of national allegiance, it seems reasonable to postulate an international market for the services of nation states. The 'product' is the bundle of services provided by the nation state. The 'payment' is principally the tax obligations imposed by the state. The 'price' is therefore the value of the services provided per unit of taxation.

The privileges of corporate organization are just one element in the package offered by the government. Fair adjudication when the company is in the right – coupled, perhaps, with the opportunity for bribery and corruption when the company is in the wrong – is also very valuable. The private costs of the adjudication process are an important component of transaction costs, and so the minimization of these costs is a major consideration. Freedom of contract, and immunity for *ad hoc* interventions by the government executive are important too; when the executive does intervene, e.g. by regulating markets, it should be in response to rent-seeking lobbying by the company (Krueger, 1974).

For the MNE, however, the quality of the protection afforded for its assets is almost certainly the paramount consideration. A colonial power, for example, is able to offer much better protection to firms in its dependent territories than are other nations. This suggests that an enterprising businessman seeking to operate in the colonies would seek citizenship of the colonizing nation, if he did not have it already, and would register his company under the jurisdiction of the colonial government. Likewise, if sovereignty over a colonial territory changes, it may be advantageous for entrepreneurs to seek new protectors by changing their corporate identity.

The net benefits conferred by a protector cannot be assessed without taking account of the tax liabilities involved. When entrepreneurs can shop around for protection, protectors must compete for custom by offering protection on reasonable terms. Imperial or colonial powers may demand high taxes to support high levels of military spending. Nations with little economic strength must compete by offering important legal privileges and low taxation: e.g. attracting banking by offering exceptional confidentiality, offering flags of convenience to ship owners who wish to operate with low safety standards, tax havens for those who wish to exploit opportunities for transfer pricing, and so on.

It is inevitable that from time to time rival protectors come into conflict with each other. Protectors, for example, may make rival claims to the same territory. This is particularly likely on the frontier. As noted earlier, unappropriated frontier territory is especially attractive to entrepreneurs. To begin with, entrepreneurs are operating in a legal vacuum, being entirely self-reliant where protection is concerned. Secrecy, subterfuge and the rule of force determine the appropriation of frontier territory, especially where the rival entrepreneurs are drawn from different social groups. In due course, each entrepreneur will appeal to his protector to consolidate his position by helping him to defend the territory he has acquired. If the territory is valuable, e.g. rich in minerals, he can expect vigorous protection because of the potential tax revenues involved. There is, however, a clear incentive for each protector not merely to consolidate established positions, but to attempt to expropriate property held under weaker protection. Where valuable resources are at stake, nations may easily be drawn into war. This is likely to lead to mutual expropriation of existing foreign investments even if these are nowhere near the frontier. Instability on the frontier may therefore spill over to raise protection costs elsewhere, and damage the climate for foreign investment as a whole.

The leaders of nation states have other strategic decisions to make, besides choosing the combination of protection and taxation they will offer to their entrepreneurs. Decisions relevant to the MNE concern the setting of tariffs, the management of the currency, and the 'laying off' of part of national defence to a 'superpower'. Where tariffs are concerned, the leaders face a trade-off between tariffs and taxes as sources of revenue.

Under certain circumstances, reducing tariff rates reduces tariff revenues, but increases the profitability of trade and hence increases the tax revenue yielded by a given rate of tax. Matters are complicated by the fact that selective tariff reductions affecting imports from specific countries may be more productive of taxation than general tariff reductions. A sophisticated policy of tax and tariff setting may therefore lead to the creation of customs unions and free trade areas. It is worth noting that the operations of MNEs may well affect the viability of alternative customs arrangements, so that not only do customs arrangements influence MNE behaviour, but MNE behaviour may influence the choice of customs arrangements.

National leaders must also decide upon whether to issue an independent currency which yields seignorage, or whether to back the currency, either wholly or partly, with precious metals or with the currency of another nation (or a portfolio of the same). The advantage of backing the currency is that it reduces the risks of currency instability perceived by businessmen, and so contributes to greater production and higher tax revenue. It is well known that the international financial operations of MNEs increase the economic efficiency of currency markets (in a narrow sense, at least) and so heighten the risk that mismanagement of an independent currency will lead to drastic financial readjustments. Thus the MNE reduces the viability of independently managed currencies and encourages nation states to base their currencies on a widely diversified portfolio of financial assets.

Finally, national leaders may decide that their own territory is too small and compact to warrant complete self-sufficiency in the provision of defence. This encourages the formation of defence unions, or the delegation of defence to a superpower. Entrepreneurs in industries of great strategic importance – aerospace, armaments, etc. – may perceive a distinct advantage in seeking the direct protection of a superpower. For reasons of security, the superpowers may encourage entrepreneurs to produce only within their borders. This suggests that strategically important industries will be non-multinational and will be located principally in the territories of the superpowers.

This discussion of the economic role of the nation state may seem somewhat fanciful but, in other contexts, economic theory already reaches well into the domain of public choice (Mueller, 1979). The view that nation states operate in a market environment underlines the fact that nation states are not permanent institutions. Like enterprises, some grow, while others survive only a short time. The recent economic history of Europe illustrates this very well. The break-up of the Austro-Hungarian empire made some European companies into MNEs overnight (Teichova, 1983). These MNEs promoted advances in armaments technology and the growth of strategic industries in the interwar period. Rival prospecting for raw materials to supply these industries led to international tension in the years before World War II. After the war, the map of Europe was redrawn again, and greater emphasis was placed on European political union under the aegis of the US as superpower. The conversion of military technology to civilian uses, when combined with US marketing skills, gave the US the economic power to sustain this role. It was under this protection that US companies acquired the confidence to invest in Europe on a large scale.

9.4   THE ROLE OF CULTURAL FACTORS

It is unsatisfactory to take an exclusively economic view of the nation state. The services provided by the state support cultural as well as business activities. The nation state is usually a formal constitutional structure superimposed upon an existing informal structure of social customs. The rule of law under the constitution merely consolidates a culture enforced through respect for tradition. (The main exception to this generalization is that some constitutions are based on a concept of 'natural law'.)

Where the law is based on tradition, the prevailing system of property rights may not always appear rational from an economic point of view. Information, for example, is the bread and butter of social discourse, but certain kinds of information have also developed into important economic commodities. The legal system in most countries still reflects the attitudes to information that evolved in a pre-commercial and pre-industrial age. Even in the most developed economies, many legal questions regarding the appropriability of information have still to be resolved. Many of the transaction costs in the market for information – discussed in the literature on licensing – arise ultimately not from the limitations of legal draftsmanship or technical problems of enforceability, but from the inappropriateness of social conventions regarding information as perceived from an economic point of view. Differences between developing countries and developed countries over the appropriability of technology probably owe just as much to different cultural attitudes as they do to economic conflict over the price at which the technology should be transferred.

Because the nation state has typically evolved to protect a social group whose members share a common culture, the territorial boundaries between nation states reflect the interplay of several different factors. Cultures tend to develop on a tribal or ethnic basis, with regional variations reflecting adaptation to differences in the physical environment.

Culture is transmitted by the movement of people, and in particular by large-scale migrations. Mass migration may represent a direct response to economic incentives: the 'push' due to the exhaustion of resources in established settlements, for example, and the 'pull' of new opportunities on the territorial frontier. Natural disasters and social upheavals may also cause mass migration. Physical geography is important in determining when and where resources become exhausted and – to a lesser extent – where new ones are discovered. It is also an important influence on the network of migration flows as, at each location, it affects the relative costs of migrating to different destinations.

Once again, recent European history illustrates the point. Jewish intellectuals, pushed out of Germany by Nazi persecution, and attracted by the frontier philosophy of the US, took with them the scientific skills which helped the US to achieve technological supremacy in World War II and in the decades afterwards. It is arguable, for example, that US direct investment in West Germany in the 1960s was only transferring back to Germany the know-how that had been lost to it in the inter-war period.

The MNE is playing an increased role in the international movement of people, and hence in the dissemination of culture. Within the MNE, high-level personnel – managers, engineers, consultants – move internationally on assignments varying from a day or so to a lifetime. What is particularly significant is that these personnel tend to meet only other personnel from the same firm, or from other MNEs. Thus the 'internal labour market' of the MNE tends to create a new social grouping. The pressures of economic survival acting on the firm tend to confer on this group cultural values which are attuned very closely to the pursuit of profit.

From a social point of view, the MNE has already begun to function as a major agent of social change. Economic theories tend to focus upon how the behaviour of the MNE is determined by its response to the environment. In historical perspective, however, the relation between the MNE and its environment is a two-way interaction, with the culture developed and transmitted by the MNE becoming a major influence on the environment in which it operates. It is this two-way interaction between firm and environment, in which both economic and cultural factors play their part, that generates the process of business growth that is recorded in history.

Bibliography

Abegglen, J. C. (1973) *Management and Worker: The Japanese Solution*, Tokyo: Sophia University.

Alchian, A. A. and Demsetz, H. (1972) Production, Information Costs and Economic Organization, *American Economic Review*, 82, 777–95.

Alford, B. W. E. (1973) *W. D. & H. O. Wills and the Development of the UK Tobacco Industry*, London: Methuen.

Aliber, R. Z. (1970) A Theory of Direct Investment. In C. P. Kindleberger (ed.) *The International Corporation*, Cambridge, Mass.: MIT Press, 17–34.

Altshuler, A. et al. (1984) *The Future of the Automobile*, London: Allen and Unwin.

Automotive Industry Data (1983) *Joint Venture and Collaboration Agreements*, Lichfield, Staffs: AID.

Babbage, C. (1832) *On the Economy of Machinery and Manufacturers*, London: Charles Knight.

Bain, J. S. (1956) *Barriers to New Competition*, Cambridge, Mass.: Harvard University Press.

Ball, M. (1980) The Contracting System in the Construction Industry, Department of Economics, Birkbeck College, University of London, Discussion Paper No. 86.

Baranson, J. (1981) *The Japanese Challenge to US Industry*, Lexington, Mass.: Lexington Books.

Barker, T. C. (1960) *Pilkington Brothers and the Glass Industry*, London: Allen and Unwin.

Barker, T. C. (1977) *The Glassmakers*, London: Weidenfeld and Nicolson.

Barker, T. C. (1985) Pilkington: The Reluctant Multinational, mimeo.

Batra, R. N. and Ramachandran, R. (1980) Multinational Firms and the Theory of International Trade and Investment, *American Economic Review*, 70, 278–90.

Baumol, W. J. (1968) Entrepreneurship in Economic Theory, *American Economic Review* (Papers and Proceedings), 58, 64–71.

Baumol, W. J., Panzar, J. C. and Willig, R. D. (1982) *Contestable Markets and the Theory of Industry Structure*, New York: Harcourt Brace Jovanovich.

Beamish, P. M. (1984) The Role of Joint-Equity Ventures in the Theory of the Multinational Enterprise. In B. M. Wolf (ed.) *Proceedings of the International Business Division of the Administrative Sciences Association of Canada*, 5(8), 32–41.

Beaton, K. (1957) *Enterprise in Oil: A History of Shell in the United States*, New York: Appleton–Century–Crofts.

Bennathan, E. and Walters, A. A. (1960) *The Economics of Ocean Freight Rates*, New York: Praeger.

Bhaskar, K. (1979) *The Future of the UK Motor Industry*, London: Kogan Page.

Boddewyn, J. J. (1983a) Foreign Direct Divestment Theory: Is it the reverse of FDI Theory? *Weltwirtschaftliches Archiv*, 119, 345–55.

Boddewyn, J. J. (1983b) Foreign and Domestic Divestment and Investment Decisions: Like or Unlike? *Journal of International Business Studies*, Winter 1983, 23–35.

Brooke, M. Z. (1985) *Selling Management Service Contracts in International Business*, Eastbourne: Holt Rinehart Winston.

Brooke, M. Z. and Remmers, H. L. (1978) *The Strategy of Multinational Enterprise: Organisation and Finance*, 2nd edn, London: Pitman.

Brown, B. D. (1978) Is Multinational Enterprise in Retreat? Foreign Divestment in the Multinational Investment Cycle: The US Experience, mimeo.

Brown, W. B. (1976) Islands of Conscious Power: MNCs in the Theory of the Firm, *MSU Business Topics*, 24, 37–45.

Brown, W. B. (1984) Firm-Like Behaviour in Markets: The Administered Channel, *International Journal of Industrial Organisation*, 2, 263–76.

Bruce, A. (1986) State-to-Private Sector Divestment: The Case of Sealink. In J. Coyne and M. Wright (eds) *Divestment and Strategic Change*, Deddington, Oxon: Philip Allan, 202–44.

Buckley, P. J. (1981) A Critical Review of Theories of the Multinational Enterprise, *Aussenwirtschaft*, 36, 70–87. Reprinted in P. J. Buckley and M. C. Casson (eds) *The Economic Theory of the Multinational Enterprise: Selected Papers*, London: Macmillan, 1–19.

Buckley, P. J. (1983a) Macroeconomic versus International Business Approach to Direct Foreign Investment: A Comment on Professor Kojima's Interpretation, *Hitotsubashi Journal of Economics*, 24, 97–100.

Buckley, P. J. (1983b) New Theories of International Business: Some Unresolved Issues. In M. C. Casson (ed.) *The Growth of International Business*, London: Allen and Unwin, 34–50.

Buckley, P. J. (1985a) New Forms of International Industrial Cooperation. In P. J. Buckley and M. C. Casson (eds) *The Economic Theory of the Multinational Enterprise: Selected Papers*, London: Macmillan, 39–59.

Buckley, P. J. (1985b) Testing Theories of the Multinational Enterprise: A Review of the Evidence. In P. J. Buckley and M. C. Casson (eds) *The Economic Theory of the Multinational Enterprise: Selected Papers*, London: Macmillan, 192–211.

Buckley, P. J. (1985c) The Economic Analysis of the Multinational Enterprise: Reading versus Japan, *Hitotsubashi Journal of Economics*, 26, 117–24.

Buckley, P. J. and Casson, M. C. (1976) *The Future of the Multinational Enterprise*, London: Macmillan.

Buckley, P. J. and Enderwick, P. (1984) *The Industrial Relations Practices of Foreign-owned Firms in British Manufacturing Industry*, London: Macmillan.

Buckley, P. J. and Enderwick, P. (1985) Manpower Management in the Domestic and International Construction Industry, mimeo, Bradford: University of Bradford Management Centre, and Belfast: University of Belfast Department of Economics.

Business International (1976) *International Divestment: A Survey of Corporate Experience*, Geneva and New York: Business International.

Calvet, A. (1981) A Synthesis of Foreign Direct Investment Theories and Theories of the Multinational Firm, *Journal of International Business Studies*, 12, 43–60.

Casson, L. (1960) *The Ancient Mariners: Seafarers and Sea Fighters of the Mediterranean in Ancient Times*, London: Gollancz.

Casson, M. C. (1979) *Alternatives to the Multinational Enterprise*, London: Macmillan.

Casson, M. C. (1982a) *The Entrepreneur: An Economic Theory*, Oxford: Martin Robertson/Blackwell.

Casson, M. C. (1982b) The Theory of Foreign Direct Investment. In J. Black and J. H. Dunning (eds) *International Capital Movements*, London: Macmillan. Reprinted in P. J. Buckley and M. C. Casson (eds) *The Economic Theory of the Multinational Enterprise: Selected Papers*, London: Macmillan, 113–42.

Casson, M. C. (1984) The Theory of Vertical Integration: A Survey and Synthesis, *Journal of Economic Studies*, 11(2), 3–43.

Casson, M. C. (1985) Multinational Monopolies and International Cartels. In P. J. Buckley and M. C. Casson (eds) *The Economic Theory of the Multinational Enterprise: Selected Papers*, London: Macmillan, 60–97.

Casson, M. C. in association with Barry, D., Foreman-Peck, J., Hennart, J.-F., Horner, D., Read, R. A. and Wolf, B. M. (1986) *Multinationals and World Trade: Vertical Integration and the Division of Labour in World Industries*, London: Allen and Unwin.

Casson, M. C., Barry, D. and Horner, D. (1986) The Shipping Industry. In M. C. Casson and associates, *Multinationals and World Trade: Vertical Integration and the Division of Labour in World Industries*, London: Allen and Unwin, 343–71.

Caves, R. E. (1982) *Multinational Enterprise and Economic Analysis*, Cambridge: Cambridge University Press.

Caves, R. E. (1971) International Corporations; the Industrial Economics of Foreign Investment, *Economica*, New Series, 38, 1–27.

Caves, R. E. and Mehra, S. (1985) Entry of Foreign Multinationals into US Manufacturing Industries, mimeo.

Champernowne, D. G. (1953) The Economics of Sequential Sampling Procedures for Defectives, *Applied Statistics*, 2, 118–30.

Chandler, A. D. Jr (1962) *Strategy and Structure*, Cambridge, Mass.: MIT Press.

Chandler, A. D. Jr (1977) *The Visible Hand: The Managerial Revolution in American Business*, Cambridge, Mass.: Harvard University Press.

Chopra, J., Boddewyn, J. J. and Torneden, R. L. (1978) US Foreign Divestment: A 1972–1975 Updating, *Columbia Journal of World Business*, Spring 1978, 14–18.

Clark, L. (1980) The Organisation of the Labour Process in Construction: Subcontracting in the Building Industry, In *The Production of the Built Environment: Proceedings of the Second Bartlett Summer School*, July 1980, 3–53.

Clark, R. (1979) *The Japanese Company*, New Haven, Conn.: Yale University Press.

Coase, R. H. (1937) The Nature of the Firm, *Economica* (New Series), 4, 386–405.

Commons, J. R. (1934) *Institutional Economics: Its Place in Political Economy*, New York: Macmillan.

Contractor, F. J. (1981) *International Technology Licensing*, Lexington, Mass.: Lexington Books.

Contractor, F. J. (1983) Technology Licensing Practice in US Companies: Corporate and Public Policy Implications, *Columbia Journal of World Business*, 18(3), 80–8.

Corley, T. A. B. (1985) The Nature of Multinationals, 1870–1939, mimeo.

Coyne, J. (1986) Direct Divestment by Management Buy-Out: Variant and Variety. In J. Coyne and M. Wright (eds) *Divestment and Strategic Change*, Deddington, Oxon.: Philip Allan, 140–65.

Coyne, J. and Wright, M. (eds) (1986) *Divestment and Strategic Change*, Deddington, Oxon.: Philip Allan.

Crossley, C. and Greenhill, R. (1977) The River Plate Beef Trade. In D. C. M. Platt (ed.) *Business Imperialism: An Inquiry based on British Experience in Latin America*, Oxford: Clarendon Press, 284–334.

Davenport-Hines, R. P. T. (1985a) Glaxo as a Multinational before 1963, mimeo.

Davenport-Hines, R. P. T. (1985b) Vickers as a Multinational before 1945, mimeo.

Davidson, W. H. (1980) The Location of Foreign Direct Investment Activity: Country Characteristics and Experience Effects, *Journal of International Business Studies*, 12, 9–22.

Davies, P. N. (1978) *Sir Alfred Jones: Shipping Entrepreneur Par Excellence*, London: Europa.

Deakin, B. M. in collaboration with Seward, T. (1973) *Shipping Conferences: A Study of their Origins, Development and Economic Practices*, Cambridge: Cambridge University Press.

Dixit, A. K. and Stiglitz, J. E. (1977) Monopolistic Competition and Optimum Product Diversity, *American Economic Review*, 67, 297–308.

Dubin, M. (1975) Foreign Acquisitions and the Growth of the Multinational Firm, Doctoral thesis, Graduate School of Business Administration, Harvard University.

Duncan, A. J. (1974) *Quality Control and Industrial Statistics*, Homewood, Ill.: Richard D. Irwin.

Dunning, J. H. (1958) *American Investment in British Manufacturing Industry*. London: Allen and Unwin.

Dunning, J. H. (1977) Trade, Location of Economic Activity and the Multinational Enterprise: A Search for an Eclectic Approach. In B. Ohlin, P. O. Hesselborn and P. M. Wijkman (eds) *The International Allocation of Economic Activity*, London: Macmillan.

Dunning, J. H. (1981) *International Production and the Multinational Enterprise*, London: Allen and Unwin.

Dunning, J. H. (1983) Changes in the Structure of International Production: The Last 100 Years. In M. C. Casson (ed.) *The Growth of International Business*, London: Allen and Unwin, 84–139.

Dunning, J. H. (1985a) The Eclectic Paradigm of International Production: An Up-date and a Reply to Its Critics, mimeo.

Dunning, J. H. (1985b) *Japanese Participation in British Industry*, Beckenham, Kent: Croom Helm.

Dunning, J. H. and Cantwell, J. (1982) Joint Ventures and Non-Equity Foreign Involvement by British Firms with Particular Reference to Developing Countries: An Exploratory Study, University of Reading Discussion Papers in International Investment and Business Studies, No. 68.

Dunning, J. H. and McQueen, M. (1982) The Eclectic Theory of the Multinational Enterprise and the International Hotel Industry. In A. M. Rugman (ed.) *New Theories of the Multinational Enterprise*, Beckenham, Kent: Croom Helm, 79–106.

Dunning, J. H. and Rugman, A. M. (1985) The Influence of Hymers' Dissertation on the Theory of Foreign Direct Investment, *American Economic Association Papers and Proceedings*, 75, 228–32.

Eaton, B. and Lipsey, R. G. (1978) Freedom of Entry and the Existence of Pure Profit, *Economic Journal*, 88, 455–69.

Ellis, F. (1978) The Banana Export Activity in Central America 1947–1976, Ph.D. thesis, Institute of Development Studies, University of Sussex.

Fellner, W. (1949) *Competition among the Few: Oligopoly and Similar Market Structures*, New York: Alfred A. Knopf.

Foreman-Peck, J. (1986) The Motor Industry. In M. C. Casson and associates, *Multinationals and World Trade: Vertical Integration and the Division of Labour in World Industries*, London: Allen and Unwin, 141–74.

Franko, L. G. (1971) *Joint Venture Survival in Multinational Corporations*, New York: Praeger.

Franko, L. G. (1973) Joint International Business Ventures in Developing Countries: Mystique and Reality, Geneva: Center for Education in International Management, Working Paper.

Franko, L. G. (1982) Use of Minority and 50-50 Joint Ventures by US Multinationals as an Indicator of Trends in 'New Forms' of International Investment, Paper presented to the Meeting on Changing International Investment Strategies: The 'New Form' of Investment in Developing Countries, Paris, 15–19 March, Paris: O.E.C.D. Development Centre, CD/R (82) 1–35 Working Document.

Friedmann, W. G. and Kalmanoff, G. (1961) *Joint International Business Ventures*, New York: Columbia University Press.

Gabriel, P. R. (1967) *The International Transfer of Corporate Skills: Management Contracts in Less Developed Countries*, Cambridge, Mass.: Harvard University Press.

Gaffikin, F. and Nickson, A. (1984) *Jobs Crisis and the Multinationals: Deindustrialisation in the West Midlands*, Nottingham: Russell Press.

Gordon, R. J. (1982) Why US Wage and Employment Behaviour Differs from that in Britain and Japan, *Economic Journal*, 92, 13–44.

Graham, E. M. (1974) Oligopolistic Imitation and European Direct Investment in the United States, Doctoral thesis, Graduate School of Business Administration, Harvard University.

Graham, E. M. (1978) Transnational Investment by Multinational Firms: A Rivalistic Phenomenon, *Journal of Post-Keynesian Economics*, 1, 82–99.

Graham, E. M. (1985) Intra-Industry Direct Foreign Investment, Market Structure, Firm Rivalry and Technological Performance. In A. Erdilek (ed.) *Multinationals as Mutual Invaders: Intra-industry Direct Foreign Investment*, Beckenham, Kent: Croom Helm, 67–88.

Gray, P. (1984) The Growth of Intra-firm Trade and the Evolving Pattern of World Trade, mimeo.

Greenhill, R. (1977) Shipping. In D. C. M. Platt (ed.) *Business Imperialism 1840–1930: An Inquiry Based on British Experience in Latin America*, Oxford: Clarendon Press, 119–55.

Grunberg, L. (1981) *Failed Multinational Ventures: The Political Economy of International Divestments*, Lexington, Mass.: Lexington Books.

Hamel, G. and Prahalad, C. K. (1985) Do You Really Have a Global Strategy? *Harvard Business Review*, 63(4), 139–48.

Harrigan, K. R. (1985) *Strategies for Joint Ventures*, Lexington, Mass.: Lexington Books.

Hennart, J-F. (1982) *A Theory of Multinational Enterprise*, Ann Arbor: University of Michigan Press.

Hennart, J-F. (1985) Comment on Graham. In A. Erdilek (ed.) *Multinationals as Mutual Invaders: Intra-industry Direct Foreign Investment*, Beckenham, Kent: Croom Helm, 88–93.

Henriques, R. (1960) *Marcus Samuel: First Viscount Bearsted and Founder of the 'Shell' Transport and Trading Company 1853–1927*, London: Barrie and Rockliff.

Hillebrandt, P. (1985) *Economic Theory of the Construction Industry*, 2nd edn, London: Macmillan.

Hirsh, S. (1976). An International Trade and Investment Theory of the Firm, *Oxford Economic Papers*, 28, 258–70.

Hladik, K. J. (1985) *International Joint Ventures: An Economic Analysis of US – Foreign Business Partnerships*, Lexington, Mass.: Lexington Books.

Hood, N. and Young, S. (1982) *Multinationals in Retreat: The Scottish Experience*, Edinburgh: Edinburgh University Press.

Horst, T. O. (1971) The Theory of the Multinational Firm: Optimal Behaviour under Different Tariff and Tax Rates, *Journal of Political Economy*, 79, 1059–72.

Horst, T. O. (1974) The Theory of the Firm. In J. H. Dunning (ed.) *Economic Analysis and the Multinational Enterprise*, London: Allen and Unwin, 31–46.

Hymer, S. H. (1976) *The International Operations of National Firms: A Study of Direct Investment*, Cambridge, Mass.: MIT Press (previously unpublished doctoral dissertation, 1960).

Hymer, S. H. (1979) The Multinational Corporation and the International Division of Labour. In R. B. Cohen, N. Felton, J. van Liere and M. Nkosi (eds), *The Multinational Corporation: A Radical Approach; Papers by Stephen Herbert Hymer*, Cambridge: Cambridge University Press.

Hymer, S. H. and Rowthorn, R. (1970) Multinational Corporations and International Oligopoly: The Non-American Challenge. In C. P. Kindleberger (ed.) *The International Corporation*, Cambridge, Mass.: MIT Press, 57–91.

Inman, R. P. (ed.) (1985) *Managing the Service Economy: Prospects and Problems*, Cambridge: Cambridge University Press.

Iacocca, L. with Novak, W. (1985) *An Autobiography*, London: Sidgwick and Jackson.

Ireland, N. J. (1983) Monopolistic Competition and a Firm's Product Range, *International Journal of Industrial Organisation*, 1, 239–52.

Jaffee, S. (1986a) *The Kenyan Horticultural Export Sector: An Economic and Institutional Analysis of Alternative Marketing Channels*, Report submited to USAID/Kenya.

Jaffee, S. (1986b) Invisible Hands, Visible Hands and Iron Fists: A Conceptual Framework for Analysing Agricultural Export Marketing Systems in Africa, mimeo.

Jensen, M. C. and Meckling, W. (1976) Theory of the Firm, Managerial Behaviour, Agency Costs and Ownership Structure, *Journal of Financial Economics*, 3, 304–60.

Johnson, C. (1982) *MITI and the Japanese Miracle: The Growth of Industrial Policy, 1925–1975*, Stanford, Calif.: Stanford University Press.

Johnson, H. G. (1970) The Efficiency and Welfare Implications of the International Corporation. In C. P. Kindleberger (ed.) *The International Corporation*, Cambridge, Mass.: MIT Press, 35–56.

Jones, G. (1984) The Growth and Performance of British Multinational Firms before 1939: The Case of Dunlop, *Economic History Review*, 36, 35–53.

Jones, G. (1985a) The Multinational Expansion of Dunlop 1890–1939, mimeo.

Jones, G. (1985b) The Gramophone Company: An Anglo-American Multinational, 1898–1931, *Business History Review*, 59, 76–100.

Kamien, N. and Schwartz, (1982) *Market Structure and Innovation*, Cambridge: Cambridge University Press.

Kay, N. M. (1983) Multinational Enterprise: A Review Article, *Scottish Journal of Political Economy*, 30, 304–12.

Khoury, S. J. (1980) *Transnational Mergers and Acquisitions in the United States*, Lexington, Mass.: Lexington Books.

Killing, J. P. (1983) *Strategies for Joint Venture Success*, New York: Praeger.

Kindleberger, C. P. (1969) *American Business Abroad*, New Haven, Conn.: University Press.

Kindleberger, C. P. (1984a) Plus ça change – A New Look at the Literature. In C. P. Kindleberger, *Multinational Excursions*, Cambridge, Mass.: MIT Press.

Kindleberger, C. P. (1984b) Multinational Ship Ownership, mimeo.

Kirzner, I. M. (1973) *Competition and Entrepreneurship*, Chicago: University of Chicago Press.

Kirzner, I. M. (1979) *Perception, Opportunity and Profit*, Chicago: University of Chicago Press.

Kitching, J. (1973) *Acquisitions in Europe: Causes of Corporate Successes and Failures*, New York and Geneva: Business International.

Klein, B., Crawford, R. G. and Alchian, A. A. (1978) Vertial Integration, Appropriable Rents and the Competitive Contracting Process, *Journal of Law and Economics*, 21, 297–326.

Klein, B. and Leffler, K. (1981) The Role of Market Forces in Assuring Contractual Performance, *Journal of Political Economy*, 89, 615–41.

Knickerbocker, F. T. (1973) *Oligopolistic Reaction and the Multinational Enterprise*, Cambridge, Mass.: Division of Research, Graduate School of Business Administration, Harvard University.

Knight, F. H. (1921) *Risk, Uncertainty and Profit* (ed. G. J. Stigler), Chicago: University of Chicago Press.

Kogut, B. and Singh, H. (1985) Entering the United States by Acquisition or Joint Venture: Country Patterns and Cultural Characteristics, mimeo.

Kojima, K. (1973) A Macroeconomic Approach to Foreign Direct Investment, *Hitotsubashi Journal of Economics*, 14, 1–21.

Kojima, K. (1978) *Direct Foreign Investment: A Japanese Model of Multinational Business Operations*, London: Croom Helm.

Krueger, A. O. (1974) The Political Economy of the Rent-seeking Society, *American Economic Review*, 84, 291–303.

Lancaster, K. (1966) A New Approach to Consumer Theory, *Journal of Political Economy*, 74, 132–57.

Lancaster, K. (1979) *Variety, Equity and Efficiency*, Oxford: Basil Blackwell.

Liebenstein, H. (1978) Entrepreneurship and Development, *American Economic Review*, 58, 72–83.

Lloyd, P. E. and Strutt, J. (1983) Recession and Restructuring in the North West Region: The Policy Implications of Recent Events, Working Paper No. 13, North West Industry Research Unit, University of Manchester.

McAleese, D. and Counahan, M. (1979) 'Stickers' or 'Snatchers'? Employment in Multinational Corporations during the Recession, *Oxford Bulletin of Economics and Statistics*, 41, 345–58.

McLean, J. G. and Haigh, R. W. (1954) *The Growth of Integrated Oil Companies*, Boston, Mass.: Division of Research, Graduate School of Business Administration, Harvard University.

McManus, J. C. (1972) The Theory of the International Firm. In G. Paquet (ed.) *The Multinational Firm and the Nation State*, Toronto: Collier Macmillan.

Magee, S. P. (1977) Information and the Multinational Corporation: An Appropriability Theory of Direct Foreign Investment. In J. N. Bhagwati (ed.) *The New International Economic Order*, Cambridge, Mass.: MIT Press.

Maxcy, G. (1981) *The Multinational Motor Industry*, London: Croom Helm.

Mishan, E. J. (1976) *Elements of Cost–Benefit Analysis*, 2nd edn, London: Allen and Unwin.

Monteverdi, K. and Teece, D. J. (1982) Supplier Switching Costs and Vertical Integration in the Automobile Industry, *Bell Journal of Economics*, 13, 206–13.

Mueller, D. C. (1979) *Public Choice*, Cambridge: Cambridge University Press.

Moores, B. (ed.) (1986) *Are They Being Served?*, Deddington, Oxon.: Philip Allan.

Nelson, R. R. and Winter, S. G. (1982) *An Evolutionary Theory of Economic Change*, Cambridge, Mass.: Harvard University Press.

Ng. Y.-K. (1983) *Welfare Economics: Introduction and Development of Basic Concepts*, London: Macmillan.

Nicholas, S. J. (1983) Agency Contracts, Institutional Modes, and the Transition to Foreign Direct Investment by British Manufacturing Multinationals before 1939, *Journal of Economic History*, 43, 675–86.

Nider, J. (1968) *On the Contracts of Merchants* (trans. C. H. Reeves, ed. R. B. Shuman) Norman: University of Oklahoma Press (1966).

Oi, W. Y. and Hurter, A. P. Jr (1965) *Economics of Private Truck Transportation*, Dubuque, Iowa: William C. Brown (chapter 2 reprinted as 'A Theory of Vertical Integration in Road Transport Services'. in B. S. Yamey (ed.) *Economics of Industrial Structure*, Harmondsworth: Penguin (1973) 233–62).

Okun, A. M. (1981) *Prices and Quantities: A Macroeconomics Analysis*, Washington, D.C.: Brookings Institution.

Oman, C. (1984) *New Forms of International Investment in Developing Countries*, Paris: OECD.

Paliwoda, S. (1981) *Joint East–West Marketing and Production Ventures*, Aldershot, Hants: Gower Press.

Pearce, R. D. (1983) Industrial Diversification amongst the World's Leading Multinational Enterprises. In M. C. Casson (ed.) *The Growth of International Business*, London: Allen and Unwin, 140–79.

Pedler, F. (1974) *The Lion and the Unicorn in Africa: The United Africa Company 1787–1931*, London: Heinemann.

Penrose, E. T. (1959) *The Theory of the Growth of the Firm*, Oxford: Blackwell.

Porter, M. E. (1981) *Competitive Strategy*, New York: Free Press.

Porter, M. E. (1985) *Competitive Advantage*, New York: Free Press.

Rae, J. B. (1965) *The American Automobile: A Brief History*, Chicago: University of Chicago Press.

Read, R. A. N. (1983) The Growth and Structure of Multinationals in the Banana Export Trade. In M. C. Casson (ed.) *The Growth of International Business*, London: Allen and Unwin, 180–213.

Read, R. A. N. (1986) *The Banana Industry: Oligopoly and Barriers to Entry*. In M. C. Casson and associates, *Multinationals and World Trade: Vertical Integration and the Division of Labour in the World Industries*, London: Allen and Unwin, 317–42.

Reader, W. J. (1981) *Bowater: A History*, Cambridge: Cambridge University Press.

Redlich, F. (1956) The Military Enterpriser: A Neglected Area of Research, *Explorations in Entrepreneurial History* (Series 1), 8, 252–6.

Reingaum, J. F. (1981) Dynamic Games of Innovation, *Journal of Economic Theory*, 25, 21–41.

Reingaum, J. F. (1985) A Two-Stage Model of Research and Development with Endogenous Second-Mover Advantages, *International Journal of Industrial Organisation*, 3, 275–92.

Rhys, D. G. (1977) European Mass-Producing Car Makers and Minimum Efficient Scale: A Note, *Journal of Industrial Economics*, 25, 313–19.

Robinson, E. A. G. (1941) *Monopoly*, London: Nisbet.

Rosenberg, N. (1982) *Inside the Black Box: Technology and Economics*, Cambridge: Cambridge University Press.

Rowthorn, R. (1979) The Future of the World Economy: Introduction. In R. B. Cohen, N. Felton, J. van Liere and M. Nkosi (eds) *The Multinational Corporation: A Radical Approach; Papers by Stephen Herbert Hymer*, Cambridge: Cambridge University Press, 167–72.

Rugman, A. M. (1981) *Inside the Multinationals: The Economics of Internal Markets*, London: Croom Helm.

Rugman, A. M. (1982) Internalisation and Non-equity Forms of International Involvement. In A. M. Rugman (ed.) *New Theories of the Multinational Enterprise*, Beckenham, Kent: Croom Helm, 1–23.

Rugman, A. M. (1983a) The Determinants of Intra-industry Direct Foreign Investment, Dalhousie Discussion Papers in International Business No. 25.

Rugman, A. M. (1983b) Transfer Pricing in the Canadian Petroleum Industry, mimeo.

Rugman, A. M. (1986) New Theories of the Multinational Enterprise: An Assessment of Internalisation Theory, *Bulletin of Economic Research*, 38(2), 101–18.

Sachdev, J. C. (1976) A Framework for the Planning of Divestment Policies for Multinational Companies, Ph.D. thesis, University of Manchester Institute of Science and Technology.

Salop, S. C. (ed.) (1981) *Strategy, Predation and Antitrust*, Washington, D.C.: Bureau of Economics, Federal Trade Commission.

Schumpeter, J. A. (1934) *The Theory of Economic Development*, Cambridge, Mass.: Harvard University Press.

Scott, J. D. (1962) *Vickers: A History*, London: Weidenfeld and Nicolson.

Servan-Schreiber, J. J. (1968) *The American Challenge* (trans. R. Steel), New York: Atheneum House.

Shapiro, C. (1982) Consumer Information, Product Quality and Seller Reputation, *Bell Journal of Economics*, 13, 2–35.

Sharpston, M. (1975) International Subcontracting, *Oxford Economic Papers*, 27, 94–135.

Shubik, M. (1959) *Strategy and Market Structure*, New York: Wiley.

Shubik, M. with Levitan, R. (1980) *Market Structure and Behaviour*, Cambridge, Mass.: Harvard University Press.

Simon, H. A. (1982) *Models of Bounded Rationality and Other Topics in Economics* 2 vols, Cambridge, Mass.: MIT Press.

Simon, H. A. (1983) *Reason in Human Affairs*, Oxford: Blackwell.

Smith, V. L. (1961) *Investment and Production: A Study in the Theory of the Capital-Using Enterprise*, Cambridge, Mass.: Harvard University Press.

Spence, A. M. (1977) Entry Capacity, Investment and Oligopolistic Pricing, *Bell Journal of Economics*, 8, 534–44.

Stopford, J. M. and Turner, L. (1985) *Britain and the Multinationals*, Chichester, W. Sussex: John Wiley.

Strong, N. and Waterson, M. (1987) Principals, Agents and Information, in R. Clarke and A. McGuinness (eds) *Economics of the Firm*, Oxford: Blackwell.

Stuckey, J. A. (1983) *Vertical Integration and Joint Ventures in the Aluminium Industry*, Cambridge Mass.: Harvard University Press.

Sugden, R. (1983) Why Transational Corporations?, *Warwick Economic Research Paper* No. 22.

Swedenborg, B. (1979) *Multinational Operations of Swedish Firms*, Stockholm: Almqvist and Wiksell.

Teece, D. J. (1977) Technology Transfer by Multinational Firms: The Resource Costs of Transferring Technological Know-How, *Economic Journal*, 87, 242-61.

Teece, D. J. (1982) A Transaction Cost Theory of the Multinational Enterprise, University of Reading Discussion Papers in International Investment and Business Studies, No. 66. An abstract appears in M. C. Casson (ed.) (1983) *The Growth of International Business*, London: Allen and Unwin, 51-62.

Teece, D. J. (1985) Multinational Enterprise, Internal Governance and Industrial Organisation, *American Economic Association, Papers and Proceedings*, 75, 233-8.

Teichova, A. (1983) Outline of Certain Research Results concerning Multinationals in Interwar East-Central Europe, Paper presented to the European Science Foundation Conference on Multinationals: Theory and History, Florence, 19-21 September, 1983.

Telesio, P. (1979) *Technology, Licensing and Multinational Enterprises*, New York: Praeger.

Tomlinson, J. W. C. (1970) *The Joint Venture Process in International Business: India and Pakistan*, Cambridge, Mass.: MIT Press.

Torneden, R. L. (1975) *Foreign Divestment by US Multinational Corporations: With Eight Case Studies*, New York: Praeger.

Trebilcock, C. (1977) *The Vickers Brothers: Armaments and Enterprise 1854-1914*, London: Europa.

United Kingdom, House of Commons (1976) *Eighth Report from the Expenditure Committee: Public Expenditure on Chrysler UK Ltd., Volume 1: Report*, London: HMSO, HC 596-1 (1975-6).

United Nations Centre on Transnational Corporations (1983) *Transnational Corporations in World Development: Third Survey*, New York: United Nations.

Utton, M. A. (1985) Predatory Pricing and the Regulation of Dominant Firms, University of Reading Discussion of Papers in Economics No. 171.

Vaitsos, C. V. (1974) *Intercountry Income Distribution and Transnational Enterprises*, Oxford: Clarendon Press.

Van Den Bulcke, D. (1979) Existing Data. In D. Van Den Bulcke, J. J. Boddewyn, B. Marten and P. Klemmer (eds) *Investment and Divestment Policies of Multinational Corporations in Europe*, Farnborough, Hants: Saxon House for ECSIM, 1-59.

Van Den Bulcke, D. and Halsberghe, E. (1983) Divestment and Loss of Employment: A Comparison between Foreign and Belgian Enterprises, Paper presented to European Institute of Advanced Management Studies Workshop on 'European Unemployment and Productivity', Oslo, 16-17 December, 1983.

Vernon, R. (1966) International Investment and International Trade in the Product Cycle, *Quarterly Journal of Economics*, 80, 190-207.

Vernon, R. (1971) *Sovereignty at Bay: The Multinational Spread of US Enterprises*, New York: Basic Books.

Vernon, R. (1974) The Location of Economic Activity. In J. H. Dunning (ed.) *Economic Analysis and the Multinational Enterprise*, London: Allen and Unwin, 89–114.

Vernon, R. (1979) The Product Cycle Hypothesis in a New International Environment, *Oxford Bulletin of Economics and Statistics*, 41, 255–67.

Vernon, R. (1983) Organisational and Institutional Responses to International Risk. In R. J. Herring (ed.) *Managing International Risk*, Cambridge: Cambridge University Press, 191–216.

Vickers, J. (1985) Strategic Competition among the Few – Some Recent Developments in the Economics of Industry, *Oxford Review of Economic Policy*, 1(3), 39–62.

Wetherill, G. B. (1977) *Sampling Inspection and Quality Control*, London: Chapman and Hall.

Wilkins, M. (1970) *The Emergence of Multinational Enterprise: American Business Abroad from the Colonial Era to 1914*, Cambridge, Mass.: Harvard University Press.

Wilkins, M. (1974) *The Maturing of Multinational Enterprise: American Business Abroad from 1914 to 1970*, Cambridge, Mass.: Harvard University Press.

Wilks, S. (1984) *Industrial Policy and the Motor Industry*, Manchester: Manchester University Press.

Williamson, O. E. (1975) *Markets and Hierarchies: Analysis and Anti-trust Implications*, New York: Free Press.

Williamson, O. E. (1981) The Modern Corporation: Origins, Evolution and Attributes, *Journal of Economic Literature*, 19, 1537–68.

Williamson, O. E. (1985) *The Economic Institutions of Capitalism: Firms, Markets, Relational Contracting*, New York: Free Press.

Wilson, B. D. (1980) The Propensity of Multinational Companies to Expand through Acquisitions, *Journal of International Business Studies*, 12, 59–65.

Wolf, B. M. (1977) Industrial Diversification and Internationalisation: Some Empirical Evidence, *Journal of Industrial Economics*, 26, 177–91.

Wright, M. (1986) Demergers: The Case of Bowater. In J. Coyne and M. Wright (eds) *Divestment and Strategic Change*, Deddington, Oxon.: Philip Allan, 45–72.

Young, S. and Hood, N. (1977) *Chrysler UK: A Corporation in Transition*, New York: Praeger.

Young, S. with Lowe, A. V. (1974) *Intervention in the Mixed Economy*, London: Croom Helm.

Young, S., Hood, N. and Hamill, J. (1985) *Decision-Making in Foreign-Owned Multinational Subsidiaries in the United Kingdom*, Geneva: International Labour Office.

Index

Jacqueline McDermott